THE CHINA MOMENT: CONTEXTUALIZING INDIVIDUALISM IN CHINESE CONTEMPORARY ART

EDITED BY MI YOU, SU WEI, ANNA-LISA SCHERFOSE

编著:苏伟,由宓,安娜丽莎·舍佛赛

THE CHINA MOMENT: CONTEXTUALIZING INDIVIDUALISM IN CHINESE CONTEMPORARY ART

HATJE
CANTZ

DOCUMENTA
INSTITUT

CONTENTS

INTRODUCTION

PREFACE: WHICH MOMENT?

HEINZ BUDE

With this research exhibition in Kassel, the documenta Institut introduces itself to the public for the first time. By mounting an exhibition we aim to show both how we are conducting our research and what we are researching. In this case, the aim is to illuminate the horizon of global contemporary art, against which the individual documenta exhibitions present their version of contemporary art. The focus is not on art itself, but on the problem of the present—which calls art into being.

China is currently engaged in a hegemonic conflict with the United States, a battle in which economic power and military strength are not the only decisive factors. Imperial projects such as the "Silk Road" will only lead to hegemonic dominance if they can be integrated into a "Chinese way of life." This brings into play art, which is allied with popular culture, an understanding of life, and the ways in which people think, feel, and desire. Our research exhibition explores this, looking at the emergence and creation of contemporary art in China in the 1980s and 1990s.

It focuses on art produced in a country that wishes to leave behind the Maoist societal experiment but without denying its effects.[1] We see how something emerged in China in the 1980s and 1990s that did not yet know what it was. Very imprecisely and very awkwardly, this is called contemporary art, something that did not exist in China before, where art academies were too masterful and museum-going audiences too reverent. Confucian teachings and inherited origins were no longer considered when coming up with something new. Instead, it was better to get up and head out to see firsthand what was happening in the country and across the world. This new form of art blazed paths that led nowhere. One finds bodies without images, masses without leaders, and emblems without meaning. They are presented starkly, without a knowing wink, as statements that do not require interpretation.

In 1964, Susan Sontag counseled "against interpretation."[2] Here, she means desultorily presenting objects in their raw state. What matters is not the meaning but the material of life—not as a lighthearted game, but in dead earnest.

The people making this art did not appear to labor under an ideological complex of guilt. They stepped forth unencumbered by bitterness, free of a bad conscience. They wished to call things by their name—only the first-person pronoun "I" did not seem to offer the right frame of reference. These individuals engaged closely with Friedrich Nietzsche, Franz Kafka, Antonin Artaud, Vilém Flusser, Samuel Beckett, and Jean-François Lyotard via a dizzying number of handwritten summaries which convinced them that one cannot simply dive headlong into endless psychoanalytic family sagas after the ravages wrought by the heroes of the cultural revolution—never mind what one may have imagined in the one-child society. Rather, it was first necessary to showcase the "desire machine" (Gilles Deleuze and Félix Guattari), listen to the voices of unreason (Michel Foucault), and give space to sexuality in "polymorphous perverse" partial objects. Coined terms like "black holes," "white cubes," "fuzzy sets," and "open systems" seem to belong equally to the domains of science, philosophy, and the arts. The vast new generation in China found Ariadne's thread had been snapped, as did those taking part in global discourse in the 1980s.[3] This wasn't a complaint—it was a liberation. Triumphant collective thinking was placed in opposition to cautious and dangerous individual thought. This allowed lessons to be learned for behaviors that were both ethical and aesthetic.

In this, advocating a Marxist view of society became superfluous. The goal was no longer to speak for the masses—a proletariat set in opposition to capital—but to gain a voice of one's own. Instead of an idealizing overarching theory, the absence of the unknown is encountered in oneself and in others, enabling one to learn where one is blocked and where one's vision is obscured. Alienation and exploitation became a mere expression of repellant self-satisfaction, devoid of tenderness or affection. Even though spokespeople clearly remained vital in achieving self-expression, the ones who promoted themselves as such were no longer to be trusted. Yet a movement cannot arise without an echo, mutual attention, and a current of affect—not in art nor in society.

But perhaps this vision of a new dawn of contemporary art in 1980s China was merely a projection founded on a belief in a shared timeline. Were we truly so close then, we individuals in the grip of upheaval in Germany and in China? The term "generation" lures us into seeing commonalities across borders and attributing agency to a particular time.

We cannot forget that across millennia, China had wholly different views when it came to political savvy, social class, and amassing wealth. Moreover, modern China forged its path quite independent of the US and the Soviet Union. China is neither a postcolonial land nor a member of the Global South. The country long vacillated between styling itself as an equal in the international community and presenting itself as a dynamic, expanding colonial actor. In this, art was never merely a handsome ornament; it was a vital part of the ontology of the "Heavenly Kingdom." The official robes worn by Chinese Mandarins are themselves works of art.

Avant-garde art incontrovertibly accompanied economic liberalization between 1979 and 1997 under Deng Xiaoping. Liberalization was the guiding principle for a regime promoting openness, unshackling, and release—ideas which placed the Chinese in a state of vibration and aggregation: How to face chaos? What does order entail? What is the role of the individual?

With this exhibition, the documenta Institut debuts as a research body that not only investigates exhibitions as a central medium of contemporary art, but also uses exhibitions as an independent means for researching exhibitions. Research into exhibitions naturally draws on archival findings, observation, and conversations with individuals who conceive, organize, and mount exhibitions, as well as with exhibition visitors and art journalists, all of which is subsequently presented in essays and monographs. But at our institute, we want not only to conduct research into exhibitions but also to use exhibitions in our research, allowing audiences in Kassel and beyond to participate in the process.

Such secondary research exhibitions present objects that have put themselves on display and are only realized through the process of being exhibited. Thematically focused temporary exhibitions differ from permanent museum collections in that they have been designed to attract an audience. A museum establishes the cultural significance of its display through its role as an institution, whereas an exhibition is an event that must demonstrate the contemporary relevance of what it shows.

There are three reasons to perform research in the form of an exhibition. Firstly, exhibitions enable a multimedia depiction of the many contexts that shape an object, spanning image, writing, sound, and movement. Often art emerges in clubs, living rooms, or offices. Different chains of meaning overlap at more than one point. Freud has described the overdetermination of perceptual frameworks which develop neither linearly nor cyclically, needing instead to be conceived of in etiological simultaneity. An exhibition is perhaps better placed than a fat tome or individual image to display why a specific future turns out to be the past of today's present, while another seemingly vanishes as a past future. Walking through an exhibition, one might begin to wonder why everything needs to have a past and a future.

A second advantage is that an exhibition can capture the restlessness of an object. People might suddenly wholly embrace something or decide to present scenes or films about strange occurrences. What drives them? What do they seek to achieve? And why do things go wrong?

The third advantage ties into the provocative question of how an exhibition allows us to interpret our present: a research exhibition aims to familiarize the audience with issues surrounding a subject in order to obviate fixed terms. Such an exhibition embarks on a search for terms that test the future rather than drawing on the past.

This research exhibition offers a scenography for an epistemological situation that makes present thoughts which inhere today. To research means to explore objective possibilities intrinsic to a situation, with a changing set of actors and stories, testing out a historical variance for which no rule has yet been established. An exhibition is suitable for this purpose because it plumbs the ability to imagine using art, thus laying bare processes of thought and showing what motivates individuals and with what aims they act. The players have yet to reach an agreement, nor has anything been divided across spheres of influence or direction. Yet something is clearly in motion. Retrospectively, what we see here reveals itself as the source of a current problem in a manner that acts not as proof but as a querying of provability itself.

Back then, Germany and China saw each other as projections of their respective futures. As the era of globalization began, China sought its future in Germany, and Germany in China, with an enervated federal republic on the one hand and a burgeoning people's republic on the other. In today's multipolar world, China has squared the circle with communist capitalism, while the now-enlarged federal republic has lost its way with Rhenish capitalism. Perhaps it is once again time to dream of other things far more mysterious and delightful.

1 Julia Lovell, *Maoism: A Global History* (London: Bodley Head, 2019).
2 Susan Sontag, *Against Interpretation* (New York: Farrar, Straus & Giroux, 1966).
3 Gilles Deleuze and Michel Foucault, *Der Faden ist gerissen*, trans. Ulrich Raulff and Walther Seiter (Berlin: Merve Verlag, 1977).

THE CHINA MOMENT

MI YOU

IS THE CHINA MOMENT OVER?

In the context of Chinese contemporary art, globalization seems to have given way to regionalization, and even decoupling. There is less representation of Chinese artists in Western institutions now than before, and this is not only because of the rise of other regional and community representations, including the Chinese diaspora. There are institutions in the US that—off the record—demand curators not include artists of Chinese origin, under what is perceived as a cultural war under Trump. The experience of these shifts for an artist of Chinese origin can be palpably translated into a general sentiment: "You cannot be warmly welcomed, but you cannot be marginalized; you cannot play the minoritarian or victim card, but you cannot be complacent either." Why has the "China moment" passed so quickly? And what is to be gained in making an exhibition about Chinese art and intellectual life now?

The Chinese and Chinese-diaspora art worlds have always been too big and complex to be fully incorporated into the global contemporary art circuit—it is more convenient to have bite-sized representations. Putting to one side whether one could even speak about a country and a culture the size of China as a single entity, in the golden era of globalization, "Chineseness" was highly sought after. The global art world consumed what it understood as Chineseness: tai chi symbols overlaid on the body, traditional spiritual practices gaining a second life in the digital space, neatly arranged everyday objects, and images of factory workers toiling away. The catalogue is extensive.

More recently however, in critical contemporary art, it seems both mainland Chinese artists and Chinese diaspora artists are measured by their distance and degree of fracture to the notion of China. In other words, Chineseness gives way to more granular experiences in relation to the social and cultural environment, power, and deeper cultural feelings.

If speaking about China wholesale at the international art arena now often falls on deaf ears, even taking a minoritarian position from within China doesn't warrant a similar degree of international attention as minoritarian political art does from Global South countries. Why do certain preferences seem to exist so that, for example, artworks on environmental degradation in the Amazon are given more spotlight than similar artworks focusing on Chinese regions? A glance at scholarship focusing on Global South extractivist economies reveals how some societies become dependent on revenues from raw materials export rather than higher value-adding goods. While scholars have developed theories on dependency and peripheral capitalism that point to the power asymmetry in global trade and financial arrangements, it can seem disingenuous for Chinese cultural producers to reiterate such theories. Relativism is tacitly exercised here. The severity of these issues is viewed against the state's capacity in alleviating them. Thus, despite China's large population in poverty, its size and influence in the global economy mean that its internal struggles are often overlooked. Even environmental calamities are less noteworthy compared to similar crises happening in countries with weaker state capacities. Another case of relativism is the constant evocation of neoliberalism in Western critical humanities and art circles—particularly in privatizing companies formerly in public ownership, deregulation, and small governments—as a generalized source of the world's problems. Therefore, it is difficult to square the argument for China, where the state can be said to position itself as a defense against neoliberalism.

For many Chinese artists working in the 2020s, it is hard to exercise moral blackmailing by following the Western critical art approach, where one side claims moral rights, and the other side is left to acknowledge power structures through endless self-criticism. As long as this performance of critique continues, art theory and production does not have to offer real solutions. The de-coupling of the global artworld from China is not only in statistical terms of artist representations, but more so in the intellectual space for Chinese artists: there's no easy target to blame and no simple formula for blackmailing, because the phenomenally high state capacity of China puts it in the odd position that it is both immanent to the problem and offers its antithesis. If one blames an extractivist economy for environmental degradation or the violation of workers' rights, in China, the state is the solution. If one blames neoliberal economy, in China, the state is the solution. This means their orbit of thinking cannot revolve around blaming others, but must be adjusted to address more complex questions.

Never Let a Crisis Go to Waste: When the glitter of the "China Moment" fades is the exact moment we should reckon with the flawed logic of the global art world in the preceding decades The global art world has thrived from the infrastructures of peak globalization and has consequently internalized value-systems that are embedded in the idea of globalization. This includes taking the alignment between liberal democracy as the only acceptable form of state, the expectation of the state to be progressive and deliver public good, and general economic stability as a given, rather than a historical contingency. Together with the crisis of globalization comes the existential crisis of the global artworld: I've called this condition "art in a multipolar world." Our intellectual inertia in the art world is typically reflected in various truisms: what we believe is what we choose to see and what we think others should think and follow to achieve an end. All of these are thrown off balance when the liberal international order and neoliberal globalization is shattered. In these times, I contend that cultural producers shouldn't merely reproduce the moral geographies of geopolitics, which follow the logic of friend and foe. We need to work out the precepts of art as it shifts and is formulated in relation to post-globalization multipolarity, the malleability of the role of the state, and the permeation of value pluralism. The art world is shifting in correlation with—though often slower than—things outside it, and this will influence how art is talked about, and crucially, how it is made.

The exhibition *The China Moment* hopes to present intellectual inquiries following this line of thinking. Many questions about China remain unasked, because the golden age of globalization meant difficult questions could be brushed aside or glossed over. Now more than ever, both sides—the Western and the Chinese art worlds—stand to gain something if instead of quietly accepting present predicaments, each could ask themselves earnest questions.

AN INTELLECTUAL CONTEXTUALIZATION

We should take a moment to look at questions that we didn't ask about China and Chinese art previously.

The exhibition is organized around an intellectual-history exploration into the notion and implications of individualism. The show is then guided by a few questions distilled from the political and sociological texts in this volume that help the audience kick start their rethinking process. These questions include: Why do the tactics and demands of the 1989 student movement appear more traditional than the 1919 student movement, the initial moment of China's modernization? Are leftists in China and leftists in the West the same leftists? Only when we engage with a contextualized interrogation between art and systems of thought can we unpack some of these contradictions in thinking and dilemma in our choices.

Starting in the 1980s, the Western art world embraced Chinese artists who were sporting political art, often in the form of actionist art, which in their reading gestured some kind of revolt against the system. A similar pattern could be found in socialist countries in the late Soviet era. However, twenty years later, some of these very artists have become reactionary, statist and nationalist. This, too, is not an isolated phenomenon and could be observed in Eastern Europe and Russia. Is political and economic opportunism the only explanation to this phenomenon, or are we missing fundamental reckonings with what constitutes the political? In retrospect, it seems that a newly gained sense of individualism and freedom found its expression in the individualist and actionist art, a reaction against a perceived system more than anything else.

Central to this research exhibition is the question of individualism. Yang Guoqiang's essay in this volume carefully maps the genealogies and subtleties of a concept which has been taken for granted in the West as a legacy of the liberal project. But for latecomer modernities, it may present a kaleidoscope of concepts and contexts. Yang delineates three forms of individualism in the intellectual history of the early twentieth century in China. Individualism could be read as a confrontation with and opposition to the state, which harbingers an extreme, anarchistic inclination, as represented by the thinking of Chen Duxiu, one of the founders of the Chinese Communist Party (CCP). Another second form of individualism follows a liberal and humanist tradition, spearheaded by the writer and later politician Hu Shi, himself educated at Columbia University under John Dewey, which advocated for individual self-cultivation and a more cautious approach to radical social transformation. And lastly, individualism could arise from earnest engagement between the masses, community, and the self, as the towering modernist writer Lu Xun represents through his life and work. This last offers arguably the most profound reflection on the social form and culture of the collective, the community, and the masses, where the individual can never be fully extricated from the web of the community with all its promise of warmth but also its backwardness and irrationality. It is also one that recognizes the conditions of China and the importance but also limits of Western thinking and calls for discursive and critical individualism emphasizing freedom of thought. Each of the three types of individualism has left its mark in the 1990s and 2000s on the intellectuals and the artists. Hence by reading the history of Chinese contemporary art in the 1990s and 2000s through the intellectual-historical lens of individualism we can gain insights into what was at stake. Readers may turn the pages to Yang Guoqiang's text, through whose insights they can make up their own minds on how artistic endeavors respond to a certain strand of individualism. What follows here is a compressed survey through the broader intellectual landscape of China, primarily in the 1990s and 2000s, which situates the other texts in the book.

THE STATE

The first variation of individualism may seem reactive because it is set against a larger, purportedly omnipresent structure such as the state. There is no circumvention of the question of the state in an intellectual engagement with China—and it should not be one resting on negation rather than interrogating with viable paths forward. I have said earlier how in the 2020s, Chinese contemporary artists are finding it difficult to talk about, let along take a position on the state. Certainly, it was not easier during the previous decades. However, there was much less moral policing from the international art world.

The status of China as an "avant-garde nation" that had practiced actually existing socialism and has stridden the path of economic modernization without significantly changing its one-party political system makes it a good place for assessing the fundamental claims put forward by different pundits and activists coming from Western-liberal, New Left, and conservative perspectives.

The progressives in the West, and increasingly, their liberal and conservative counterparts, have been quite ready to nominally accept the return of state intervention and public ownership of industries. But what about economies that are taken to be an alternative to neoliberalism? Chinese liberal scholar Qin Hui—whose essay is included in this volume—points out while Leftists in Western welfare states should oppose globalization, Leftists in China should welcome it, but simultaneously push for reform, so that it can benefit the Chinese working class and the disadvantaged.[1]

To be sure, liberals were in the intellectual mainstream in China from the 1980s well into the 2000s, with many promoting neoliberalism as the path for the country's economic development. The Chinese New Left was bitter about the neoliberal swing of the country in the 1990s and early 2000s. Where they could, they stood with underprivileged communities such as migrant workers and peasants, through both street-activism and policy suggestions in consultation sessions. Over time, state capacity proved not only to be the driving force of economic rebuilding, but was targeted increasingly to address social equity;[2] examples include state-sponsored poverty alleviation programs which have effectively eradicated absolute poverty;[3] the state's steps to protect gig workers' labor rights;[4] and, contrary to common assumptions, data privacy.[5]

Leading New Left thinker Wang Hui—another author included in this volume—points out the indispensable role that the socialist past has played in the reform period, highlighting the legacy of land collectivization and the political mobilization of the masses.[6] Families, clans, and spatial-governance relations were organized into new social relations in communes during the socialist period, on the foundation of which rural reform in the 1980s was organized. It is only through socialist political mobilization that the idea that the socialist state represents the interests of the majority of people is generally accepted. Without such acceptance, it would have been difficult for the different social strata to believe that the reforms promoted by the state represented their interests—why would anyone buy into Deng Xiaoping's "let some get rich first" without cynicism?

Recent theoretical debates focus more on the Chinese (economic) development model that delivers prosperity.[7] China's staggering economic growth is due to the government's policy directives and its related entities—namely, state-owned enterprises and banks that are deeply involved in both the production process and the allocation of economic resources. After decades of high-speed development, local government debt has been exposed to risks.[8] But it has also produced assets such as infrastructures and industrial firms. There are doubts nonetheless—and not just from the liberals—as to whether this system promotes innovation in science and information technology. Ecological degradation is a grave consequence, but the resolve to address it is often coupled with optimism rather than despair, unlike in the West.

Focusing on the economic side of things does occlude relevant issues. After China firmly withstood the shockwaves of the 2007–08 global financial crisis, some scholars have increasingly gained confidence and propped up the models of Chinese development and modernization not only as an analytical discourse but as a normative one.[9] If this reflects the zeitgeist and serves ideological discourse both domestically and internationally, it does not become a self-fulfilling prophecy without facing academic scrutiny in China. One could debate, for example, whether the Chinese model is ontologically extant, or whether it pertains to a wider condition of path independence—in other words, whether the set of policies will necessarily lead to growth.[10] Or one can view these developments in the context of from where state legitimacy is derived. Dingxin Zhao—whose text is included in this book and whose other illuminous texts find their way into various footnotes here—applies a state-society model in his research on historical and contemporary China, which encompasses the behavior and capacity of the state; the nature of society as seen through, for example, the intermediate associations of social groups; and the linkages between state and society. For Zhao, the latter entails three differing conceptions of legitimacy: legal-electoral, ideological, and performance legitimation, based on a critical expansion of Max Weber's model of traditional, charismatic, and rational-legal legitimacy.[11] The Mao era enjoyed ideological legitimation, the economic boom era performance legitimation. It seems today's discourse production feeds into re-ideologization.

THE PEOPLE

If reacting against the system or state is too simplistic and cannot account for all the contradictions surrounding the state, the second version of individualism—following the humanist tradition—presents other conundrums. Dewey holds that the individual in a democratic society must think critically and creatively, and, through communication with others, build strong democratic communities of shared experiences and emotions. All of which should be enabled or strengthened by art.[12] The liberal context, under which art can serve as a form of civic education, is not a given in China, which shouldn't preclude the practitioners from building projects that strive toward a more liberal society and nuanced understandings of what it means as the intermediary and local levels. These projects, as presented in the exhibition and beyond the exhibition, are more vulnerable than the more sloganist political and actionist kind. The state can view it as dissensus while co-opting some of the topics onto its own, or worse as promoted by foreign NGOs, but the same critique can equally be voiced by the leftists. Meanwhile the practitioners may come to a bottleneck, where accumulated good-doing does not guarantee a way forward for the society to evolve given its structural resistance to change. Nevertheless, some have an acute sense of responsibility in building a basic civil education in the absence of active civil society.

Individualism in its third vocation concerns the masses and the collective. It follows neither a liberal line of thinking nor a socialist impulse of revolt. The missing conceptual translation on the topic of the public and masses is evident. For example, the public awakening and political advocacy that Joseph Beuys called into being through art found its way to China as early as the 1980s, where the public nature of Beuys's art was introduced as a conceptual strategy, inspiring a number of contemporary artists to work with the society, or the *socius*, as conceptual creations. However, in the 1980s and 1990s, most independent contemporary artists in China were wary and hostile to the previous era's political mobilization through artistic images; whereas the academic artists upheld the notion of publicness in art—it was nothing revolutionary for those schooled in traditional leftist idea of the masses.

It is an operationalized automatism that working with and for the common people is generally good. The community and the masses are not abstract but historically constructed. Qin Hui focuses on the Chinese peasantry elsewhere, which cannot be essentialized into the "moral peasant" or the "rational peasant": the small community is underdeveloped, but this does not mean the development of individuality. On the contrary, the underdevelopment of the "small community" is the result of the expansion of the "big community": i.e., the state with its exercise of bureaucratic top-down control and legalist administrative measures that suppressed patriarchal law and clan power in most of the historical periods.[13] A definition, and, more importantly, a practice of individualism that has worked through the collective and masses is what the third version of individualism demands.

But it is a tall order for everyone. With the rise of populism, the "common people" are once again foregrounded for political theorization and mobilization, in contrast to the minoritarian impulses of critical art producers. However, this construal resembles the tyranny of the majority debate only formally. Rather, the liberal and left's weakened position in the West is conceptual and historically rooted. Antonia Majaca traces the genealogy of liberal philosophy of Dewey and—more notably—the anti-totalitarian Hannah Arendt and their uneasy relation to the mass.[14] Wittingly or unwittingly, they manifest an elitism that traces back to Gustave Le Bon's theory of the crowd. With due respect to their intellectual legacies, we could ask this liberal position today: Is it fair to blame the common people?

But the leftist approach to the "common people" equally needs to be scrutinized. Some orthodox leftists tend to overcorrect, politicizing or glorifying the common people without sufficient evidence. In the better days of global contemporary art, it was nothing incoherent or unfashionable, and indeed even perhaps political to borrow left— even "far left"—aesthetics from a patently left country and appropriate it in the West. To instantiate a "New Left art," artists from former socialist countries, such as the art collective *Chto Delat* founded in Saint Petersburg in 2023, began to sport socialist aesthetics in Western, broadly leftist, art circles. But this position was inevitably rendered unviable after Russia's full-scale invasion of Ukraine in February 2022. For now, it serves little for a New Left position to distinguish itself from a broad liberal anti-war alliance, not to mention the preponderance of anti-war art in galleries across the West. In the Chinese context, we have seen a surge in "New Left art" that glorifies the role of the common people in the socialist time either in labor processes, or creation of alternative technology and networks.

As a result, Western leftists and liberals oscillate between the positions of blame and expectation, each side upholding its perspective as the sole explanation of today's predicaments. Their Chinese counterparts are often caught up between reduced versions of both poles. But maybe the proper position to take is to rise above the gridlock in thinking.

In order to move forward, we should start from a place of humility, one based on understanding others' views on the self, while maintaining a distance from our own perceived teleology. This calls for a moment of reflection: Can I challenge the deeply held assumption that anything I see to be ontologically necessary might be contingent? Have I considered that I could be wrong, that my references could be self-centered? Am I open to mediated positions, such as accepting that I might be right, but others are right too? Have I ruled out all alternative explanations? We can be self-critical, self-skeptical, and tactical. But we should not be cynical or intellectually resigned. To remain open to critique, to espouse contradictions, and most importantly, to resist simplified narratives—this is the position Chinese artists must deeply invest in.

Ultimately, the exhibition and the reader are not only about China; they also serve as a mirror for others to understand their societies better, whether Western liberal or an authoritarian one with certain liberties.

1 Qin Hui, "Dilemmas of Twenty-First Century Globalization: Explanations and Solutions, with a Critique of Thomas Piketty's Twenty-First Century Capitalism," *Reading the China Dream*, November 15, 2018, https://www.readingthechinadream.com/qin-hui-dilemmas.html.

2 Shaoguang Wang and An'gang Hu, *The Chinese Economy in Crisis: State Capacity and Tax Reform* (Armonk, NY: M.E. Sharpe, 2001).

3 See, for example, the Brookings Institute commentary, Maria Ana Lugo, Martin Raiser, and Ruslan Yemtsov, "What's next for poverty reduction policies in China?," https://www.brookings.edu/articles/whats-next-for-poverty-reduction-policies-in-china/?b=1.

4 See, for example, "Meituan to change delivery algorithm rules as China urges labour protection," *Reuters*, September 13, 2021, https://www.reuters.com/world/china/meituan-change-delivery-algorithm-rules-china-urges-labour-protection-2021-09-13/.

5 See, for example, "China's Draft Regulations on Generative AI, with Kendra Schaefer and Jeremy Daum," podcast transcript *Sinica*, March 11, 2023, https://thechinaproject.com/2023/03/11/chinas-draft-regulations-on-generative-ai-with-kendra-schaefer-and-jeremy-daum/.

6 Wang Hui, "The Economy of Rising China," *Reading the China Dream*, originally published in *Beijing Cultural Review*, no. 2 (2010), pp. 24–35, https://www.readingthechinadream.com/wang-hui-the-economy-of-rising-china.html.

7 See, for example, Xiaohuan Lan, *How China Works: An Introduction to China's State-Led Economic Development* (Singapore: Palgrave Macmillan, 2024); Keyu Jin, *The New China Playbook: Beyond Socialism and Capitalism* (New York: Viking, 2023). See also venture capitalist Eric Li Shimo's TED talk, "Eric X. Li: A tale of two political systems," July 1, 2013, TED, YouTube video, https://www.youtube.com/watch?v=s0YjL9rZyR0 .

8 See, for example, Zhang Yukun, Xia Yining, and Ding Feng, "In Depth: China's Trillion-Dollar Local Government 'Hidden Debt' Dilemma—Caixin Global," *Caixin Global*, September 19, 2023.

9 *Beijing Culture Review* is a bastion of rigorous scholarship on contemporary socialism and China.

10 Dingxin Zhao, 赵鼎新：路径不依赖、政策不相干——什么才是中国经济成功的关键, "Path Independence, Policy Irrelevance—What Holds the Key to China's Economic Success in Zhao," 2017.

11 See Dingxin Zhao, "State Legitimacy, State Policy, and the Development of the 1989 Beijing Student Movement", *Asian Perspective* 23, no. 2 (1999), pp. 245–84.

12 John Dewey, *Art as Experience* (New York: Minton, Balch & Company, 1934).

13 Qin Hui and Jin Yan, *Tianyuanshi yu kuangxiangqu: guanzhong moshi yu qianjindai shehui de zairenshi* [Idyllic and rhapsody: The Guanzhong model and the re-understanding of the pre-modern society] (Beijing: Central Compilation & Translation Press, 1996); Qin, *Chuantong Shilu.*

14 Antonia Majaca, "Odysseus of the Nimble Wits: The Spirits of Totalitarianism and the Cultural Cold War's Entscheidungsproblem" in *Parapolitics: Cultural Freedom and the Cold War*, eds. Anselm Franke, Nida Ghouse, Paz Guevara, and Antonia Majaca (Berlin: Haus der Kulturen der Welt and Sternberg Press, 2017), p. 123–52.

INDIVIDUALISM THROUGH THE LENS OF THE "CHINA CONUNDRUM"

SU WEI

Since 1993, the years have seen a stream of exhibitions in Western Europe and North America devoted to contemporary Chinese art and its history. The interweaving of divergent research agendas with the spectacularization of Chinese art has not only cemented its place within global contemporary art history, but has also forged many of its enduring stereotypes. Within China itself, a local historiography of the contemporary began to emerge as early as the late 1980s. This practice of self-historicization has been carried forward over the past decade by a host of Chinese art institutions, academies, and individual researchers, cultivating a distinctive landscape of the self as a historical subject.

Contemporary Chinese art has always been inextricably bound to the problematic of "China." Its fraught use and abuse in the arena of international politics and mass media have erected numerous obstacles to a genuine dialogue between China and the world. Within China itself, meanwhile, the resurgence of an extreme political conservatism and nationalism means the very desire for such a dialogue is at its nadir. This present condition stands in stark contrast to the zenith of the globalization of contemporary Chinese art, a period when its practitioners widely regarded the effacement of Chinese cultural specificity as a necessary precondition for entry. They invested their faith in the primacy and progressive nature of globally circulating ideas and capital. This conviction, yoked to an urgent desire to join a Western-centric global art system, became the primary engine for Chinese contemporary art over the past two decades.

Running parallel to this artistic dynamic, a countervailing force was gathering in the country's cultural sphere: since the new millennium, contemporary Chinese thought has come to play an increasingly vital role. Its intellectual precedent can be traced to the early twentieth century, when the thinker Liang Qichao (1873–1929), in his treatise on the revolution in modern historiography, declared that history is made by the "active agent" (*zi dong zhe*), not the "passive recipient" (*ta dong zhe*).[1] This historically grounded perspective, charged with the subject's immense discursive energy, has profoundly shaped recent scholarly engagements with the "China" problematic, spanning historiography, ethnic studies, and cultural-intellectual history. It has sparked a fervent reassessment of "China" that foregrounds subjectivity as a critical axis. Notably, however, some knowledge producers have amplified this trend by assimilating it into the state's master narrative and the Communist Party of China (CPC [commonly known as the Chinese Communist Party or CCP]) ideological frameworks, thereby inflecting it with political instrumentalism and militant undertones.

Against this backdrop, and through an engagement with contemporary Chinese thought, this exhibition, based on my research into the subject in the past two years, seeks to liberate contemporary Chinese art from the confines of a hermetic geopolitical environment and from a narrative predicated on a fixed "Chineseness," proposing to view it instead as a still-uncharted terrain within global art history. Here, I frame "China" not as an object of nationalistic historiography or cultural sociology, but as a conundrum. Contemporary Chinese art is rooted in this very conundrum, manifesting itself through manifold interactions with Chinese reality. Since the 1980s, the public and private spheres have undergone immense transformation, their boundaries and attributes continuously redefined by structural societal shifts under the guidance of the state. During this period, China's cultural spheres entered a dual phase of re-evaluation and re-enlightenment as socialist culture gradually receded. Their internal discourses had to be repositioned through multi-dimensional dialogues with both socialist and Western cultures, and through constant friction with the will of the state and sociopolitical realities. This interactive process persists to this day, generating a volatile and elusive spectrum between the broad social sphere and the individual domains of practitioners. Stalled political reforms and China's deep imbrication within the globalized economic structure have only made this conundrum more pronounced. As such, contemporary Chinese art continues to play a vital yet contested role in this ongoing transformation—a process marked as much by possibility as by uncertainty.

1. TO WHAT IS "INDIVIDUALISM" LINKED?

"Individualism" is the central theme of this research-based exhibition. While the concept may have lost its critical purchase in Western knowledge production, it has been transposed onto non-Western contexts—especially regions like China where a socialist history suppressed it. In this process, "individualism" has been imbued with universalist connotations, yet the context and impetus for its revival during a period of cultural transition remain underexplored. Through a series of artist case studies, historical archives, and public programs, this exhibition examines the manifestations of "individualism" both inside and outside the Chinese art world. It aims to reveal the trajectory of contemporary Chinese art as it navigates its complex interactions with the state's will, the socialist legacy, globalization, and the discourses of contemporary Chinese thought. "Individualism" here is thus a relational concept, its meaning and scope in constant flux with the currents of China's historical process.

Within the discourse of contemporary Chinese art, "individualism" is a concept seldom invoked but widely treated as a given. This situation has its roots in the 1980s, when a seismic shift in the public-private domains meant the state-owned economy and cultural system lost their absolute authority to define the "private." At that moment, the "individual" urgently needed to be redefined by cultural practitioners who had newly regained command over cultural resources. By the end of the decade, a clearer path for the growth of "individualism" had begun to emerge.

This trajectory was dramatically accelerated by Deng Xiaoping's 1992 Southern Tour speeches, which unleashed a tidal wave of commercialization across Chinese society. The pro-democracy movements of the late 1980s flickered out like a spent meteor, swiftly consumed by a new zeitgeist defined by commerce. In response, two generations of artists at the turn of the 1990s had to rapidly reorient themselves, not only to confront a nascent, often crude market economy but also to seek a new urgency beyond lofty idealism. This urgency found its full expression in the burgeoning individual consciousness of artists.

Beyond this shifting social landscape, Chinese contemporary art's inroads into the global art system also expanded the horizons of individual consciousness. After participating in a series of international exhibitions in 1993—including the *China Avantgarde* exhibition in Berlin, the Venice Biennale, and the 1994 São Paulo Biennial—some artists began to come to terms with the foundational tenets of contemporaneity: individual practice, an ethos of self-organization, and a certain intellectuality suspended above social convention. Each of these represents an expansion of what individualism had meant.

This particular strain of individualism, however, diverged from conventional understandings; it emerged from distinct antecedents within Chinese intellectual history. The historian Yang Guoqiang (b. 1948) has traced the genealogy of the formation of "individualism" in early-twentieth-century China, discussing the "individual" through three relational modes, each embodied by prominent intellectuals: in opposition to the state (Chen Duxiu, 1879–1942); in distinction from society (Hu Shi, 1891–1962); and in confrontation with the masses (Lu Xun, 1881–1936). From within the opposition to the state arose an anarchically inclined individualism. From the conscious demarcation of boundaries with modern society came a form of liberal individualism, influenced by John Dewey, that gained currency among intellectuals. And from reflections on how Chinese and Western cultural traditions are embedded in popular culture, a speculative and critical humanistic individualism was proposed and enshrined by China's twentieth-century intellectuals.[2]

Following this tripartite logic, the "individualism" of the 1990s returned in a new guise. First, as Chinese artists entered the global art system, the individualist spirit as a countering force to statism reappeared in transnational imaginings and practices. Second, with no established arts infrastructure, practitioners relied heavily on self-organization and negotiation with official and private institutions; many existed in a semi-underground state, separate from ordinary social life, a suspension of social identity that enabled a liberal-style individualism to re-emerge. Third, facing the rise of a modern mass society stimulated by the market economy, practitioners began to adopt a mode of thinking akin to that of critical intellectuals, allowing them to address the tensions between art and popular culture, East–West differences, and modern consumer society.

These artists drifted between the academy, official institutions, the crude art market, and the underground, exhibiting their work in public museums, new hotels, diplomatic compounds, and alongside abandoned railway tracks. This itinerant state, known as "*mangliu*" (literally "blind flow" or drifters), persisted throughout the 1990s and spawned a variety of parasitic strategies for survival and practice. When investors brought Chinese contemporary art into the international art market in the early 2000s, some of these strategies evolved into a full embrace of local and global art systems and their commercial operations. The 2001 exhibition *Fuck Off*, initiated by Ai Weiwei, can therefore be seen as a prescient, self-reflexive warning against this impending condition.

2. VEIL OF IGNORANCE: A CONTEST OF VALUE AND ARTISTIC STANCE

Before the gallery industry emerged in the early 2000s, Chinese artists were generally skeptical about the capacity of art to embody cultural and social value, believing that an artistic stance rooted in the "individual" was more trustworthy. Such an attitude has a history. A major 1988 debate in the newspaper *Fine Arts in China (zhong guo mei shu bao)* on the "Purification of Language" reflected an anxiety about the ontology of art, focusing on whether it possesses a language independent of social change. This anxiety over the essence of art evolved in the 1990s, as more artists took "conceptuality" as their foundation, attempting to transcend narrow cultural and social values in order to establish an artistic stance rather than an ontology. This turn was partly a reaction against the popularity of Political Pop, which its critics saw as bearing too much mundane cultural and social expression. They hoped "conceptuality" could break through this perceived iconographic superficiality. Yet this critique often rested on a fascinating misreading: for a Political Pop artist like Wang Guangyi (b. 1957), the primary concern was precisely how to suspend the value judgments of different societies and cultures. Adopting an intentionally crafted "ignorant" posture, he sought to critique the disciplining of human existence by social systems and cultural customs, thereby forging his artistic stance.

In the early 1990s, this search for an authentic stance led artists from across China to gather—and come to dwell—in Beijing's East Village and the Yuanmingyuan (the Old Summer Palace) "Painters' Village." In an era of highly restricted social mobility, their way of life demonstrated a defiance of social norms and the official art apparatus. But that was not the whole story. For a small number of artists like Datong Dazhang (1955–2000), this precarious existence triggered a radicalized "individual" consciousness, one that demanded artistic practice through spiritual and physical asceticism, forcing a complete separation from one's native environment. Through "self-exile," it interrogated the very grounds of the individual. This was markedly different from the progressive, reflective path of the enlightenment atmosphere in the 1980s, and gave birth to an alternative artistic stance—one that necessitated the transcendence over artistic professionalism and production-oriented art. The work of this small handful of artists has long been understudied, but is receiving increasing attention today. Their practices sometimes venture into territories of a generation's spiritual history that are difficult to confront, issuing a warning in a language of raw, savage force to a mainstream that embraced "individuality" in crude universalist terms.

Furthermore, even the most underground existence in China entailed negotiation with the official institution and establishment. Where documentary film is concerned, for instance, the careers of some directors began precisely when official media like China Central Television (CCTV) briefly opened their doors to independent creators. These directors generally adopted a pragmatic attitude, even leveraging such professional, official connections to gain access to expensive filming equipment. Through the lenses of these initiators of China's underground documentary movement, ordinary people and the "nameless" on the margins of society became the focus. What ultimately emerges is a dialogue between two distinct forms of individuality: the filmmaker's, defined by his or her creative agency, and the subject's, defined by its suppressed social existence—a conversation that unfolds entirely within the fraught context of negotiation with the establishment.

Meanwhile, in the Chinese intellectual sphere, the primary object of critique was an elitist humanism: the very intellectual tradition that had first supplied individualism with its critical armory, yet which individualism itself would ultimately outgrow. Denounced as revisionist by socialist culture and severely repressed between 1949 and 1979, it underwent a full-fledged revival in the 1980s. With the rise of popular culture in the 1990s, however, it was positioned as the antagonist in a fierce debate surrounding the "humanistic spirit." If the intellectuals of the 1980s were still engaged in propagating elite cultural values to the public, this public intellectual stance underwent a dramatic transformation in the 1990s. The journal *The Scholar* (*xue ren*), founded in the early 1990s, led a trend toward the professionalization and academization of public intellectuals. At the same time, the question of whether and how intellectuals should participate in China's national modernization sparked the great debate between the New Left and the Liberals in the mid-to-late 1990s. Looking back, the chasm separating state-driven projects from intellectual practice had already begun to yawn open, and it would become even more pronounced after the new millennium.

3. FREE WILL WITHOUT A REFERENT

In the early 2000s, propelled by an abrupt influx of capital, the gallery industry boomed in China. The first wave of galleries, born in Beijing and Shanghai, were often established as non-profit spaces or art centers. This dual identity served to establish aims beyond the commercial while also facilitating applications for foreign funding. A new variety of artistic practice emerged in the wake of such changes, one that fused an experimental spirit with visual spectacle and a reliance more on material production and physical space of exhibition. As a result, practitioners were no longer content with a semi-underground existence and multimedia experiments. More diverse art practices began to appear, a diversity that would characterize the subsequent fifteen to twenty years.

It must be stressed that this pluralistic development was predicated upon a provisional suspension of any foundational political or cultural premises. The alignment with globalism, then at its peak, served to mitigate the unresolved problems of 1990s "individualism" in a climate of fluidity and relativism; consequently, the urgent task of forging an authentic subjectivity, rather than mere cultural signifiers, was deferred. This imperative would not re-emerge until the subsequent economic cooling, though a few wary practitioners had anticipated the crisis from the start. At this critical juncture, with very few exceptions, nearly everyone practiced—or believed they did—under the guidance of a free will generated by the free market, striving to obtain the endorsement for legitimate passage into globalism.

In the intellectual arena, this phenomenon found a critical echo in Wang Hui's (b. 1959) concept of "depoliticized politics." Responding to heightening social stratification, he addressed a key deficit among Chinese cultural workers: their lack of political subjectivity and their inability to analyze and imagine the reality of China. In his analysis, an overly hasty farewell to "revolution" and socialism—which severed the "short twentieth century" (1911–76) from the new era since 1980s and cultivated a yearning for Western-style democracies premised on individual rights—led to the loss of political subjectivity in the intellectual sphere of China. This proposition, controversial even today, simultaneously uncovered the problems of China's art world. A generalized free will proved to be a double-edged sword: driven by the market and globalism, it stripped away many cultural and political signifiers and further opened up the borders of art, but it also led practitioners on to a brief departure from the conundrum of Chinese subjectivity. It lifted art into an aerial sanctum, floating above local history and political reality, carrying with it the vaunted values of pluralism. For Chinese contemporary art at that moment, however, this detachment and pluralism could be an idyllic pasture, they could also be a slow-acting poison, leaching the substance from the very grounds of subjectivity.

4. THE "CHINA" BEHIND THE "INDIVIDUAL"

The creative "individual" of the 1990s matured rapidly, defined by a dual antagonism that became the very essence of the decade's avant-garde: a tension with a transitional Chinese society and a critical consciousness aimed at mass culture. Yet, in a striking paradox, the individual's most direct antagonist—the state and its discourse—remained largely lurking in the background, elided from dominant art discussions. This profound blind spot was not corrected but extended into the first decade of the twenty-first century, an era defined by the ascendant logic of globalism.

The intellectual sphere, however, tells a different story. Beginning with the New Left/Liberal debate in the mid- to late 1990s, Chinese thinkers have consistently placed "China" as a set of problematics at the very core of their inquiry. To this day, with the exception of researchers who harbor illusions about statism, they have undertaken profound explorations in re-assessing the "revolutionary" legacy, examining the formation of "China" through the interplay of modern intellectual history and present reality, and re-narrating it through the intersection of area studies and global perspectives. These intellectual maneuvers, possessing a keen sense of reality and a synoptic consciousness, inherit the literary spirit of the early twentieth-century writer Lu Xun, continuously deconstructing and reconstructing the image of China from the crucible of present urgencies.

An essay on the socialist literary system by the literary historian Hong Zicheng (b. 1939), included in this volume, serves as a case in point.

Throughout his long career, Hong has consistently investigated the socialist literary legacy. As someone who personally experienced that system, he combines intense self-critique with precise analysis to reveal its inherent "integral quality" (*zheng yi xing*)—its nature as a totalizing system in which art, politics, and private life were fused. In mapping this monolith, he charts a historical path for understanding the creative "individual" of today, a figure forged in a complex dialectic of resistance and negotiation with this seamless ideological whole.

Regarding the "China conundrum," there also exist unperceived dark spots and zones forbidden by official ideology. A minority of creators on the margins of professionalized knowledge and art production have paid attention to this. They place China in an ethical position to be interrogated, probing the self-contradictions, violence, and absurdity in the operations of that discourse. At the same time, they reveal the emotional and psychological structures and subjective states of the "internal others" within "China." In his poem "Diary of Hope," the poet Wang Wei (b. 1975) adopts the perspective of a "cosmopolitan without a world" to forge a poetic method: bringing to completion the truncated lives of individuals who resist state violence or have perished in the resurgence of ultra-leftist politics. His vision opens up a more arduous and deeply dialectical path, one that imagines a "China" whose very possibility is located in the improbable.

These intellectual currents have spurred a reflexive reconstruction of the "China" problematic within the art industry, placing Chinese curators in a complex position regarding globalism. With their artists gaining widespread acceptance in Western institutions, curators have been searching for an alternative mode of self-historicization—one that can enter the global dialogue without resorting to the increasingly familiar and threadbare national/state narrative. This challenge has, in turn, given rise to several key research paths: appropriating methods from other cultural fields to create an interdisciplinary perspective; starting from an urgency of the here and now to re-examine art history since the 1980s, or even to search for historical clues from the 1949–79 period; and extracting cross-contextual perspectives from working experiences in both Chinese and Western contexts. The profound implication of this methodological turn is that in thickening the history and narratives of "China," it also complicates the figure of the artist as an individual. These practices, therefore, rarely treat the artist as a unique or isolated phenomenon; rather, they place the individual within a multi-dimensional network of knowledge production, ripe for continuous analysis and reconstruction.

EPILOGUE: THE SELF-AWARE INDIVIDUAL AND ITS SHADOW, A CONFRONTATION WITH NIHILISM

In this essay, I have sought to link the manifestation of "individualism" within the trajectory of contemporary Chinese art to the different historical appearances of the "China conundrum." In doing so, I have framed the artistic freedom gained by the "individual" as a product of a specific Chinese context in which "everything must be re-evaluated." This context is scaffolded by a series of critical historical junctures: the fierce negation of the socialist cultural legacy in the late 1970s; the comprehensive linguistic turn within art and the failure of the democracy movement in the late 1980s; the surge of the market economy in the 1990s; the cooptation of contemporary art by global art mechanisms in the 2000s; and, over the last decade, the proliferation of "communal" practices born of a disillusionment with institutionalization and market myth-making. In the wake of each event, the "individual" was forced to renegotiate its position, revealing yet another facet of its complex character.

In the shadows of these moments, however, nihilism has always loomed as a specter. Its impulse often arose from a primal, almost spiritual desire for an "artistic autonomy" that could transcend the coordinates of history and reality. In this guise, it functioned as a hidden sanctuary, preserving art's transcendent quality and opening a space for alternative aesthetics for the "individual." Yet this sanctuary, when it becomes an absolute, reveals its true nature. Here, nihilism is not merely a rejection of values but a philosophical stance wherein the rejection of all constraints (political, historical, social) becomes an end in itself, hollowing out the very purpose it initially sought to protect. In this form, it appears as a hypocritical moral guise, becoming a pretext to evade the "China conundrum" and the anxieties of subjectivity.

This evasive turn is what gives nihilism in the Chinese context its specific charge: the negation of history. One need not forget that the CCP itself regards "historical nihilism" as a reaction against its official historical narrative. In the realm of contemporary art, this nihilism is the philosophical exhaustion that follows when a reigning value—in this case, the unmoored, free individual of the global market—devalues itself, revealing its own emptiness. It is the symptom of a historical dead end, a recognition that the path of simply embracing globalism has exhausted its creative and critical energy.

Therefore, for China's art practitioners, dealing with this nihilism is not a choice but a historical necessity. The key challenge is not to simply "bid farewell" to old positions, but to activate a consciousness within a self-aware individual—a reflexive turn inward to examine the very foundations of one's own artistic freedom. One must ask, "What historical forces shaped this 'individualism' I practice? Was its celebrated detachment from politics a form of genuine freedom, or a form of complicity that led to this very void?" This act of rigorous self-interrogation is what transforms nihilism from a terminal diagnosis into a creative starting point. It forces the artistic "individual" to confront and re-submerge themselves within the complex strata of the "China conundrum." The goal is to transform "China" from an essentialized background to be escaped into a dynamic method and field—a field where internal contradictions are constantly revealed, capable of generating new forms of thought and sensibility. It is only by first confronting the void that a new and more grounded path can be forged for the regrowth of individualism.

1 Liang Qichao, "Zhongguo Shi Xulun" [On the Narration of Chinese History], in *Yinbing Shi Wenji* [Collected Works from the Ice-Drinker's Studio], vol. 3, Taiwan Zhonghua Shuju, 1983.

2 For details, see Yang Guoqiang's article "On Individualism in the New Culture Movement (excerpts)" in this collection, pp. 155–67.

INDIVIDUALISM IN CHINESE CONTEMPORARY ART

1. **INDIVIDUALISM AS REACTION**
   个人主义:反应
2. **INDIVIDUALISM AS PARTICIPATION**
   个人主义:参与
3. **INDIVIDUALISM AS RE-ANIMATION OF HUMANISM**
   个人主义:重新激活人文主义
4. **INDIVIDUALISM AS INTERROGATION OF THE MASS**
   个人主义:对大众的质询

ARTISTS

1. DATONG DAZHANG 大同大张
   JIANG JIE 姜杰
   KAN XUAN 阚萱
   LIN YILIN 林一林
   MA LIUMING 马六明
   WANG GUANGYI 王广义
   WU WENGUANG 吴文光
   XIN KEDU – NEW MEASUREMENT GROUP 新刻度小组
   ZHUANG HUI 庄辉
2. CHEN SHAOXIONG 陈劭雄
   HONG HAO & YAN LEI 洪浩&颜磊
   NI HAIFENG 倪海峰
   ZHOU TIEHAI 周铁海
3. CAO FEI & OU NING 曹斐&欧宁
   HAN LEI 韩磊
   LIVING DANCE STUDIO 生活舞蹈工作室
   HIROSHI OHASHI 大桥宏, WANG MOLIN 王墨林, TONG SZE HONG 汤时康, ZHAO CHUAN 赵川
   RENT COLLECTION COURTYARD “收租院”
   SUI JIANGUO 隋建国
   WANG BING 王兵
   WANG YOUSHEN 王友身
   XIAO LU 肖鲁
   ZHAO YINOU 赵银鸥
   ZHENG GUOGU 郑国谷
4. WANG TUO 王拓

1. INDIVIDUALISM AS REACTION
个人主义：反应

DATONG DAZHANG
I Saw Death, 1998
Photograph
Variable dimensions

In *I Saw Death* we see Datong Dazhang himself, staring into the lens with intense focus, his mouth covered in white toothpaste, and his hand extended outward pointing beyond the frame and towards the viewer. In December 1998, the artist mailed this photograph to a group of friends, accompanied by the handwritten message "I saw death."

Born Zhang Shengquan in 1955 in the Shanxi province, Datong Dazhang was a self-taught artist who remained largely outside institutional contexts. In the late 1980s, he co-founded the underground art collective WR (*Wu Ren*, "Five People"), organizing a series of unofficial exhibitions in open-air settings, including one at the Yungang Grottoes. The group took part in the 1989 *China/Avant-Garde* exhibition at the National Art Museum in Beijing, staging *Mourning*, a quiet procession through the museum in white burial cloths and a symbolic funeral for Chinese modern art as it was institutionalized by the state. After increased censorship and the closure of one of their exhibitions in 1993, the group dissolved and Dazhang moved further into mail art and ephemeral practices.

Over the following years, Dazhang developed a highly personal and symbolically charged practice. He often worked through gestures that invoked philosophical questions around death, sacrifice, and spiritual transformation. In *Crossover* (1996), he planned to kill a sheep after carrying it across a river, referencing Buddhist and Daoist ideas of "crossing over." Ultimately, he released the animal and discarded the knife as fellow artist Song Dong, who thought the killing was too brutal, prevented Dazhang from carrying it out. Dazhang, on the other hand, regarded the performance as a failure. By the late 1990s, Dazhang's health had declined, and he became increasingly withdrawn. He filled his home with notes, quotations, and markings—transforming it into a kind of lived archive. Among the materials he returned to was Sylvia Plath's line of her poem *Lady Lazarus*: "Dying is an art, like everything else. I do it exceptionally well."[1] Dazhang's actions remained deeply internal, shaped by personal reflection and a sense of private necessity.

On the first day of the year 2000, Datong Dazhang ended his life in his home, which friends described as a "garbage palace." He left behind a note affirming what he had predicted years earlier: that he would die at the age of forty-five. His death marked a turning point in China's contemporary art scene—both as a moment of loss and as a rupture that signaled the end of a more fragile, experimental era.

1 Sylvia Plath, *Ariel* (London: Faber & Faber, 1965), p. 15.

Datong Dazhang (b. 1955, Hebei Province – d. 2000, Beijing), born Zhang Shengquan, he was conscripted into the army in 1970 and later worked in Guiyang and Datong before turning toward art in the mid-1980s. In 1987, he initiated the WR Group, organizing several open-air exhibitions in Datong. He took part in the landmark *China/Avant-Garde* exhibition in Beijing in 1989 with his performance *Mourning*. During the early 1990s he developed mixed-media paintings and staged independent exhibitions in Beijing, one of which was shut down before its opening. From 1993 to 1998, his "Mail Art" project circulated performance plans and conceptual sketches among China's art circles, while works such as *Death Lottery* (1994), *100 Days of No Sex* (1995), and *Crossing* (1996) expanded his experimental practice. He withdrew from the public in 1999 and ended his life on January 1, 2000.

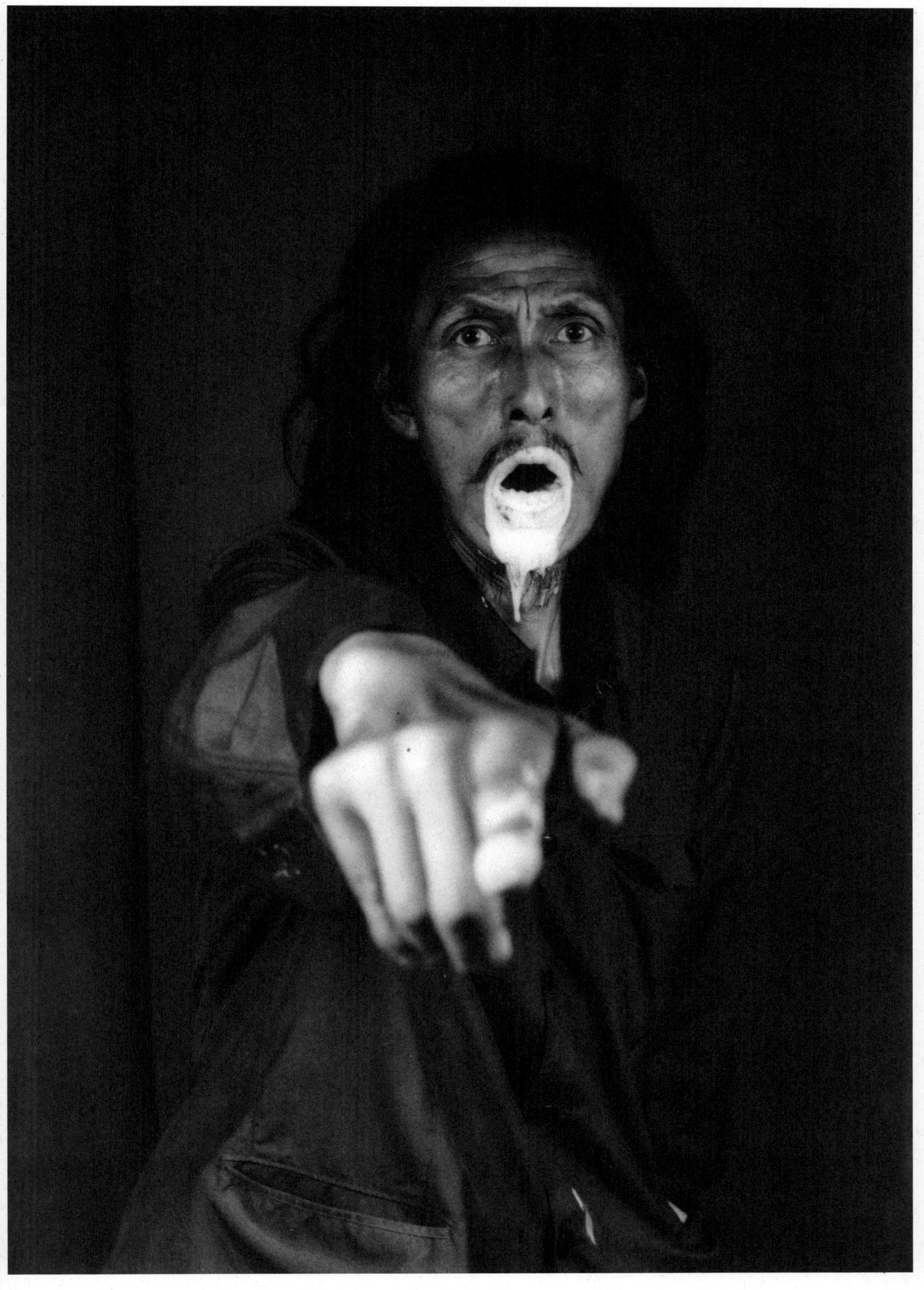

JIANG JIE

Long March – Xiao Shuxian 2002–Nowadays, 2002–2018

23 photographs
Variable dimensions

In 2002, curators Lu Jie and Qiu Zhijie executed the large-scale artistic project *Long March – A Walking Visual Display*. With a group of artists and artworks—one of them a sculpture of a baby made of fiberglass by Jiang Jie—they retraced the historical route of the Red Army's Long March and created a series of site-specific exhibitions, performances, and public dialogues across rural China.

Following the Long March's route, Lu Jie and Qiu Zhijie arrived in Moxi, a small town at the foot of the Hailuogou Glacier. They were awakened early by a knock at the door from a man who introduced himself as Xiao Honggang, the founder of the "Glacier Museum of Strange Rocks." He insisted they visit his collection and led them to his home, where conversation over food turned from population policies and rare stones to sculpture and meaning.

When Xiao learned about Jiang Jie's baby sculptures—fragile figures evoking vulnerability, constraint, and emotional ambiguity—he was transfixed. Lu Jie and Qiu Zhijie offered to entrust him with one of the sculptures. The Xiao family agreed to adopt it, naming it "Xiao Shuxian." A family photograph was taken at the front door, and the new "child" embraced by parents and siblings. A receipt of guardianship was signed, and the sculpture was placed in the household glass cabinet. This was the beginning of a relationship that would continue for decades.

The work *Long March – Xiao Shuxian 2002–Nowadays* is composed of twenty-three photographs taken over the years, documenting Xiao Shuxian's presence in the life of the Xiao family. Against the backdrop of Jiang Jie's critical investigations into life under China's One-Child Policy, the work stages a subtle tension: a sculpture born from artistic inquiry becomes embedded in the factual reality of a family.

Jiang Jie's practice often centers on the body as a site of contradiction. Her sculptures show infants rendered with the emotional registers of adulthood, which thereby appear caught between dependency and refusal. In *Xiao Shuxian*, these themes reach a temporal depth as the sculpture remains unchanged, while the family ages, children grow up, and political contexts shift. In this constellation, the body of the baby stands as a fixed point around which time turns.

Unlike her previous works, which place the individual in a contemporary social frame, this project inserts the figure into a living historical arc. The Xiao family's changing life is documented not as a private archive, but as a public record that reflects a generation of rural teachers, state policies, and post-revolutionary afterlives.

If Jiang Jie's earlier babies could be perceived as metaphors for fragility or disempowerment, *Xiao Shuxian* becomes a witness. Through repetition and quiet ritual, the photographs unsettle the boundaries between fiction and biography, art and adoption, permanence and change. The work not only commemorates a single performance; it extends performance into life itself.

Jiang Jie (b. 1963, Beijing) graduated from the Arts and Crafts School of Beijing (1984) and the Central Academy of Fine Arts (1991), where she is now Associate Professor in the Department of Sculpture. She has exhibited at the Yokohama Triennale (2005); Chengdu Biennale (2005, 2023); Wuhan Biennale (2022); and Anren Biennale (2017), and in major institutions including the Powerlong Museum (Shanghai); Pingshan Art Museum (Shenzhen); Today Art Museum (Beijing); Musée d'Art Contemporain de Lyon; Kuppersmühle Museum (Duisburg); National Museum of Contemporary Art (Oslo); and 4A Centre for Contemporary Asian Art (Sydney).

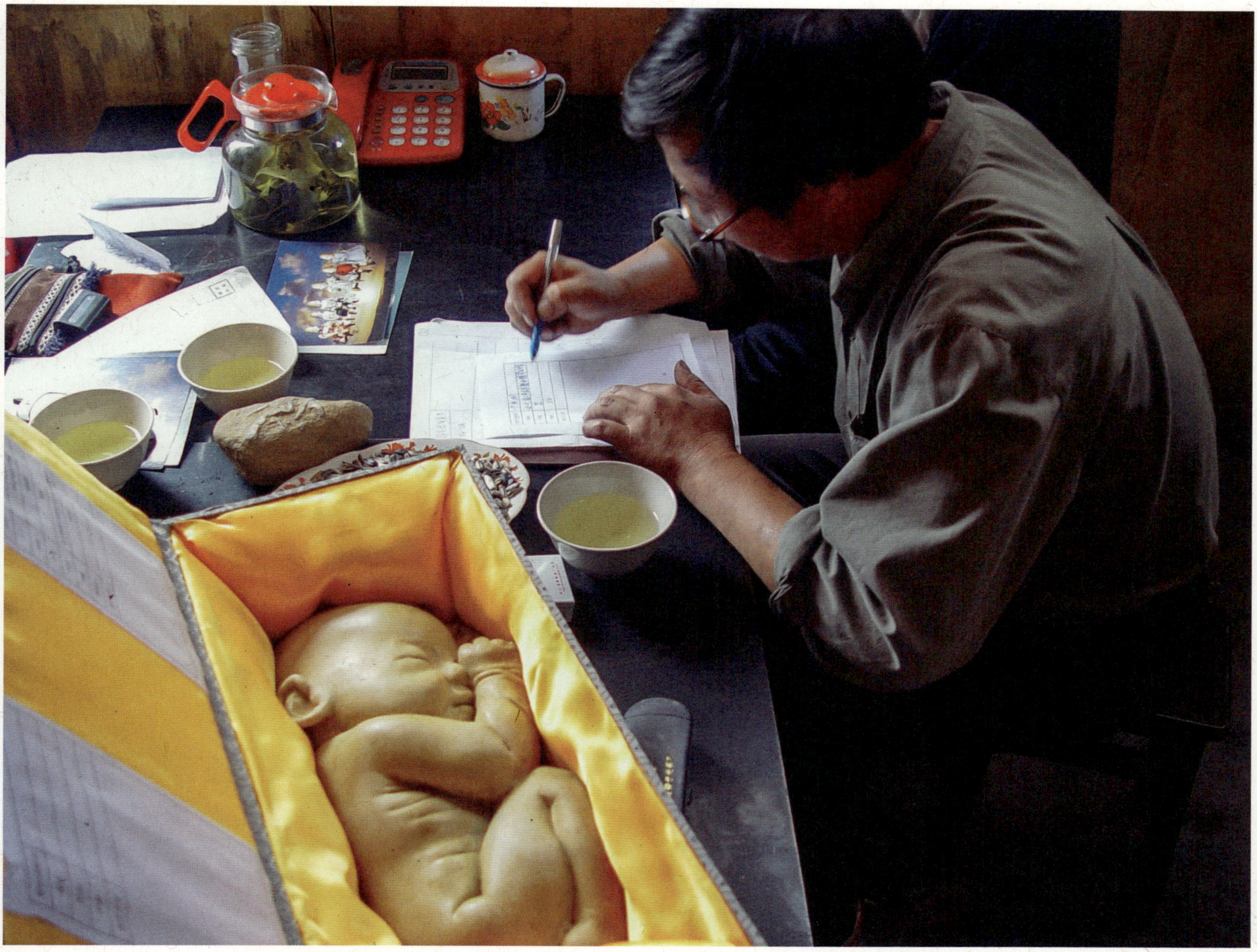

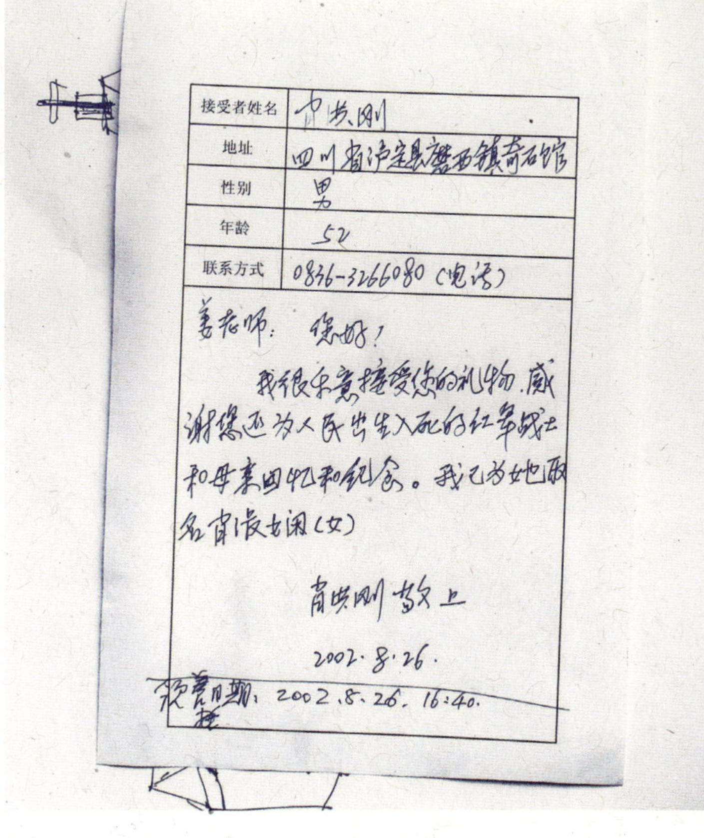

二万五千里文化传播中心

接受者姓名	肖兴刚
地址	四川省泸定县磨西镇奇石馆
性别	男
年龄	52
联系方式	0836-3266080（电话）

姜老师：您好！

我很乐意接受您的礼物，感谢您还为人民出生入死的红军战士和母亲回忆和纪念。我已为她取名肖长娟（女）

肖兴刚 敬上

2002.8.26.

领货日期：2002.8.26. 16:40.

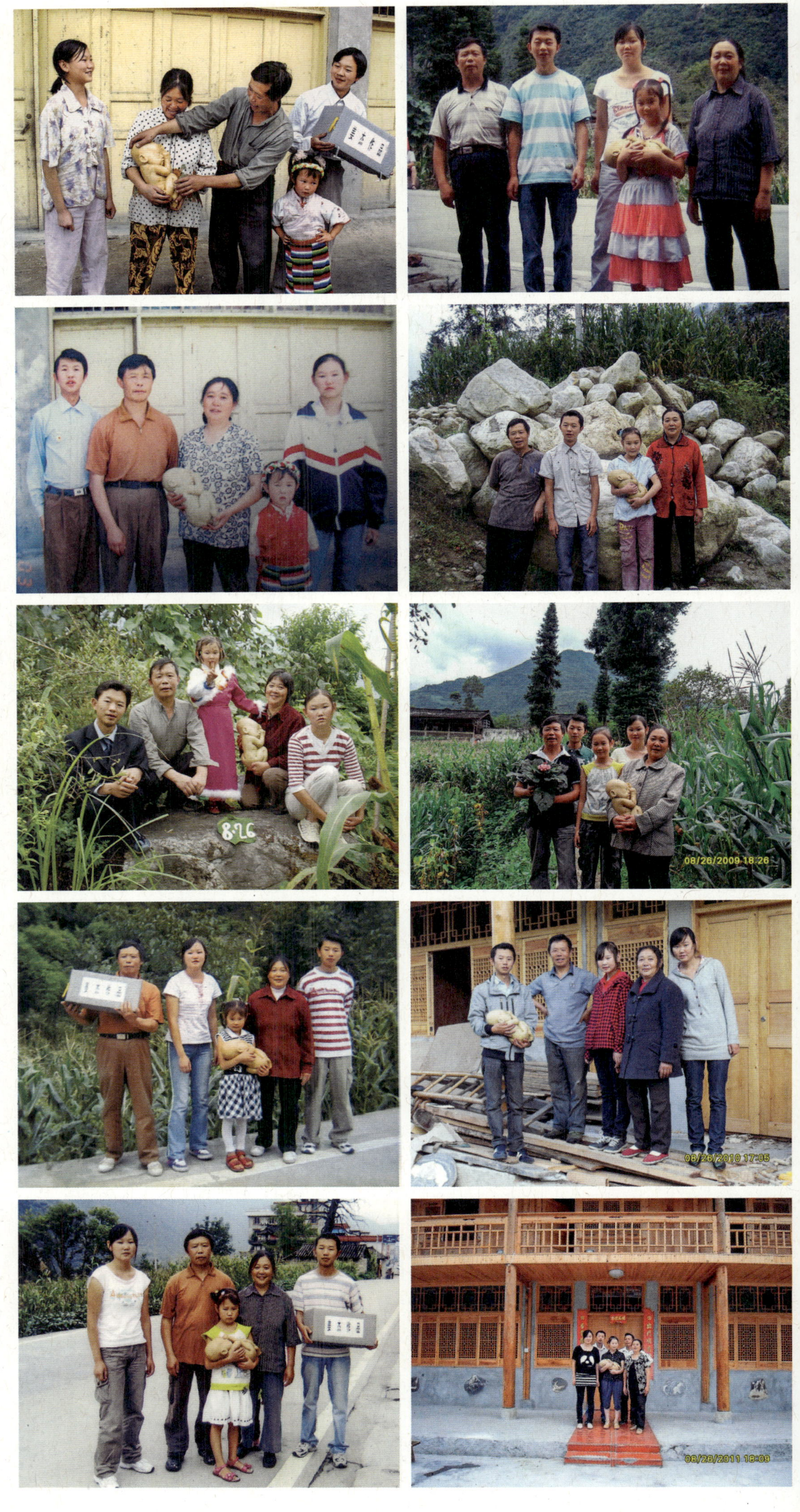
8.26
08/26/2009 18:26
08/26/2010 17:05
08/26/2011 18:09

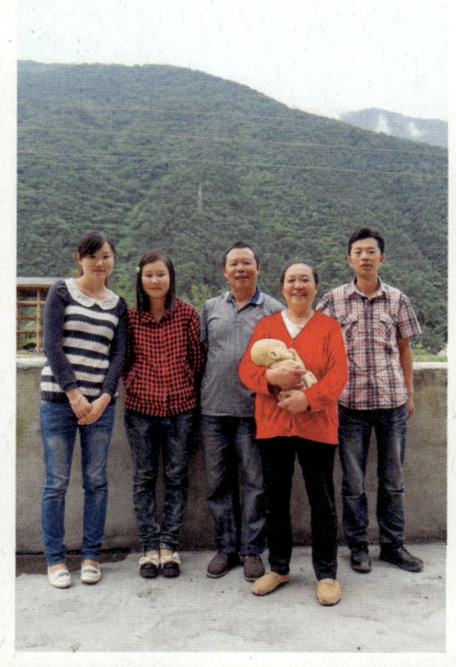
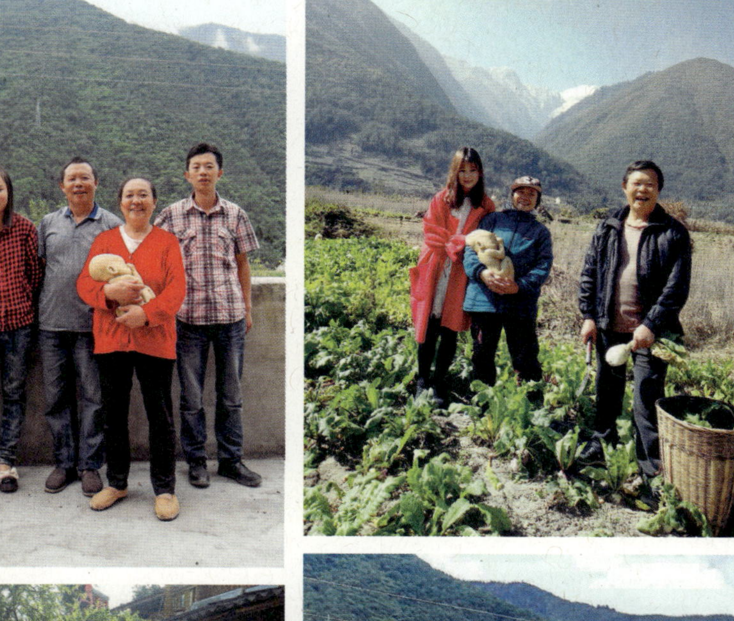
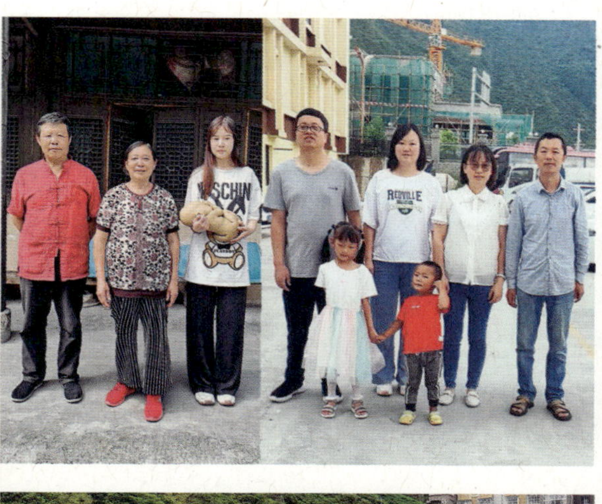
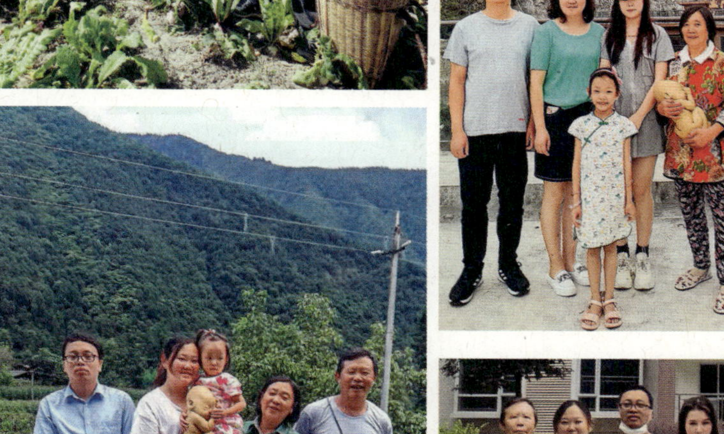
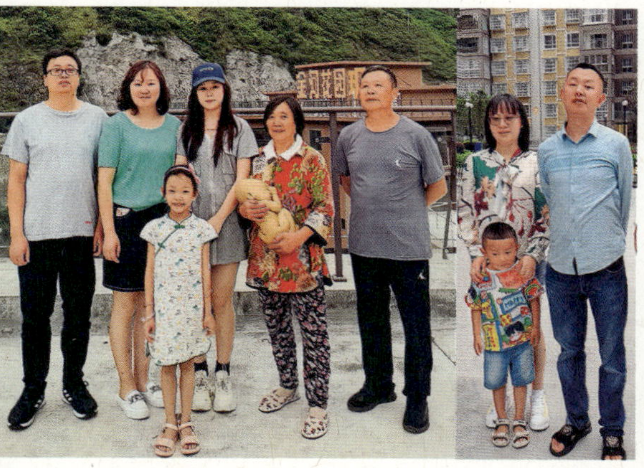
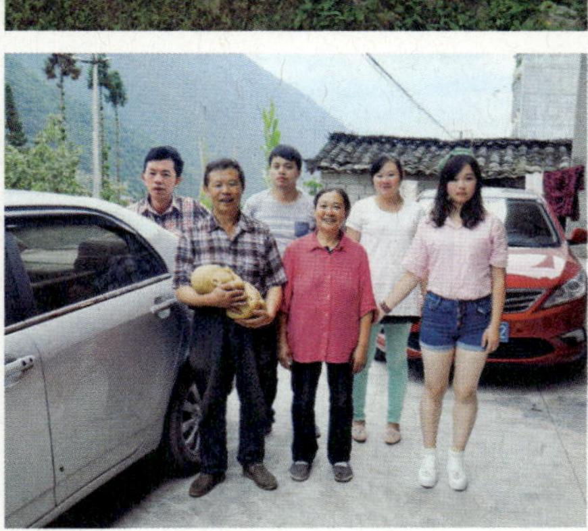
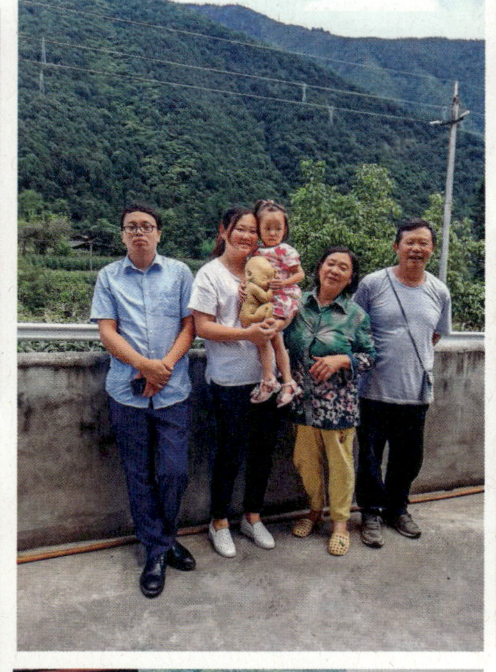
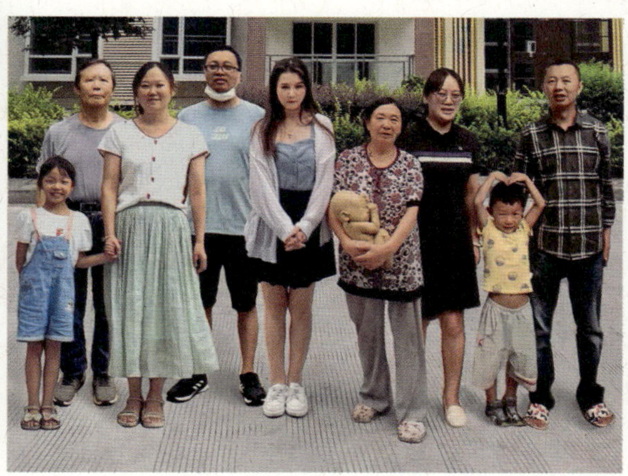
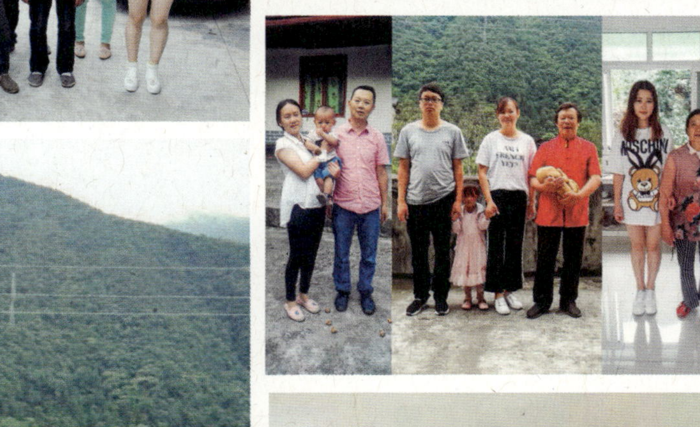
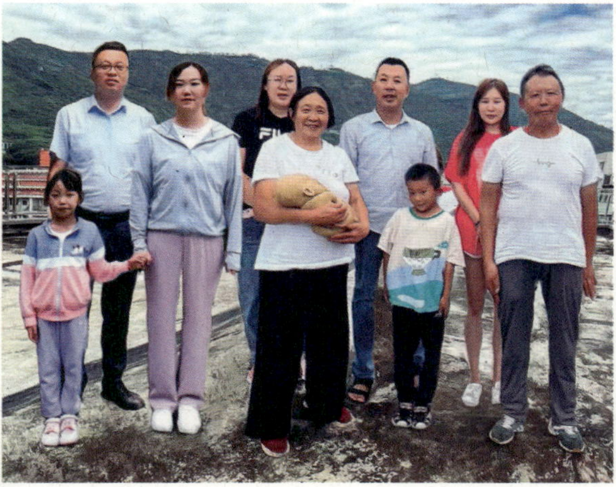
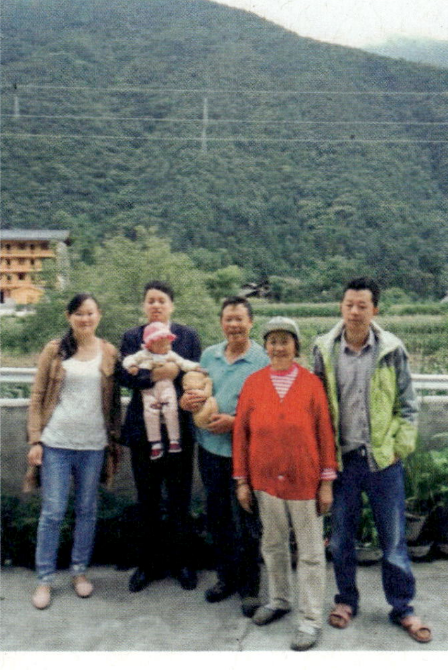
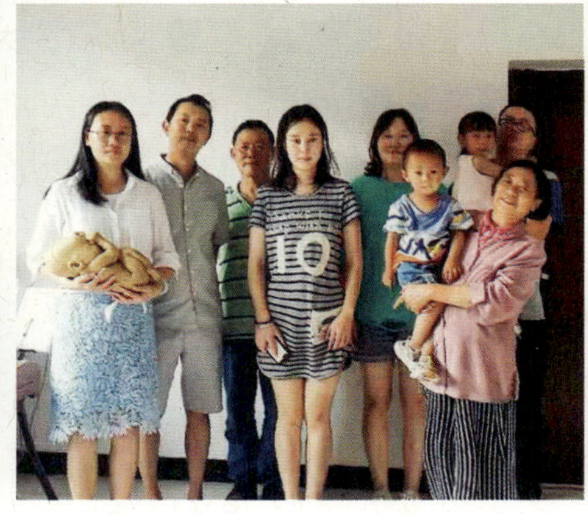
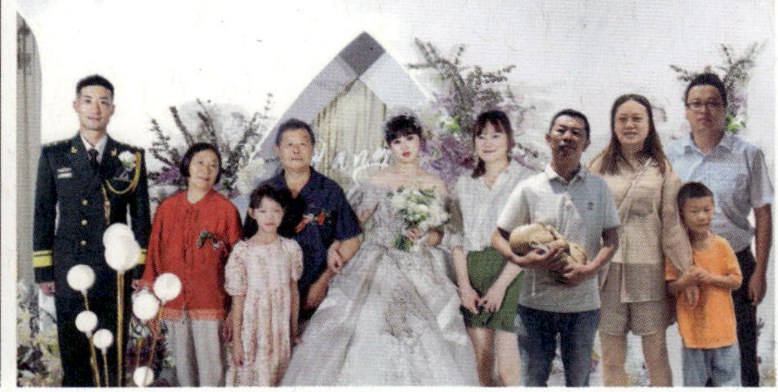

KAN XUAN

Ai!, 1999

Single-channel video (color, sound)
1:22 min

In her early video *Ai!*, Kan Xuan runs through a pedestrian underpass at Beijing's Fuxingmen station, one of the city's busiest transit hubs. The camera, handheld and unsteady, initially adopts her perspective: sprinting through a near-empty corridor, shouting her own name, answering herself each time with a determined, rising "Ai!" ("Here!"). Moments later, the view shifts and we now see the artist herself, moving against the swelling tide of commuters, repeating her call.

As the crowd thickens, the camera captures both her movement and the crowd's reaction. Some passersby turn and stare, others step aside. Most simply keep walking. Together with Kan Xuan, the camera pushes through the crowd, at times losing sight of her entirely. The contrast between the single body and the collective flow becomes a choreography and a quiet confrontation between individual subjectivity.

Shot with lo-fi directness, the work draws power from its rawness, embracing the textures of everyday life: fluorescent lights, worn floor tiles, the clatter of footsteps. What might initially seem absurd—a woman calling her own name in public—emerges as a profound act of self-address, a small rupture in the city's unceasing tempo.

Ka Xuan's call can be understood both as literal and existential. She summons herself in a crowd that neither answers nor obstructs. If there is resistance here, it is not against the people, but against anonymity and the loss of one's own name, voice, or presence in the crowd. "Kan Xuan!" is a call to the self, repeated until it reverberates with tension, humor, even desperation.

Ai! is a joke with serious undercurrents. It is also a subtle response to the psychological pressures of life in a rapidly modernizing China, where mass movement and collective conformity have become spatial facts and social ideals. In this sea of bodies, Kan carves out a space to insist on being felt, heard, seen. The artist appears as someone searching; for herself, for connection, for a kind of recognition that need not come from others. The call "Ai!" is not only a reply—it is a holding on. In this, *Ai!* belongs to a larger conversation about individualism in contemporary art, not as self-expression, but as a reaching toward coherence in the blur of the crowd.

The piece runs just over a minute, but its effect is lasting. There is no resolution. The crowd does not part; the tunnel remains crowded; Kan Xian does not reach the end of it. But in that brief span, Kan's voice cuts through, and for a moment, an individual among the crowd emerges, persistently calling herself into being.

Kan Xuan (b. 1972 Xuancheng, Anhui Province) is based between Beijing and Amsterdam. She studied at the China Academy of Art in Hangzhou (1993–97) and is a former resident at the Rijksakademie van beeldende kunsten (2002–03). Her work has been presented in solo exhibitions at UCCA, Beijing (2012); IKON museum, Birmingham (2016); Guangdong Times Museum, Guangzhou & Berlin (2019), among others. Group exhibitions include M+, Hong Kong (2024); Hammer Museum, Los Angeles (2023); Guggenheim Museum, New York (2018); Venice Biennale (2007 & 2013); Gwangju Biennale (2011); and Istanbul Biennale (2007). She is the recipient of the Contemporary Chinese Art Award (2014) and the Award of Art China (2020).

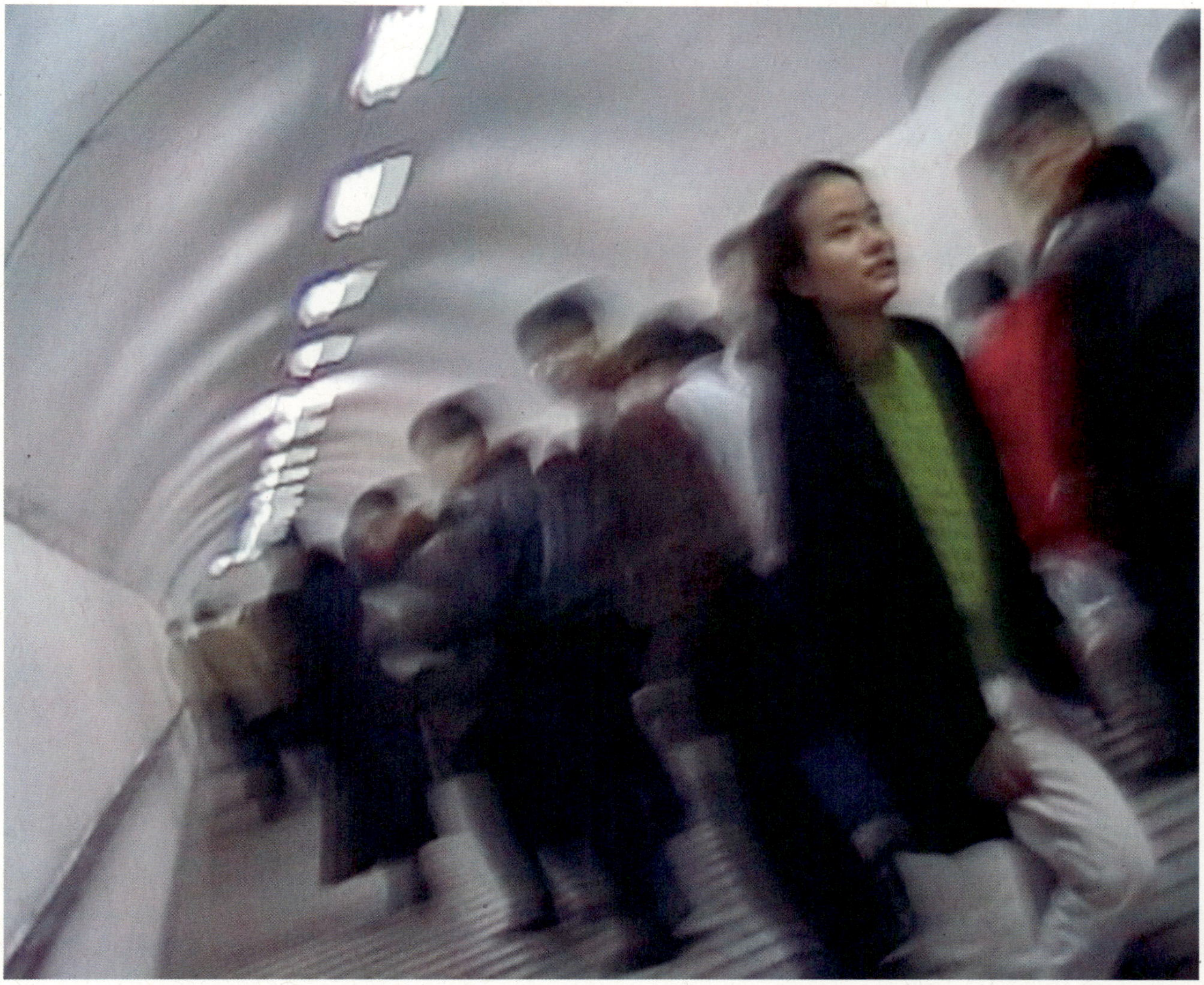

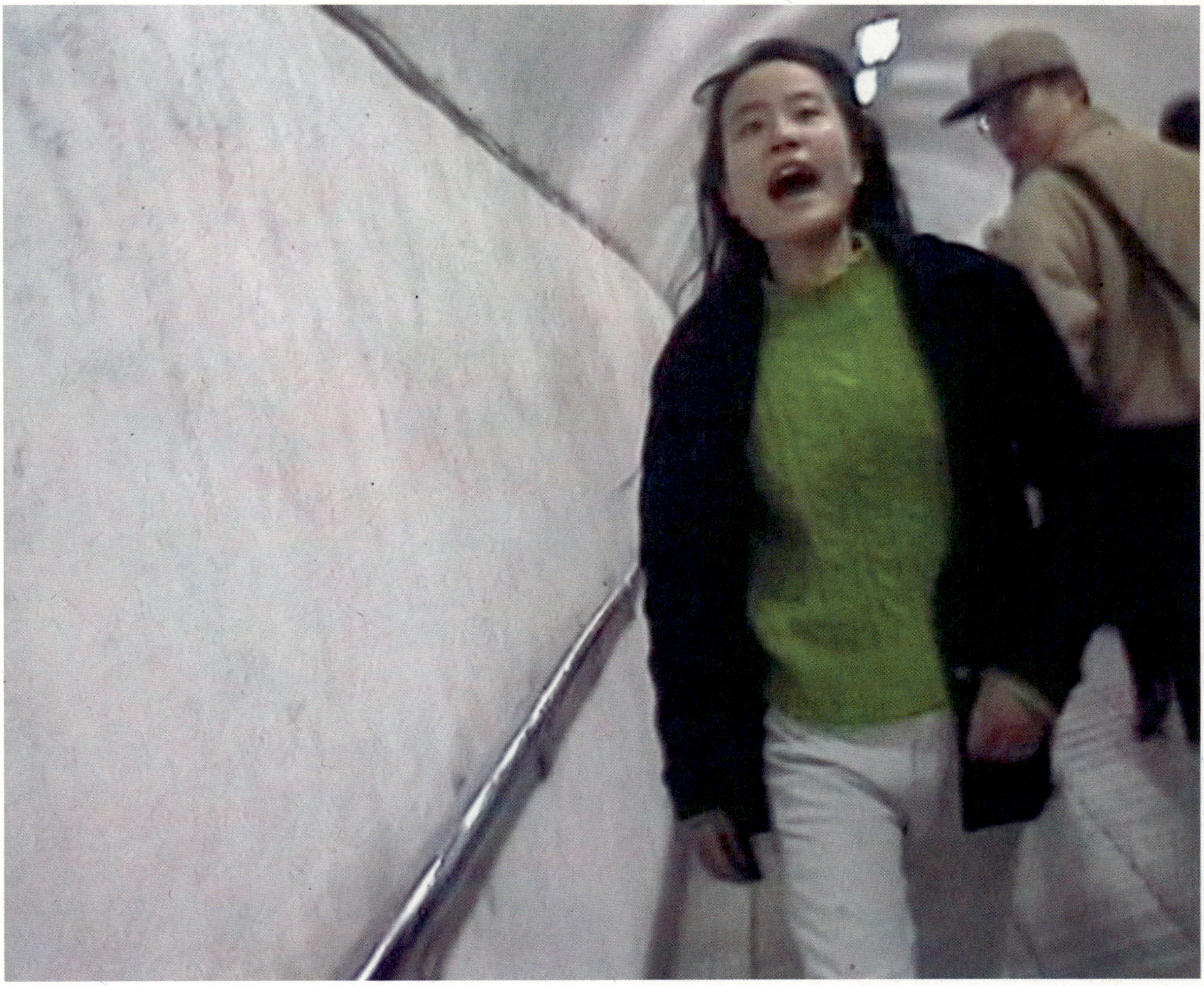

LIN YILIN

Safely Maneuvering Across Lin He Road, 1995

Single channel video (color, sound)
34:30 min

On a hot afternoon in 1995, artist Lin Yilin began stacking bricks on one side of Lin He Road, a major street in the rapidly transforming city of Guangzhou. By taking them from one end of the stack and carrying them to the front, he slowly and methodically moved the wall he had built, gradually walking it across the road. Over 90 minutes, this absurd, repetitive gesture transformed a temporary stable architectural object into a slow-moving interruption and Lin's labor became a quiet act of resistance, momentarily pausing the relentless flow of urban life.

In this simple action, Lin exposed the fragility of the systems that shape our everyday surroundings. The documentation video of his performance shows cars swerving and one can hear them honk while pedestrians walk by and some stop to watch. Lin managed to suspend the usual rhythm of the city, if only briefly. His brick wall was neither a protest nor a monument, but a self-imposed obstacle that compelled others to notice, adjust, and reroute and thereby to test the power of the individual in the backdrop of a changing world.

Performed at a time when China's urban centers were undergoing rapid development, *Safely Maneuvering Across Lin He Road* challenges the viewer to consider who shapes the city and at what cost. Lin Yilin, a founding member of the Big Tail Elephant Working Group, used performance to confront the physical and ideological effects of modernization, merging sculpture, endurance, and street theater.

Lin uses his own body as an intervention; the brick wall both protects and needs to be protected in its mobile and provisional state. With no clear goal other than its own persistence, the wall reclaims space not through dominance but through movement and time. The artist's body repeating the same task again and again, asserts an individual rhythm against the high-speed flow of cars, commerce, and capital.

"Safety was a big problem in China's road traffic in the 1990s,"[2] he recalls, and Lin titled the work only after completing it. That anxiety lingers in the performance itself, but so does its quiet determination which creates moments of disruption and stillness in the turbulent flow of urban life. Lin Yilin creates a pause, a temporary space in which individual agency becomes both visible and possible.

2 Nonny de la Peña, "Nonny de La Peña in Conversation with Lin Yilin," *Asia Art Archive*, September 18, 2017, https://aaa.org.hk/en/like-a-fever/like-a-fever/nonny-de-la-pea-in-conversation-with-lin-yilin.

Lin Yilin (b. 1964 Guangzhou), lives and works between New York and Guangzhou. He studied at the Guangzhou Academy of Fine Arts and co-founded the Big Tail Elephant Group in 1990. His work has been featured in major international exhibitions, including *Cities on the Move* (1997); the 2nd Johannesburg Biennale (1997); the 1st Taipei Biennale (1998); the 4th Gwangju Biennale (2002), the 50th and 56th Venice Biennales (2003, 2015); documenta 12 (2007); the 10th Lyon Biennale (2009); and the 12th Havana Biennale (2015). Lin's work has been shown and collected by institutions such as the Guggenheim Museum, MoMA PS1, Kunsthalle Bern, MAXXI in Rome, and M+ in Hong Kong.

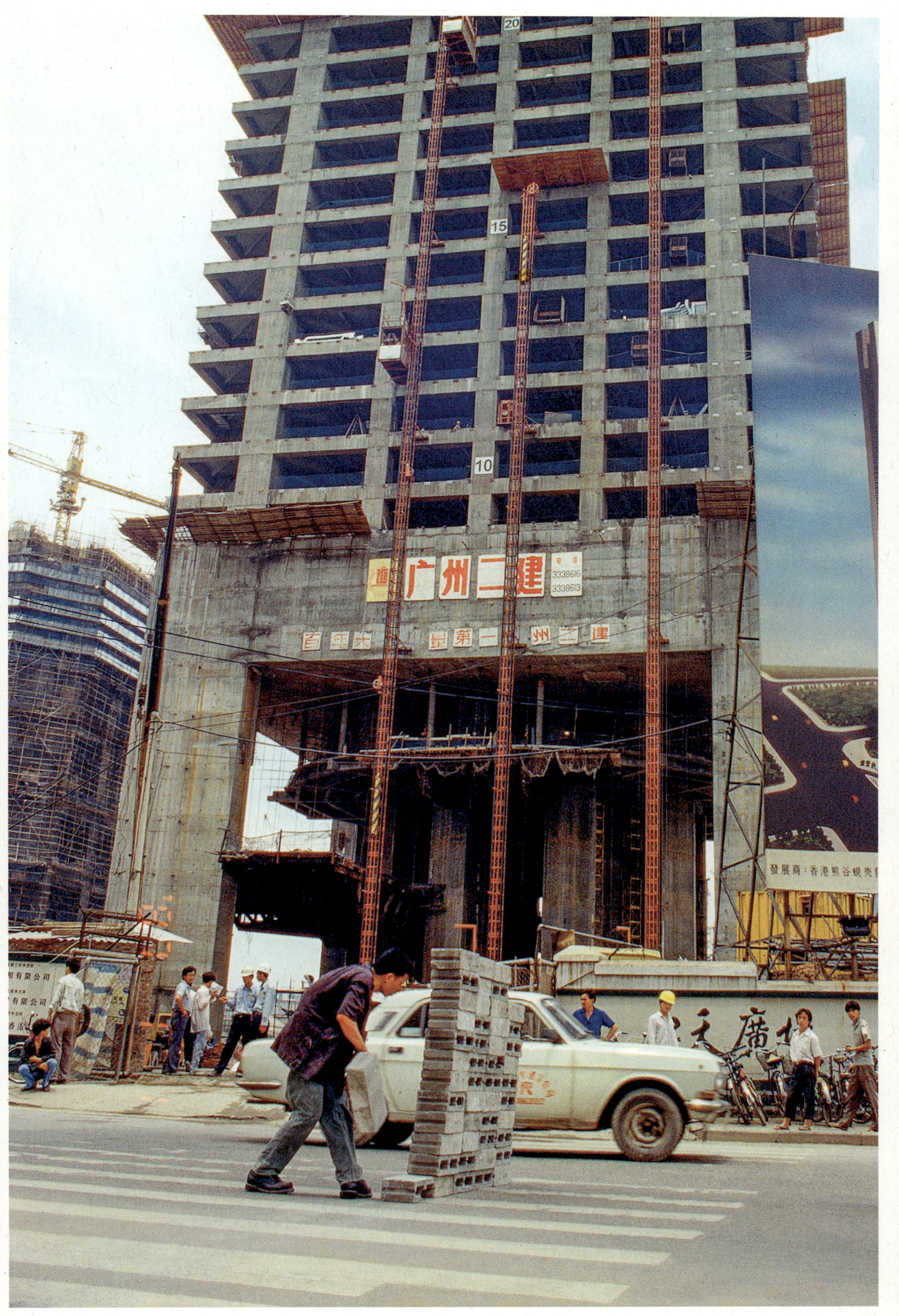
20
15
10
广州二建
电话
3338616
3338613
發展商：香港

MA LIUMING

Fen-Ma Liuming I, 1993

Photograph
120 × 79 cm

In *Fen-Ma Liuming* (1993), Ma Liuming introduces one of the most iconic personae in Chinese performance art. The photograph shows the artist sitting barefoot and composed, wearing a floral dress, scarf, and earrings. Shot from below, the image captures Fen-Ma Liuming looking calmly downward into the camera.

Ma's alter ego emerged in the early 1990s during his time in the Beijing East Village, an artist colony on the outskirts of the city. Known for its experimental practices and rejection of official art channels, the East Village became a catalyst for performance-based work that used the body as its primary material. Trained as a painter, Ma turned toward performance in search of a more direct, embodied language. Fen-Ma Liuming was born from a spontaneous gesture: persuaded by friends to try on make-up and a skirt, Ma was startled by his own reflection. "The inspiration he gave me was beyond my entire education," he later said, describing the persona as if it had an independent existence.

This persona was not simply a character, but a continuous practice. Through Fen-Ma Liuming, Ma staged performances that questioned the stability of identity, confronting gender as a system of signs. One such performance, documented in a series of black-and-white photographs, shows Fen-Ma Liuming walking the Great Wall of China. Wearing make-up and long, flowing hair, Ma walked naked and barefoot along the rough stones until his feet began to bleed. Occasionally encountering passersby, he remained silent. The video begins with him applying lipstick and brushing his hair against the wind. The historic structure of the Great Wall is here juxtaposed with a body that eludes categorization.

The work drew immediate attention from the authorities. In 1994, Ma was arrested and imprisoned for two months. The experience marked a shift in his tone. Earlier performances explored ambiguity—pleasure and pain, softness and resistance. Later works reflected a growing sense of constraint, surveillance, and interior struggle. Fen-Ma Liuming continued to appear internationally, but with increasing introspection.

Art historian Yuko Hasegawa observes that while Fen-Ma Liuming's face appears "mask-like" and contrasts with Ma Liuming's real body, fully exposed to the audience.[3] This tension between formal stillness and raw presence became a defining quality of Ma's work. He often cited the principles of Yin and Yang, aiming to balance inner and outer states, visibility and withdrawal.

In later years, performances as Fen-Ma Liuming continued as a series of "sleep" works, which the artist performed at numerous institutions. On site he would take a sleeping pill and remain unconscious. This way Fen-Ma Liuming slept at the opening of the Istanbul Biennale in the middle of the audience. On some occasions, the audience was invited to touch or interact with him while he was asleep. *Fen-Ma Liuming* opens a space for embodied questioning instead of protest or a confession. The persona embodies oppositions such as artist and subject, male and female, sane and mad which are neither affirmed nor denied. Apparent contradictions and dichotomies are placed side by side, asserting the possibility of remaining undefined.

3 Yuko Hasegawa, "Ma Liuming: The Politics of Non-Differentiation," in *Ma Liuming: Performances, Paintings, Sculptures*, ed. Eleonora Battiston and Liuming Ma (Bologna: Damiani, 2007), p. 27.

Ma Liuming (b. 1969, Huangshi, Hubei Province) studied at the Hubei Academy of Fine Arts (1987–91) and has lived and worked in Beijing since 1993. His work has been featured in major exhibitions at the Guggenheim Museum, New York; Tate Modern, London; Centre Pompidou, Paris; the Hirshhorn Museum, Washington, D.C.; Haus der Kunst, Munich; the Victoria & Albert Museum, London; San Francisco Museum of Modern Art (SFMOMA); and the 48th Venice Biennale. He has also shown at the Busan, Chengdu, Gwangju, and Nanjing Biennales, as well as UCCA Beijing, Minsheng Art Museum, and Taikang Art Museum.

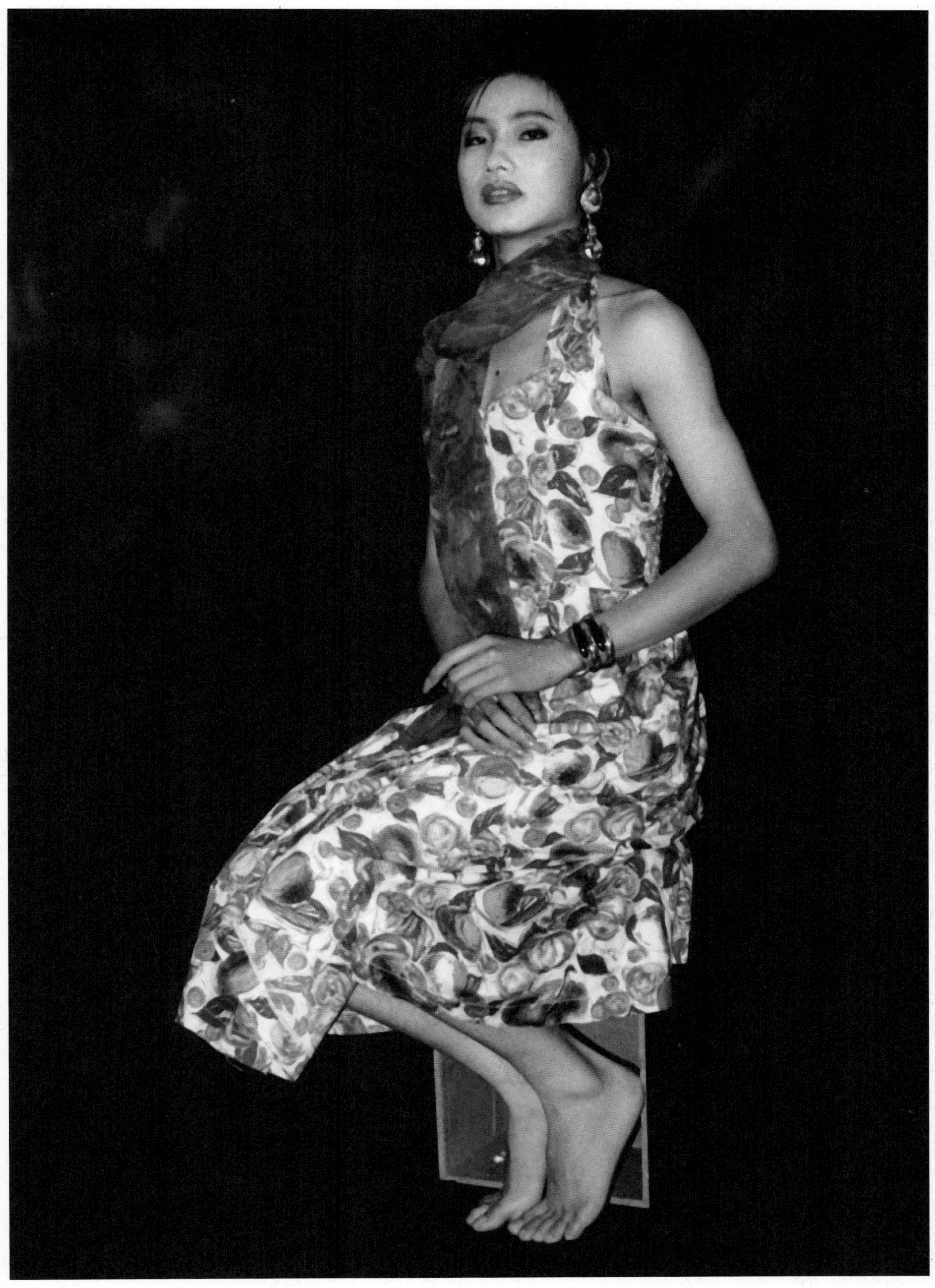

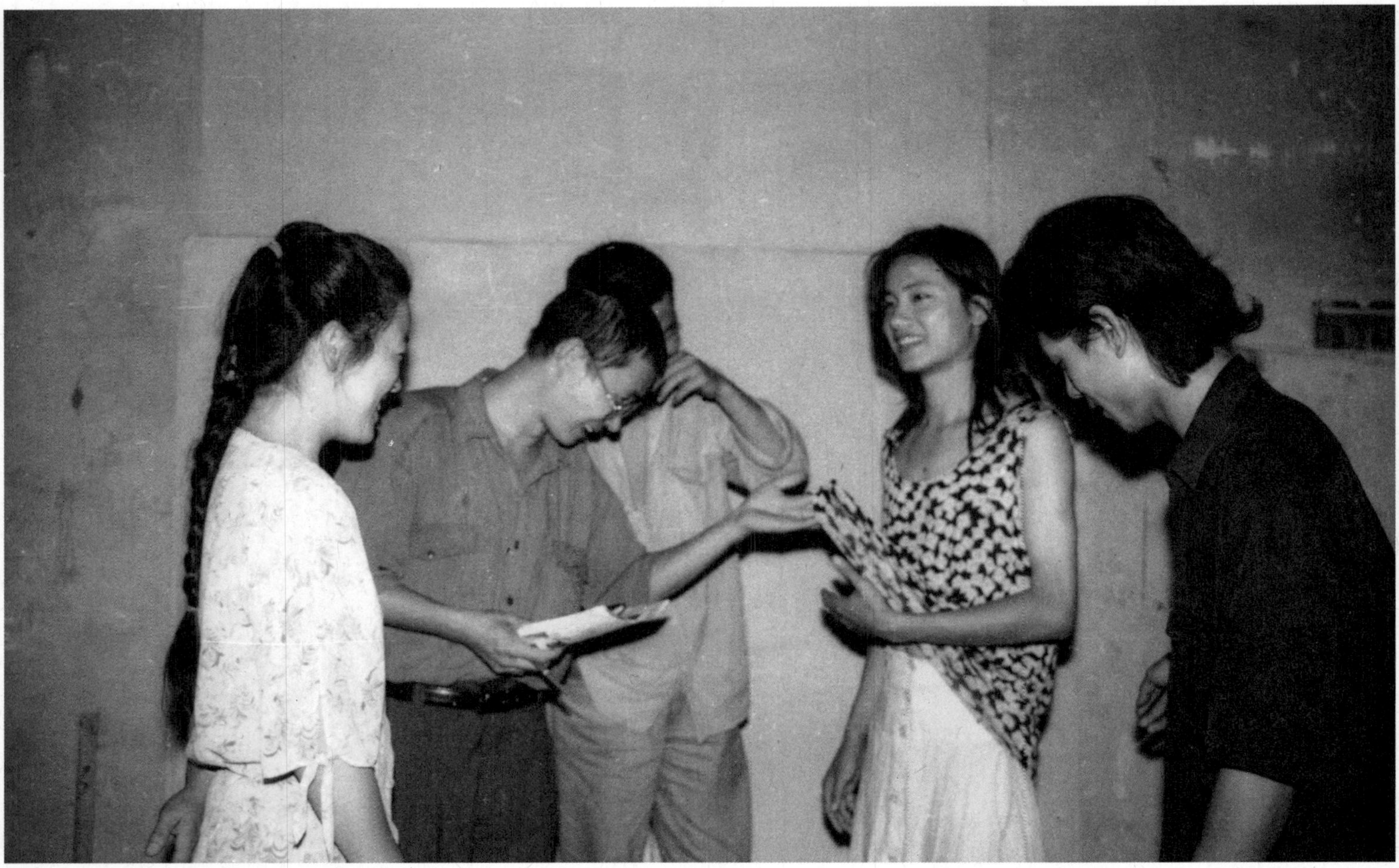

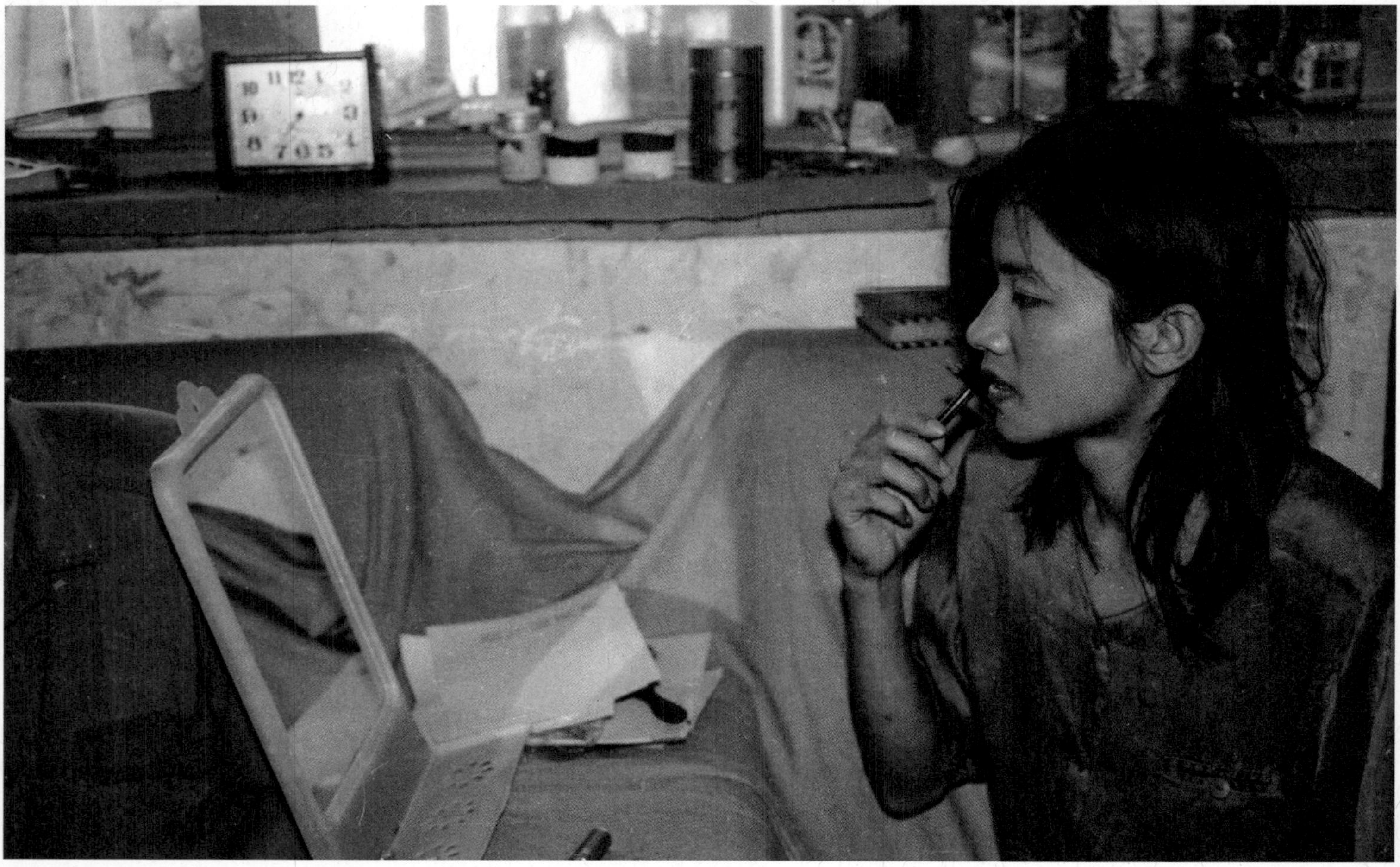

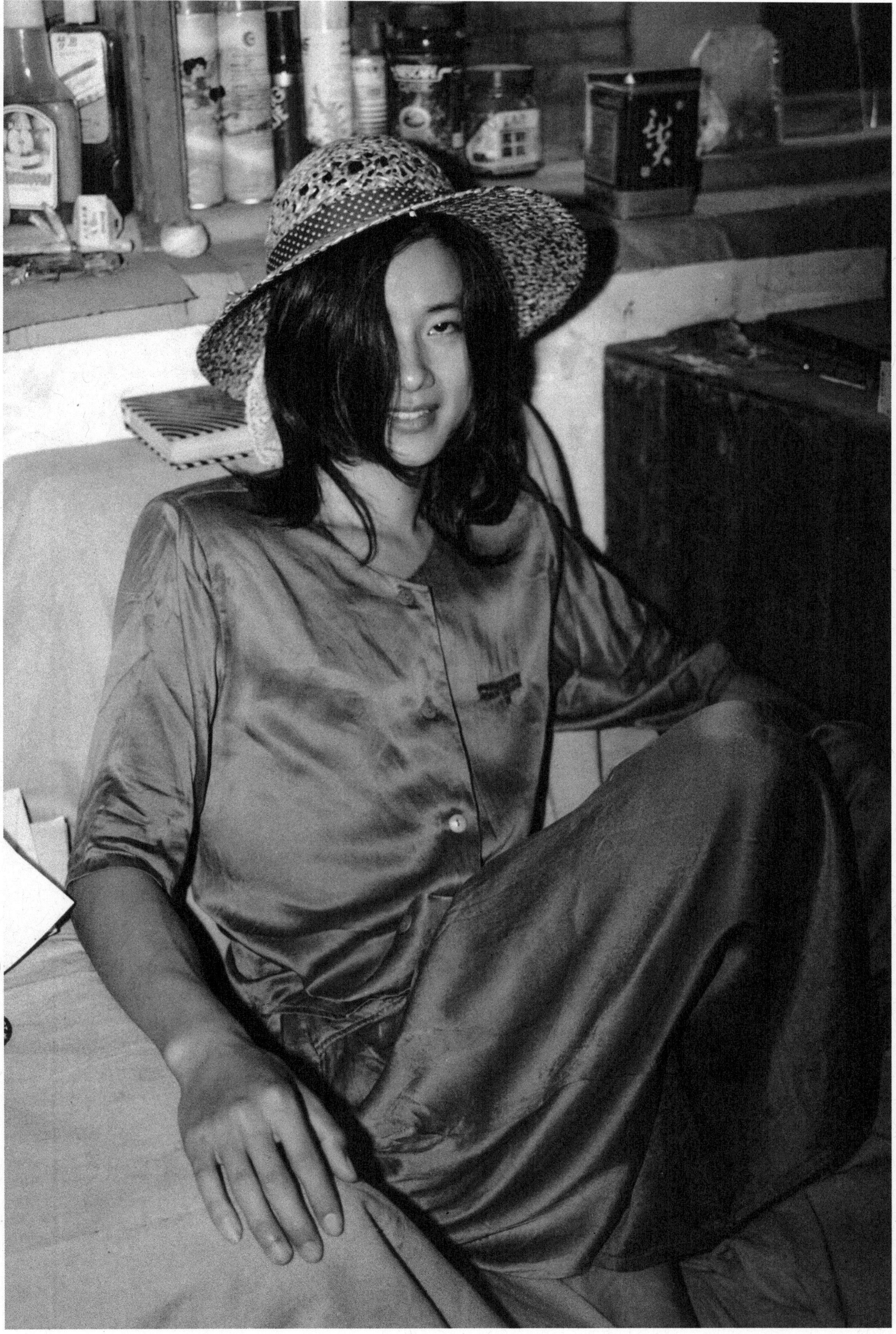

WANG GUANGYI

Study for *Cold War Aesthetics*, 2007

Acrylic and felt-tip pen on photocopy, 30 × 21 cm

Study for *Quarantine—All Food is Potentially Poisonous*, 1996

Acrylic and ball-point pen on paper, 37.5 × 26 cm

Wang Guangyi developed an artistic practice that critically examines political imagery, power, and ideology. His youth was defined by the Cultural Revolution and its visual language, and after studying at the Zhejiang Academy of Fine Arts in Hangzhou, where he first came into intensive contact with Western art history and philosophy, he began to combine the political symbols of socialism with the aesthetics of Western consumer culture.

Wang Guangyi became known in particular for his iconic series *Great Criticism*, in which he confronts brand logos of Western corporations with images of Maoist propaganda. However, his work goes far beyond this approach, which is often referred to as "Political Pop." At the heart of his work is an interest in the mechanisms that generate political, social, and cultural power through images. The personal confrontation with the ideological influences of his own biography plays just as much a role as the reflection on global processes of exchange and influence.

A decisive turning point in Wang Guangyi's career came after his participation in several groundbreaking international exhibitions in the early 1990s, including *China Avantgarde* in Berlin, the Venice Biennale, and the São Paulo Biennale. These experiences not only gave him a new understanding of the international art scene but also led to a fundamental reassessment of his own artistic role.

Wang made a conscious effort to dissociate himself from the label "pop artist." He was irritated by the reduction of his works to a cultural commentary that merely expressed political meanings in iconic images. Instead, he developed a deeper concept of globalization not limited to the concept of East versus West. He juxtaposed his own experiences as an actor within the global art system with his return to everyday life in China, without, however, adopting a definitive cultural position. Instead, Wang chose to deliberately suspend his political and cultural evaluations in order to pursue a conceptual strategy that maintains a systematic distance from reality. As part of his artistic process, he produced numerous studies that can be understood as thought models, methodical preliminary considerations, and precursors to later works.

The studies from the 1990s and 2000s collected here document Wang Guangyi's search for a new artistic strategy that purposefully distances itself from direct image criticism. They are conceptual sketches and methodical approaches to themes that have had a lasting influence on his work: control over the body and society, the symbolism of the Cold War, and the paranoid structures of ideological systems.

His cycle *International Politics* (1993), a series of canvas pieces depicting international leading political figures in interaction, is an observation on ideological gestures of international politics. In the study for the work, Wang Guangyi develops an abstract visual vocabulary to capture the complexity of international power relations. Instead of just depicting people, as in the final work, traces of his earlier visual language can still be seen in this study: an iconic sales stand for Chupa Chups lollipops, which also serves as an advertising pillar for a newspaper article. Interestingly, in the work's final execution, Wang bids farewell to the last traces of Political Pop.

With *Blood Test—Everyone is a Potential Virus Carrier* (1996), Wang transfers control over the body into a medical scenario: every person appears potentially suspicious, every trace becomes an indication of a threat, portraying the paradoxical relationship and psychological reality of the controller and the controlled who mutually monitor each other. The final version of *Blood Test—Everyone is a Potential Virus Carrier* consists of ready-made objects such as vegetables, fruits, supermarket shelves, and hygiene posters; the study here serves as a draft of just such a poster.

His *Quarantine—All Food is Potentially Poisonous* (1996) addresses the political dimension of mistrust and social hygiene in a similar way. Everyday, seemingly harmless consumer goods are under general suspicion. The study for *Quarantine—All Food is Potentially Poisonous* gives a good impression

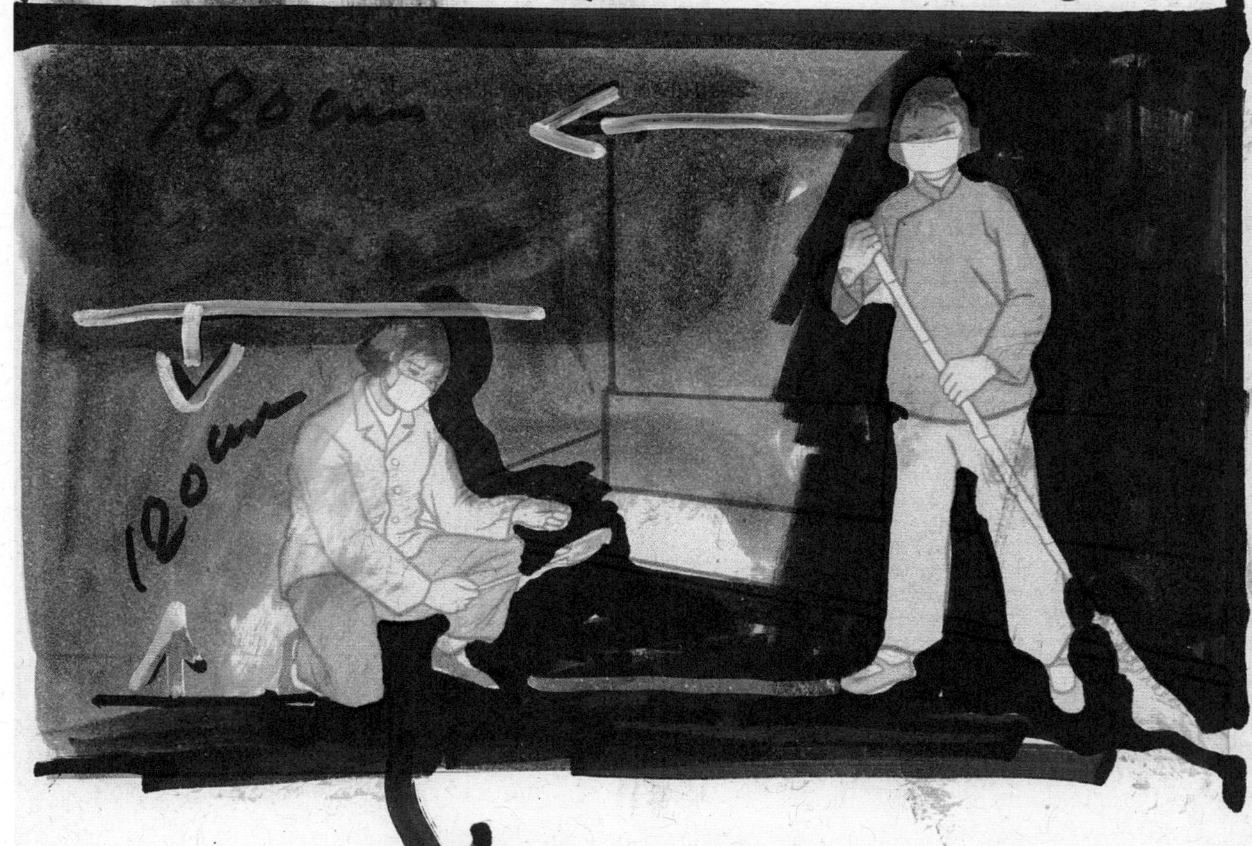
所有关于哲学和政治的本质问题，
就是寻找敌人。
180cm
120cm
冷战美学，
2008 王广义
今天世界的政治格局仍然是
冷战时期埋下的种子的结果。

of the later-realized installation for which the artist recreated a small neighborhood supermarket decorated with propaganda posters—warnings about the dangers of poor hygiene taken from a quarantine station. This juxtaposition with the usual supermarket products confronts anxieties and fears related to hygiene and public health, particularly those associated with the end of the Cold War. Wang interweaves these reflections on everyday control—the fear of the invisible that could penetrate the body from the outside—with the paranoia that pervades both political and economic systems.

Wang Guangyi's series *Cold War Aesthetics* (begun in 2007) continues his critical engagement with the visual grammar of ideological power. Drawing on the imagery and rhetoric of the Maoist era (1949–76), the series reanimates the visual vocabulary of that period, particularly the didactic aesthetics of military training manuals and heroic portrayals of workers and peasants. The installation combines human-like sculptures with large backdrops, creating a theatrical, immersive environment. The sculptures evoke the rigid, codified gestures and postures of Cold War propaganda, yet their staging introduces a performative, almost uncanny dimension. The contrast between the lifelessness of the figures and the heroic fervor of the imagery behind them produces a space of critical distance: a tableau where the aesthetics of discipline and ideological control are exposed as constructs rather than truths. This large-scale project blends the symbolic systems of the Cold War with a contemporary lens that questions their lasting effects. Wang's approach does not merely replicate the aesthetics of the past, but rather recontextualizes them, revealing the tensions between collective ideals and individual agency, between propaganda and its afterlife in the present. The two studies for *Cold War Aesthetics* give an insight into Wang's conceptual thought processes as well as practicalities about the execution of the final work. The drawing shows the dimensions of the sculptures and considerations for using dry ice to create fog.

Wang Guangyi is interested in the codes of power that function beyond concrete images—an aesthetic of control articulated through structure, scheme, and system. His studies offer a glimpse into a conceptual laboratory that he would later expand into large-scale paintings, sculptures, and installations. They mark a moment when he began to understand his artistic practice as conceptual research—beyond direct critique, beyond fixed political positions. These works combine personal reflections on ideological influence with a broader investigation into the mechanisms of global image production.

In the later-executed sculptures, the individual is never at the center. Instead, the human figure appears as part of a larger system, a visual representative of structural functions such as defense, discipline, or ideological coordination. Wang references the compositional strategies of propaganda posters and instructional diagrams where the individual is subsumed under collective purpose. In this way, the figures are not portraits but avatars: de-individualized, schematic, and performative.

Wang Guangyi's work confronts the limited space left for individuality within political and visual regimes of control. His studies explore how subjectivity is shaped, assigned, and instrumentalized within those frameworks. Individualism, in this context, becomes a question of how one navigates structure, not how one escapes it. These drawings are therefore more than preparatory sketches. They constitute a field of artistic inquiry—an effort to visually chart the relationships between art, politics, and power, while asking what kind of subject, if any, can emerge within them.

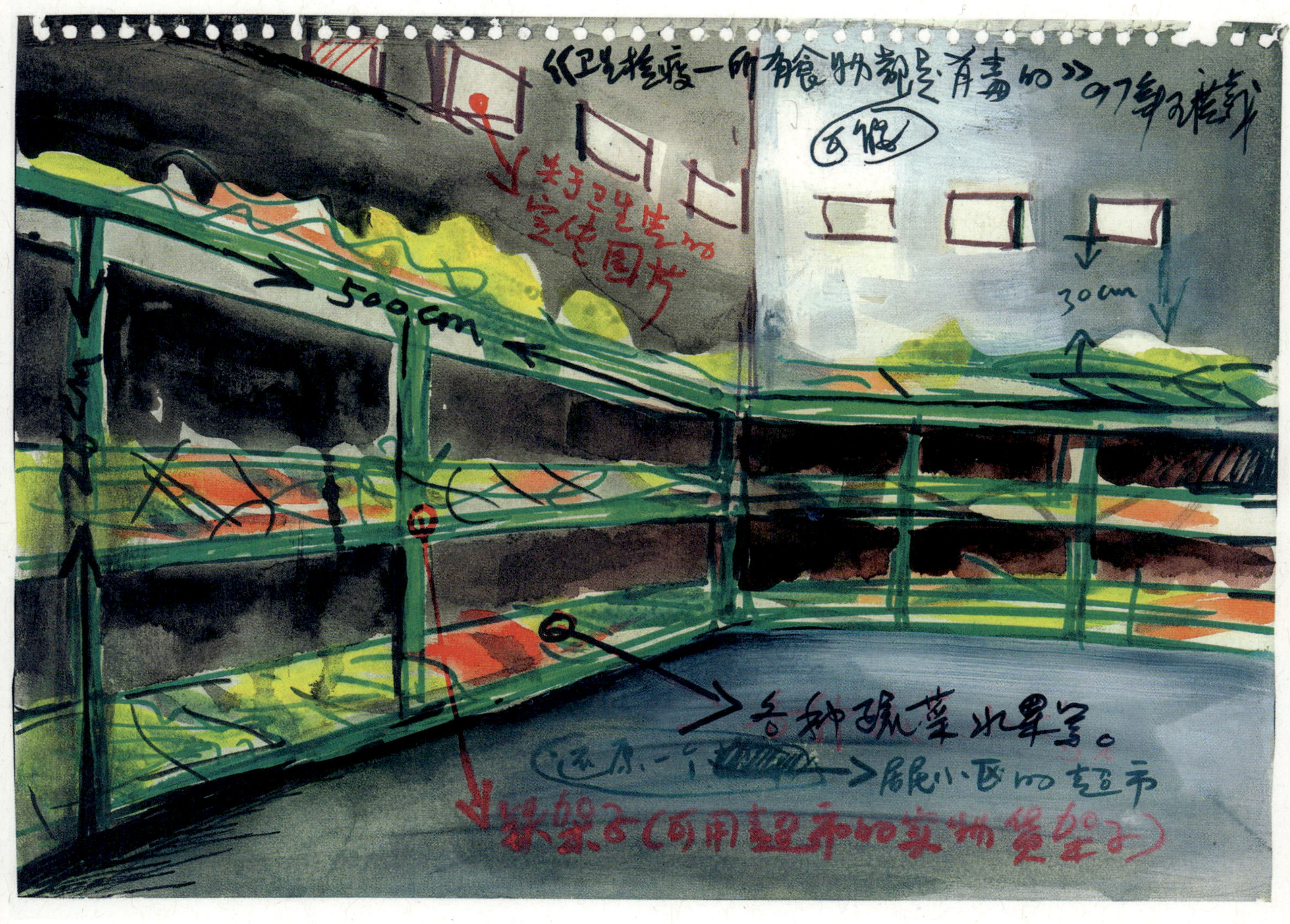

Wang Guangyi (b. 1957, Harbin) graduated from the China Academy of Art, Hangzhou (1984) and lives and works in Beijing. Recent solo exhibitions include *Wang Guangyi. Obscured Existence* (Palazzo Pitti, Florence, 2023) and *Think of the Long Trip Home: Sketches by Wang Guangyi* (Tsinghua University Art Museum, Beijing, 2024). He has shown at the Venice Biennale (1993); São Paulo Biennial (1994); and Busan Biennale (2016), and in major institutions including the Solomon R. Guggenheim Museum, New York and Bilbao; Centre Pompidou, Paris; Tate Modern, London; Museum Ludwig, Cologne; MAC Marseille; and OCT Contemporary Art Terminal, Shenzen. His work is in collections such as SFMOMA, San Francisco, the Ford Foundation, New York, M+ Hong Kong, and the National Gallery of Armenia.

WU WENGUANG

Diary: Snow, November 21, 1998, 1998

Video (color, sound)
12 min

On November 21, 1998, a group exhibition titled *It's Me*, curated by Leng Lin, was scheduled to open at the Imperial Ancestral Temple near Beijing's Forbidden City. It was snowing heavily that day and the area around the temple was covered in snow. Faced with a sudden cancellation notice, everyone who arrived for the opening was denied entry. In *Diary: Snow, November 21, 1998*, Wu Wenguang captures what followed: artists, curators, critics, and journalists lingering in the cold, standing in small groups outside the locked gates, talking, waiting, and reflecting.

Shot from Wu Wenguang's handheld camera, the video begins en route to the venue. Snow-covered roads slide past the car window as Wu speaks casually about friends and recent encounters. When the camera arrives at the scene, the observational tone remains unchanged. Despite the exceptional circumstances that might have provoked extreme reactions from the participating artists, the atmosphere remains calm. The camera just captures people, left outside, talking in the snow. The camera, too, is left out, barred like the others while the art is locked in. What might have been a chronicle of an exhibition becomes, instead, a quiet record of its erasure.

Wu Wenguang's video is one of the few surviving on-site documents of the exhibition *It's Me*, but its significance lies beyond historical record. As Yan Xiaoxiao notes, Wu's work marks a turning point—not just in Chinese independent documentary, but in the artist's own practice. In the years that followed, Wu turned his camera more insistently on himself and his surroundings, developing a diaristic, self-reflective mode of filmmaking that departed from conventional reportage. In *Diary: Snow, November 21, 1998*, the seeds of that shift are already visible.[4] The subject of the film is less the cancellation itself than the moment that cancellation creates: a space of waiting, a collective pause in which nothing happens, but much is felt.

The exhibition *It's Me* had been intended as a self-referential, even introspective response to the pressures of a globalizing art world. Rather than claiming fixed cultural positions, its artists sought to affirm fluid, transnational subjectivity. In this light, Wu Wenguang's film takes on added resonance. The camera doesn't document a protest or assert an argument. It lingers with a group of individuals caught between personal expression and systemic constraint, between artistic intention and political suppression.

Diary: Snow, November 21, 1998 resists any form of narrating spectacle or dramatizing resistance. By quiet and close observation and by physically joining the group of people denied entry, it reveals quiet forms of endurance and makes the viewers a part of it.

4 Ding Liu et al., *The 7th Shenzhen Sculpture Biennale: Accidental Message: Art is Not a System, Not a World* (Lingnan Fine Arts Publishing House, 2012).

Wu Wenguang (b. 1956, Yunnan Province) studied Chinese Literature at Yunnan University (1978–82) and moved to Beijing in 1988. A pioneering figure in Chinese independent documentary, his work has been shown at the Museum of Modern Art (MoMA), New York; Centre Pompidou, Paris; Yamagata International Documentary Film Festival; International Documentary Film Festival Amsterdam (IDFA); San Francisco International Film Festival; and Open City Documentary Festival, London. In 2005, he founded the Village Documentary Project to encourage rural villagers to document their own lives. In 2010, he initiated the Folk Memory Project, which records personal histories of famine survivors across China.

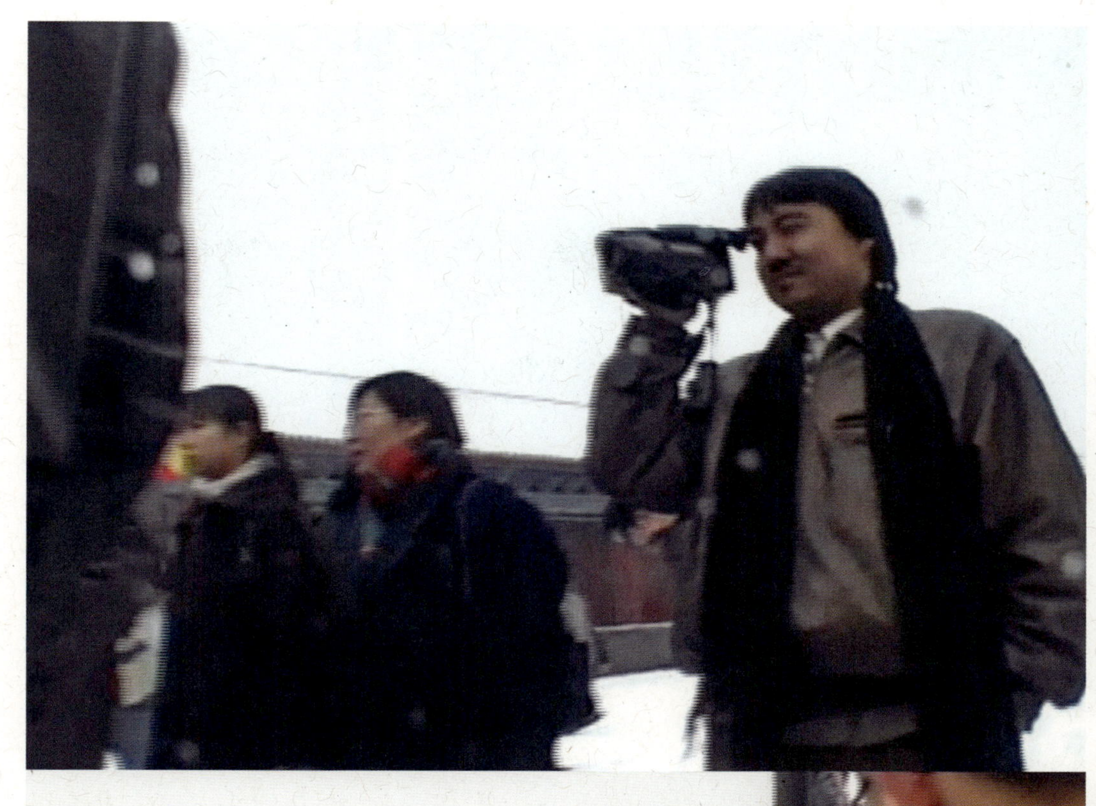

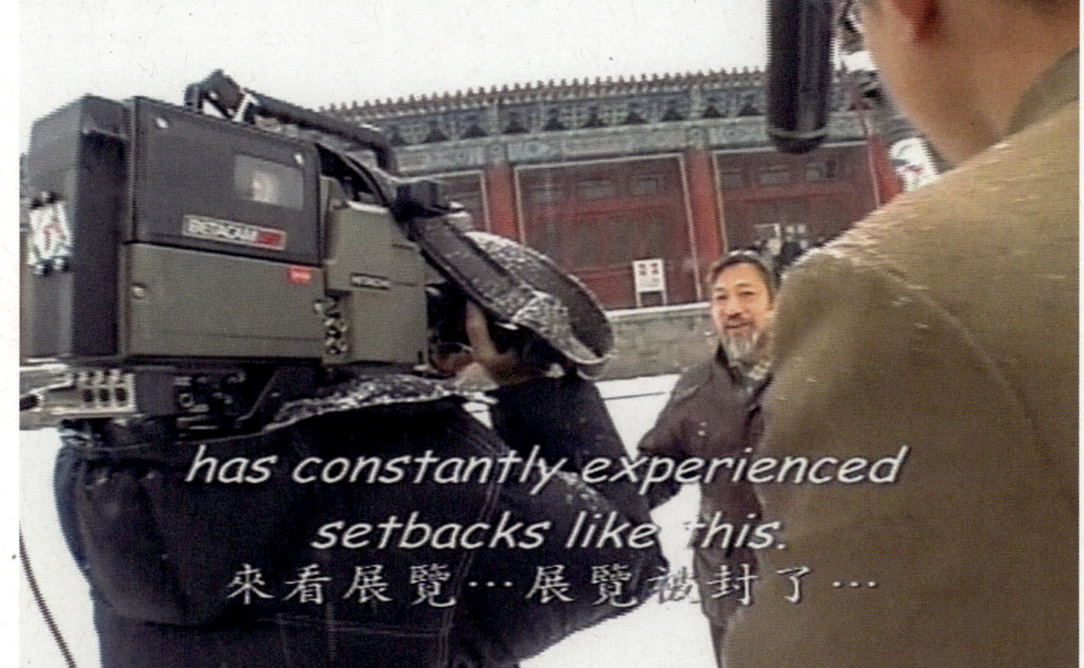
has constantly experienced
setbacks like this.
來看展覽…展覽被封了…

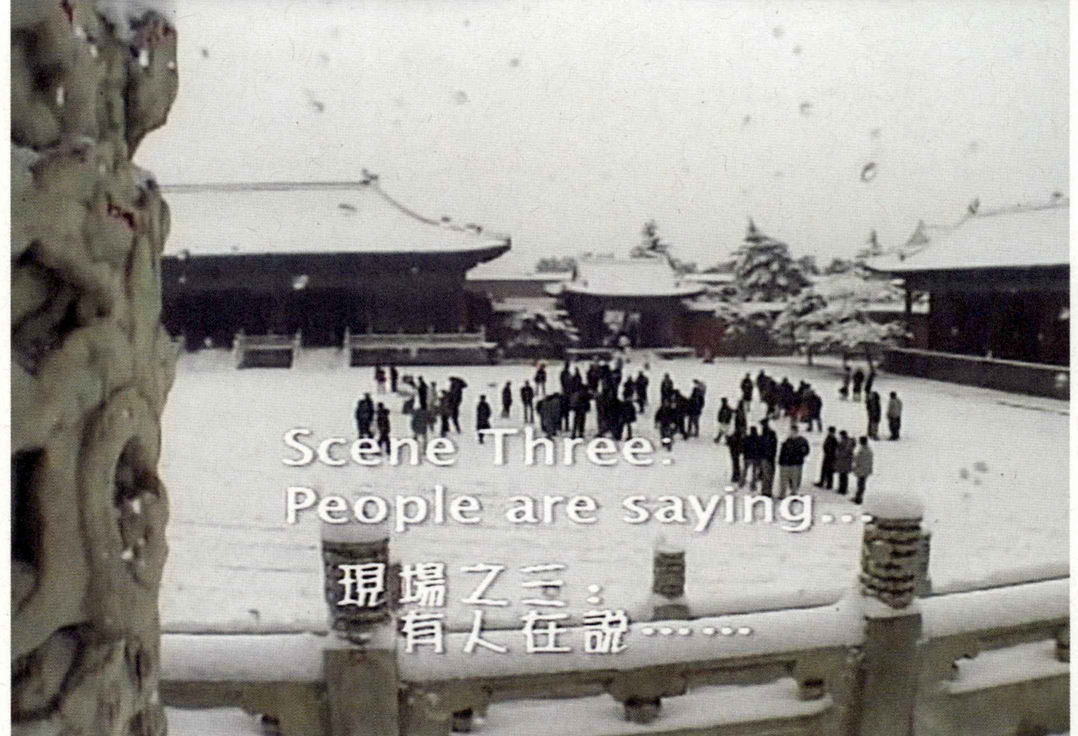
Scene Three:
People are saying...
現場之三：
有人在說……

XIN KEDU – NEW MEASUREMENT GROUP
The Analysis (I), 1990

Founded in 1989, the New Measurement Group (新刻度小组) (Chen Shaoping, Gu Dexin, and Wang Luyan) developed a conceptual practice that sought to neutralize individual expression in favor of systemic logic. What emerged was a radical experiment in the erasure of authorship and the critique of subjectivity itself.

The group understood the world as defined not by emotional or intuitive experience but by the quantitative relationships between objects. Measurement as a precise, repeatable, and impersonal currency became their artistic method and language. They rejected any expression grounded in personal feelings or psychological response, insisting on diagrams, charts, and procedural rigor. Every decision in their collaborative process, from the choice of materials to working methods, was governed by collectively determined rules.

From 1990 to 1995, the New Measurement Group produced five books, *Analyst I–V*, each one a distillation of their method. They entail analyses of spatial relations, behavioral patterns, and object logic transformed into abstract, graph-like visuals. These publications served as the primary outputs of the group and were exhibited internationally. What looked at first like design or data visualization was in fact a philosophical proposition: that art could operate without the artist, or at least without the ego of the artist.

Yet, paradoxically, this rigorously impersonal approach is also a statement of individualism—one that pushes against the social and ideological systems that assign identity, meaning, and visibility to the artist. In a context where contemporary Chinese art was increasingly entangled in global markets and personal narratives, the New Measurement Group's refusal of both became a form of quiet defiance. Their rejection of authorship was not submission but resistance and a confrontation with how individuality is constructed and consumed. By eliminating signature style and overt expression, they created space to interrogate the very structures that define the "individual" in art. As Liu Ding and Carol Yinghua Lu note, Qian Weikang understood the group's practice as emerging from a sharpened awareness of how the art system exercises institutional power over meaning and authorship and its tendency to reproduce hierarchies under the guise of freedom.[5]

In 1995, recognizing that even their critical system was being subsumed into the institutional art world, the group made a final gesture by destroying their remaining works. This act of self-erasure was consistent with their project and intended to eliminate the very system they had created. Most of their documents, artworks, and internal records are now lost. What survives is not only a set of publications but a rare conceptual position in Chinese art history. Against a backdrop of market expansion and rising self-expression, the New Measurement Group staged a collective retreat into logic, precision, and structure. In doing so, they shifted the focus from personal expression to the systems that shape meaning. By removing individual emotion and authorship, they redefined what artistic agency could look like and challenged the understanding of the self within larger systems.

5 Ding Liu and Carol Yinghua Lu, "Crimes Without a Scene: Qian Weikang and the New Measurement Group," *e-flux Journal*, May 2015, https://www.e-flux.com/journal/65/336470/crimes-without-a-scene-qian-weikang-and-the-new-measurement-group.

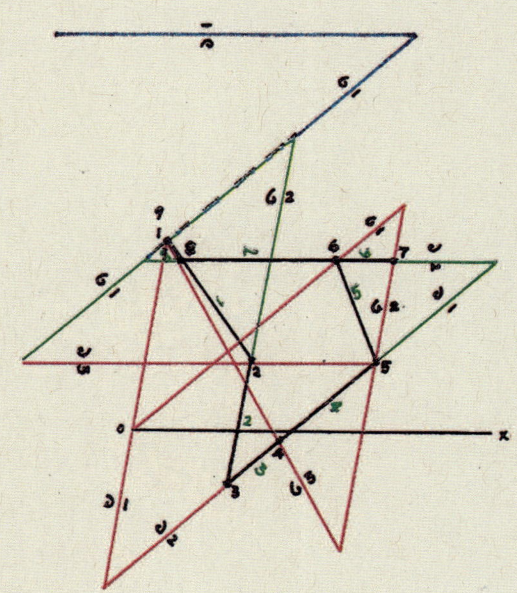

Xin Kedu (New Meausurement Group) was active from 1989 to 1996, comprising Beijing-based artists Gu Dexin (b. 1962), Chen Shaoping (b. 1947), and Wang Luyan (b. 1956). Before formally founding the group, they collaborated with Li Qiang, Wu Xun, and Cao Youlian, presenting *Tactile Art* and *Basic Existence: Point–Static Measurement* at the *China/Avant-Garde* exhibition (1989). From 1990 to 1995, they produced five issues of *Analyst*, exhibited in major shows such as *China's New Art Post-1989* at the Hong Kong Arts Centre (1993), *From the Central Kingdom: Chinese Avant-Gatrde Artists Des del País del Centre* at the Centre d'Art Santa Monica, Barcelona (1995), and *Exceptional Passage – China Avant-Garde Artists Exhibition* in Fukuoka (1991).

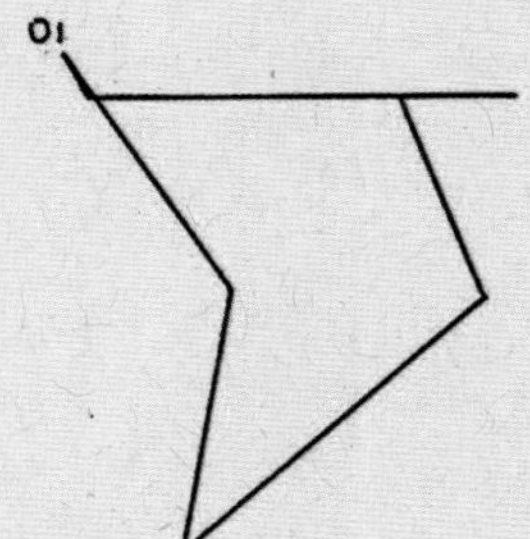

ZHUANG HUI

Longitude 109.88, Latitude 31.09, 1995–2008

Black-and-white photographs, video (color), paper
Variable dimensions

Zhuang Hui (b. 1963, Yumen, Gansu) is a conceptual artist whose diverse practice spans performance, installation, and photography. Deeply shaped by his upbringing in rural Gansu and the influence of his father, an itinerant studio photographer, Zhuang's work blends humanistic inquiry with aesthetic restraint. His practice consistently centers around specific people, sites, and events—capturing both their physical presence and their gradual disappearance in the face of modernity.

In his long-term project *Longitude 109.88, Latitude 31.09* (1995–2008), Zhuang Hui turns his attention to one of the most consequential and controversial infrastructure projects in modern China, the Three Gorges Dam. Begun in 1994 and completed in stages by 2009, the dam reshaped the landscape of the Yangtze River and its surroundings, submerging ancient towns, displacing over a million people, and dramatically altering ecosystems. Unlike many artists who responded to the project after the fact, Zhuang was present from the beginning.

In April 1995, Zhuang traveled to three locations along the future reservoir: the construction site at Sandouping in Xiling Gorge, a remote point on the riverbank in Wu Gorge, and Baidi City near the entrance to Qutang Gorge. At each site, he dug a series of shallow holes, half-a-meter deep—over one hundred in total—spaced at measured intervals. He documented each hole with large-format black-and-white photographs. The act was of a quiet, almost geological nature, and attracted little notice at the time. Zhuang did not publicly present the photos until twelve years later, in 2007, after he returned to the location—this time sending a cameraman to revisit and film the same coordinates, guided by his original maps. By then, the entire area had vanished beneath 100 meters of water and the holes had become inaccessible.

Longitude 109.88, Latitude 31.09 brings the photographs of the holes together with films of all three locations and a map of the areas the artist had revisited. In a conversation with the curator Wu Hung, Zhuang Hui describes that he sees the holes as traces that had been left a hundred meters down in the water. "A hole is not a real object, it is something without rhyme or reason,"[6] so instead of documenting houses or personal belongings or showing the changes in the water level, Zhuang offers a number of fixed points on the map where people can simply imagine the existence of the previously dug holes. This way, the work is neither a monument nor a protest but shows submerged memories. The subtle, durational approach does not give loss a shape but registers its quiet totality. The photographic documents thus preserve a moment in time that has been physically erased. The project offers no judgment, but frames a tension between what is visible and what disappears. It also suggests an alternative approach to Land Art: one in which the gesture is modest, localized, and deeply attuned to the cultural meanings of earth in Chinese society, where land is both revered and heavily exploited. Zhuang's method is deliberately unaggressive—closer to fieldwork than intervention—yet the implications of his work are vast. *Longitude 109.88, Latitude 31.09* charts not only the changing contours of the Yangtze River, but the shifting relationship between politics, memory, and the landscape in contemporary China.

6 Hung Wu et al., eds., *Displacement: The Three Gorges Dam and Contemporary Chinese Art* (Chicago: University of Chicago Press, 2008).

Zhuang Hui (b. 1963 in Yumen Town, Gansu Province), moved to Luoyang aged thirteen and began teaching himself painting. After high school, he worked at the Luoyang No.1 Tractor Factory until relocating to Beijing in 1996 to pursue art full time. His work has been shown internationally, including at the 48th Venice Biennale (1999); Centre Pompidou, Paris (2003); Tate Liverpool (2007); Hirshhorn Museum and Sculpture Garden, Washington, D.C. (2022); Kunstmuseum Bern (2005); Musée d'Art Contemporain de Lyon (2004); Deichtorhallen Hamburg (2002); and the 9th Shanghai Biennale (2012).

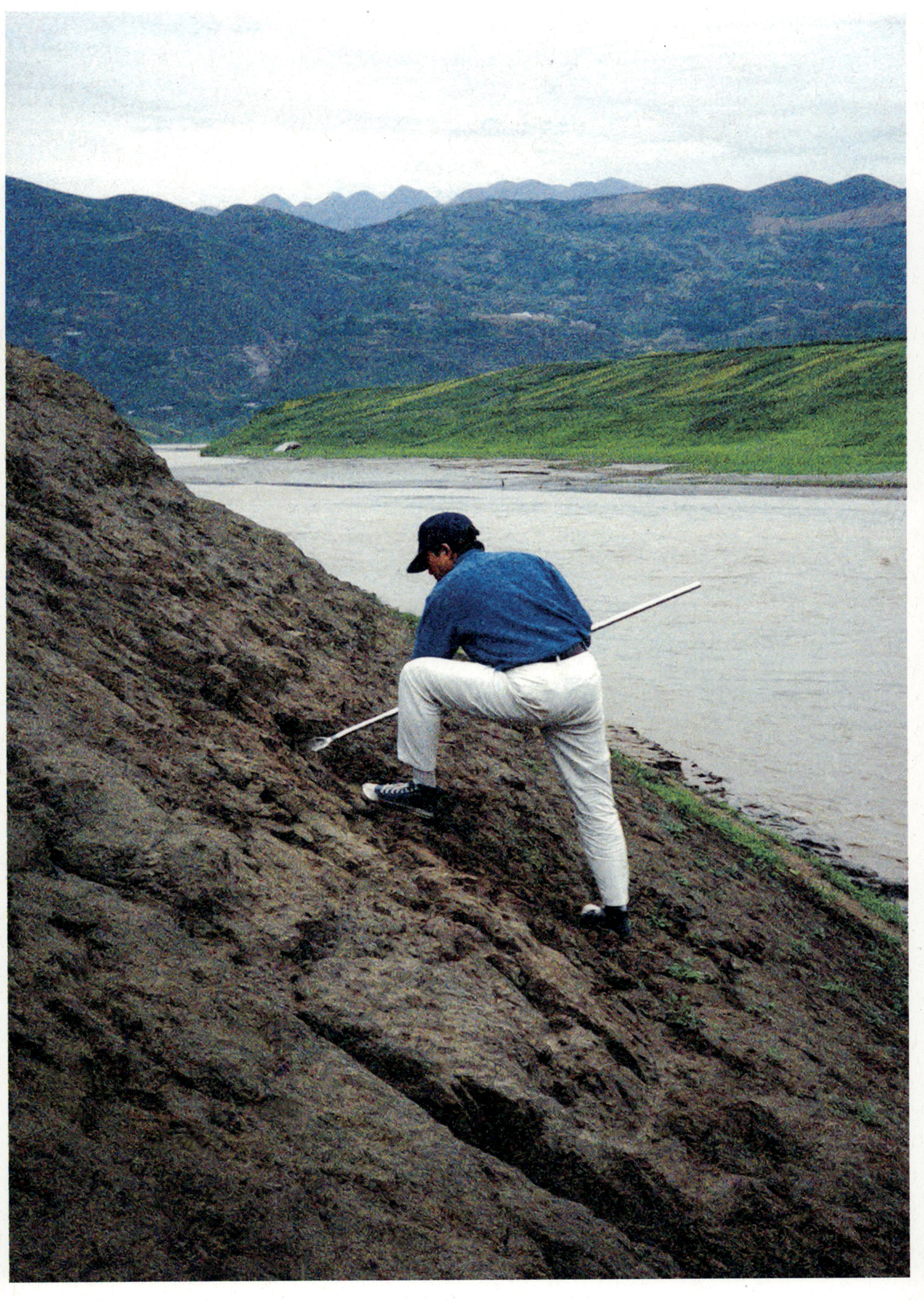

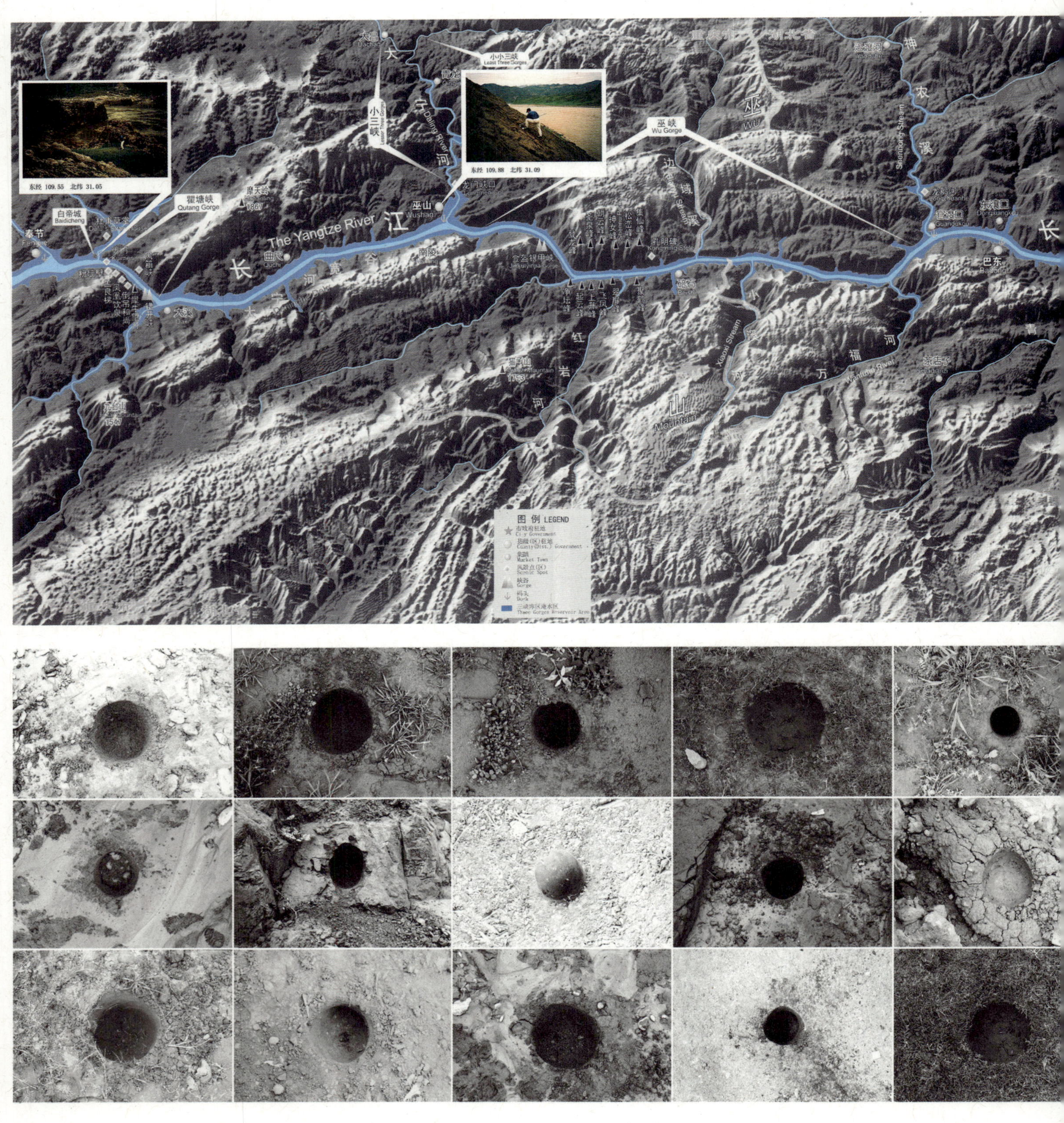

小小三峡
Least Three Gorges
巫峡
Wu Gorge
瞿塘峡
Qutang Gorge
白帝城
Baidicheng
The Yangtze River
长
江
巫山
Wushan
奉节
巴东
东经 109.55 北纬 31.05
东经 109.88 北纬 31.09
Shennong Stream
图例 LEGEND

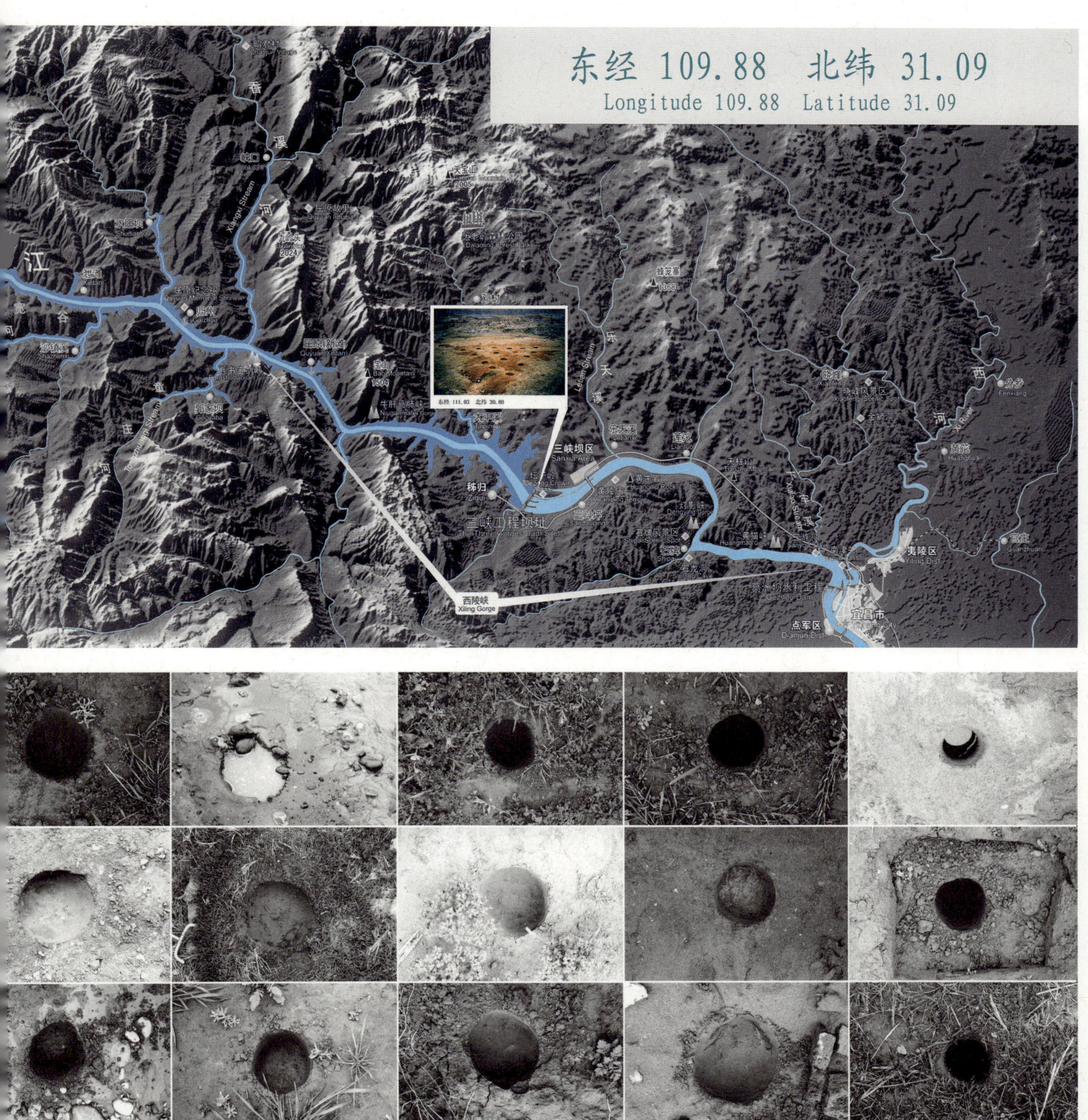
东经 109.88 北纬 31.09
Longitude 109.88 Latitude 31.09
三峡坝区
Sanxia Area
秭归
Zigui
三峡工程坝址
夷陵区
Yiling Dist
宜昌市
点军区
Dianjun Dist
西陵峡
Xiling Gorge

2. INDIVIDUALISM AS PARTICIPATION
个人主义：参与

CHEN SHAOXIONG

72.5 Hours of Electricity Consumption, 1992

Daylight lamp, bulb, electricity meter, wooden frame, raincoat
Variable dimensions

With *72.5 Hours of Electricity Consumption*, Chen Shaoxiong stages a quiet, almost invisible performance: human-shaped forms made of fluorescent lights are illuminated continuously over three days, while an electricity meter records their power usage. Nothing moves or changes except the slow ticking of the meter and the gradual disappearance of time. In this work, time itself becomes both material and subject, measured not by meaning but by consumption.

Chen, based in Guangzhou at the time, was fascinated by the possibility that time could be bent or fragmented—an idea drawn from his reading of Einstein's theories. In a city driven by trade and reform but with little contemporary art infrastructure, he experienced the bustling everyday as both dull and absurd. For Chen, the fantasy of cutting out a portion of time and holding it still offered a way of turning life into something that could be observed—where art would not illustrate life but *become* it.

The installation draws on materials taken directly from that daily life: raincoats, fluorescent tubing, the soft glow of street signs. More than referencing artists like Dan Flavin or Bruce Nauman, whom Chen admired, the work pays homage to the night markets and street stalls of southern China—spaces of social encounter, alcohol, repetition, and routine. From these low-cost materials and scenes of overstimulation, Chen built something quieter: an illusion of time stolen back from purpose.

The skeletal light forms evoke anonymous figures, glowing but static—stand-ins for individual presence stripped of narrative or function. Every hour marked by the meter becomes a small rebellion against the idea that time must be used efficiently or perform significance. The piece pushes back not through a dramatic gesture, but through endurance: light as energy, energy as waste, waste as a kind of freedom.

Chen's later *Five Hours* (1993), shown outside a Guangzhou bar, made this idea even more direct: a performance in which absolutely nothing happened. He remained skeptical of spectacle—both in politics and in art—and wary of how easily ideologies could become performance. In *72.5 Hours*, this skepticism becomes form: a figure that glows without message, a presence that insists without demanding attention.

This individualism is not loud or heroic. It is stubborn, quiet, and slightly absurd—a refusal to be useful, to be explained, or to disappear. It asks what it means to be an individual not outside of daily life, but inside it, just standing there, consuming electricity, while the world rushes on outside.

Chen Shaoxiong (1962–2016, Guangdong Province) graduated from the Printmaking Department of the Guangzhou Academy of Fine Arts. His work was the subject of solo exhibitions at the Power Station of Art, Shanghai (2016), and the Seattle Art Museum (2014). He participated in major group exhibitions including the 21st Biennale of Sydney (2018); *Art and China after 1989: Theater of the World* (Guggenheim Museum, New York, 2017); Gwangju Biennale (2012); *Ink Art: Past as Present in Contemporary China* (Metropolitan Museum of Art, New York, 2013); and *Xijing Is Not Xijing* (21st Century Museum of Contemporary Art, Kanazawa, 2016). His work is held in the collections of MoMA New York, M+ Hong Kong, the Victoria and Albert Museum London, Kunstmuseum Bern, and the Power Station of Art, Shanghai. In 2013, he received the Rockefeller Foundation Bellagio Creative Arts Fellowship.

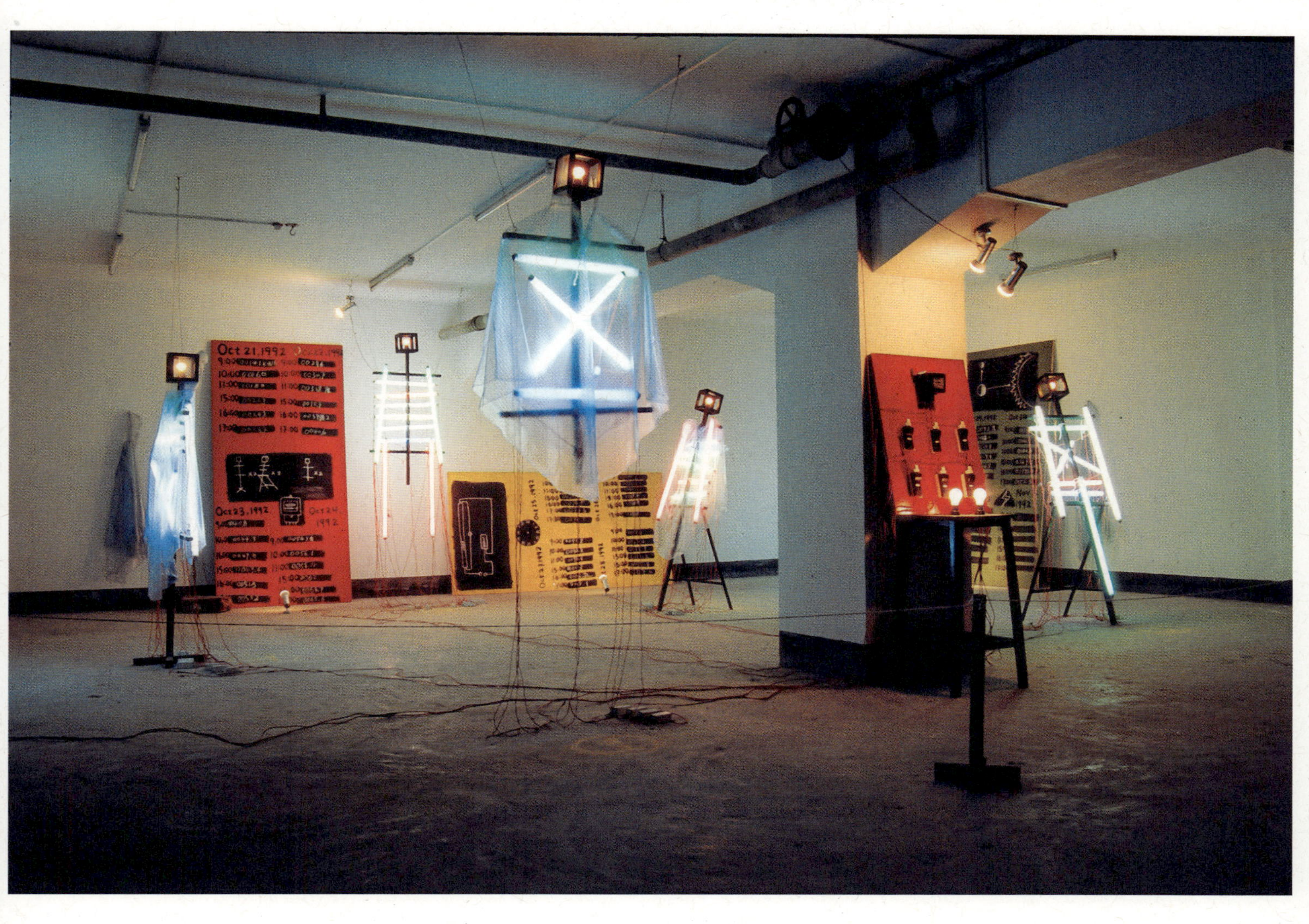

HONG HAO & YAN LEI

Invitation Letter to Documenta Kassel, 1997

Printed letter and stamped envelope
Letter: 29.7 × 21.7 cm; envelope: 11 × 22.1 cm

In 1997, when both Yan Lei and Hong Hao were in their early thirties, they orchestrated one of the most notorious conceptual pranks in the Chinese art world. Under the pseudonym *Mr. Ielnay Oahgnoh*—their names spelled backward—they mailed over a hundred fake invitation letters to fellow Chinese artists. The letters, printed on counterfeit documenta letterhead and written in formal German, invited recipients to participate in a "special section" of the upcoming documenta X in Kassel, one of the most prestigious exhibitions of contemporary art worldwide.

At the time, international recognition was rare and intensely desired in the Chinese art scene. An invitation to exhibit at documenta was seen as a symbol of having arrived—not simply as a Chinese artist, but as a participant in global discourse rather than its distant other. The fake letters struck a nerve. Some artists recognized the ruse immediately; others took it at face value and reacted with outrage once the truth emerged. The hoax caused quite a stir in the art scene and became a defining event—a daring artistic intervention with which Hong Hao and Yan Lei both amused and angered their colleagues.

Yet beyond the provocation, *Invitation Letter to Documenta Kassel* exposed deeper structural tensions. In 1997, only one artist from China was officially included in documenta X. The work critiqued not only Western curatorial exclusions, but also the fervent desire among Chinese artists to be validated by international institutions. It raised uncomfortable questions: Who gets to participate in "global" art? Who decides? And what does inclusion actually mean?

By mimicking the bureaucratic forms that confer status with the letterhead, the institutional tone, and the authoritative formatting, Yan Lei and Hong Hao revealed how easily legitimacy can be fabricated, and how eagerly it is often accepted. The piece underscored how prestige operates less through substance than through appearances, and how global art infrastructures both reflect and reproduce existing asymmetries.

Seen in hindsight, the work anticipated many of the transformations soon to shape Chinese contemporary art: the rise of biennials, the expansion of the commercial gallery system, and the strategic balancing of artistic autonomy and institutional participation. Within this complex structure, artists like Hong Hao and Yan Lei embody a pragmatic contradiction—operating both within and against the very systems they critique.

Fifteen years later, in a twist of irony, Yan Lei was formally invited to participate in documenta 13.

Hong Hao (b. 1965, Beijing), graduated from the Printmaking Department of the Central Academy of Fine Arts in Beijing in 1989 and is based in the same city. His work has been featured in solo exhibitions at Museo d'Arte Moderna di Bologna, Rencontres d'Arles, and Pace Beijing. He has participated in major group exhibitions including *China's New Art: Post-1989; Inside Out* (Asia Society and MoMA PS1); the Shanghai Biennale; Chengdu Biennale; Asia-Pacific Triennial; and *The Global Contemporary* at ZKM | Center for Art and Media, Karlsruhe. Since the 1990s, he has maintained an ongoing collaboration with fellow artist Yan Lei

Yan Lei (b. 1965, Hebei Province) graduated from the Zhejiang Academy of Fine Arts (now China Academy of Art), Hangzhou, in 1991. He has participated in major international exhibitions including the Venice Biennale (2003, 2013); documenta 12 and 13 (2007, 2012); São Paulo Biennial (2002); Gwangju Biennale; Shanghai Biennale; Guangzhou Triennial; and Istanbul Biennial. His solo exhibitions have been held at UCCA Beijing, Aspen Art Museum, and Hong Kong Arts Centre. In 2002, he was awarded the Chinese Contemporary Art Award as "Best Artist."

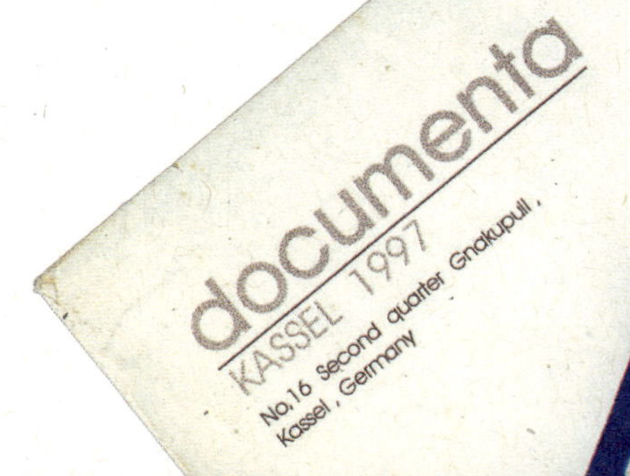

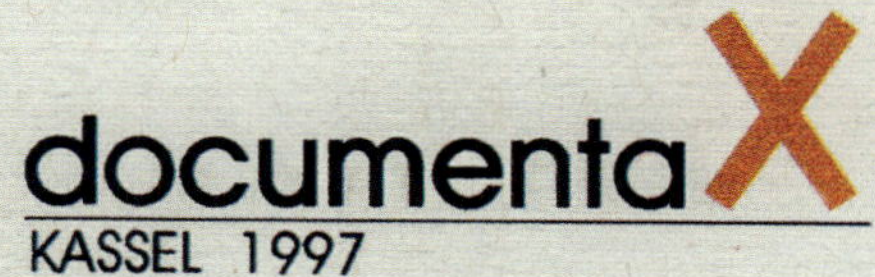

5 - 20 - 1997

Liebe(r) Frau/Herr

Tian Ming Guo

Seit 1955 gibt es die documenta in Kassel. Dieses Jahr wird die zehnte documenta statt finden und zwar vom 21. Juni an genau 100 Tage.

Der Träger der Ausstellung freut sich, Ihnen mitteilen zu können, daß dieses Jahr besondere fianzielle Mittel zur Verfügung sstehen, die für eine Sonderausstellung mit zeitgenössischer chinesischer Kunst verwendet werden sollen.

Diese Ausstellung ist ein Zeichen der Anerkennung für die besondere Stellung der zeitgenössischen chinesische Kunst in der Kunstwelt. Wir fühlen uns verpflichtet, den chinesischen Künstlern diese einzigartige Gelegenheit zu bieten. Der Titel der Ausstellung heißt "Aus der anderen Welt - chinesiche Avantgarde" - er spiegelt die galoppierende Entwicklung der chinesischen Kunst wieder.

Aus Zeitgründen können wir diese Ausstellung leider nur kurzfristig ankündigen. Schon jetzt ist es nicht mehr möglich, diese Sonderausstellung gleichzeitig mit der documenta stattfinden zu lassen. "Aus der andere Welt - chinesiche Avantgarde" wird deshalb im September 1997 eröffnet werden. Wir hoffen, daß Sie für diese Situation Verständnis haben. Der Ausstellungsort wird No.16 Second quator Gnakupul, Kassel sein.

Der Autor diese Briefes wurde zum Kurator der Ausstellung ernannt, und wird vom 30. Juni bis zum 15. Juli nach China reisen, um die Künstler zu treffen und alle nötigen Vorbereitungen vorzunehmen.
(Tel 010 6507 3384, Fax 010 6507 3363)

In der Hoffnung, Sie in China zu sehen

Hochachtungsvoll

Ielnay Oahgnoh

Kurator der Ausstellung

Ielnay Oahgnoh

...rter Gnakupuil ,Kassel , Germany TEL: 49561 - 65918 FAX: 49561 - 65103

... guo
...Lou 3403
...a Zhuang Bei Li
...jing 100027 P.R.China

HONG HAO & YAN LEI

Snow Bull, 2009

Oil on canvas
300 × 660 cm

Snow Bull is a monumental allegory of individual agency caught in the machinery of global capital. Created in the immediate aftermath of the 2008 financial crisis, the painting stages a surreal, frozen landscape in which a New York blizzard, an exploding satellite, a depiction of Lenin dressed in the suit of an art collector and the Chelsea Tower collide with collapsing economic dreams. At its center stand the artists themselves wearing cow heads and wielding fuel nozzles. They appear both like weapons and the most imposing status symbol in a moment of sky-high petrol prices. Both heroic and absurd, the two artists in the painting appear as figures of resistance and complicity, caught in the spectacle they inhabit.

This work emerges from a moment when Chinese contemporary art had reached unprecedented visibility and commercial success on the global stage. Between 2003 and 2008, the art market exerted growing pressure on artistic production, shifting the role of the artist from outsider to commodity, from cultural critic to branded identity. *Snow Bull* captures the confusion, seduction, and exhaustion of that moment. Yet rather than rejecting it outright, Hong Hao and Yan Lei embed themselves within it—posing, performing, and parodying the figure of the artist as both agent and captive.

Theirs is a deeply ambivalent form of individualism. The two artists appear as absurd antiheroes—exaggerated, costumed, stylized—not as stable subjects, but as fragmented selves navigating spectacle, crisis, and value. They do not stand outside the system they depict but insert themselves into its contradictions. In doing so, they expose how individual identity, especially in the realm of art, becomes shaped and distorted by market dynamics, institutional narratives, and geopolitical fantasies.

Snow Bull thus becomes more than a commentary on economic collapse; it is a reflection on the precarious status of the artist as an individual in an era of global circulation. By casting themselves into the center of the storm, Hong Hao and Yan Lei dramatize a paradox: the artist as both participant in and witness to the transformation of culture into capital, and the self into surface. Individualism, in this work, is not a position of autonomy—but a performance negotiated through masks, myth, and irony.

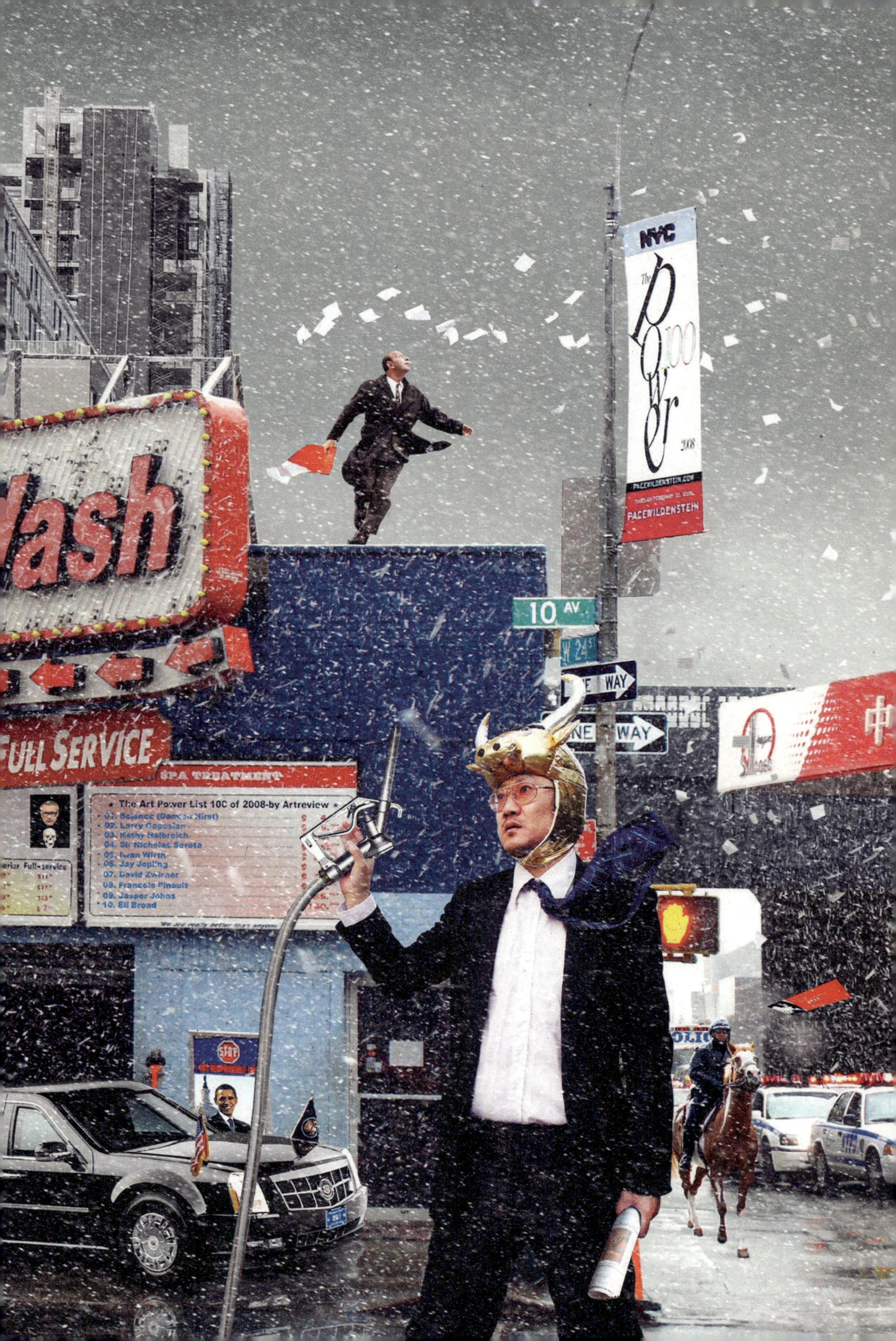
NYC
The Power 100
2008
PACEWILDENSTEIN.COM
PACEWILDENSTEIN
10 AV
W 24 ST
ONE WAY
ONE WAY
Wash
FULL SERVICE
SPA TREATMENT
The Art Power List 100 of 2008-by Artreview
01. Science (Damien Hirst)
02. Larry Gagosian
03. Kathy Halbreich
04. Sir Nicholas Serota
05. Iwan Wirth
06. Jay Jopling
07. David Zwirner
08. Francois Pinault
09. Jasper Johns
10. Eli Broad
Full-service
STOP
POLICE

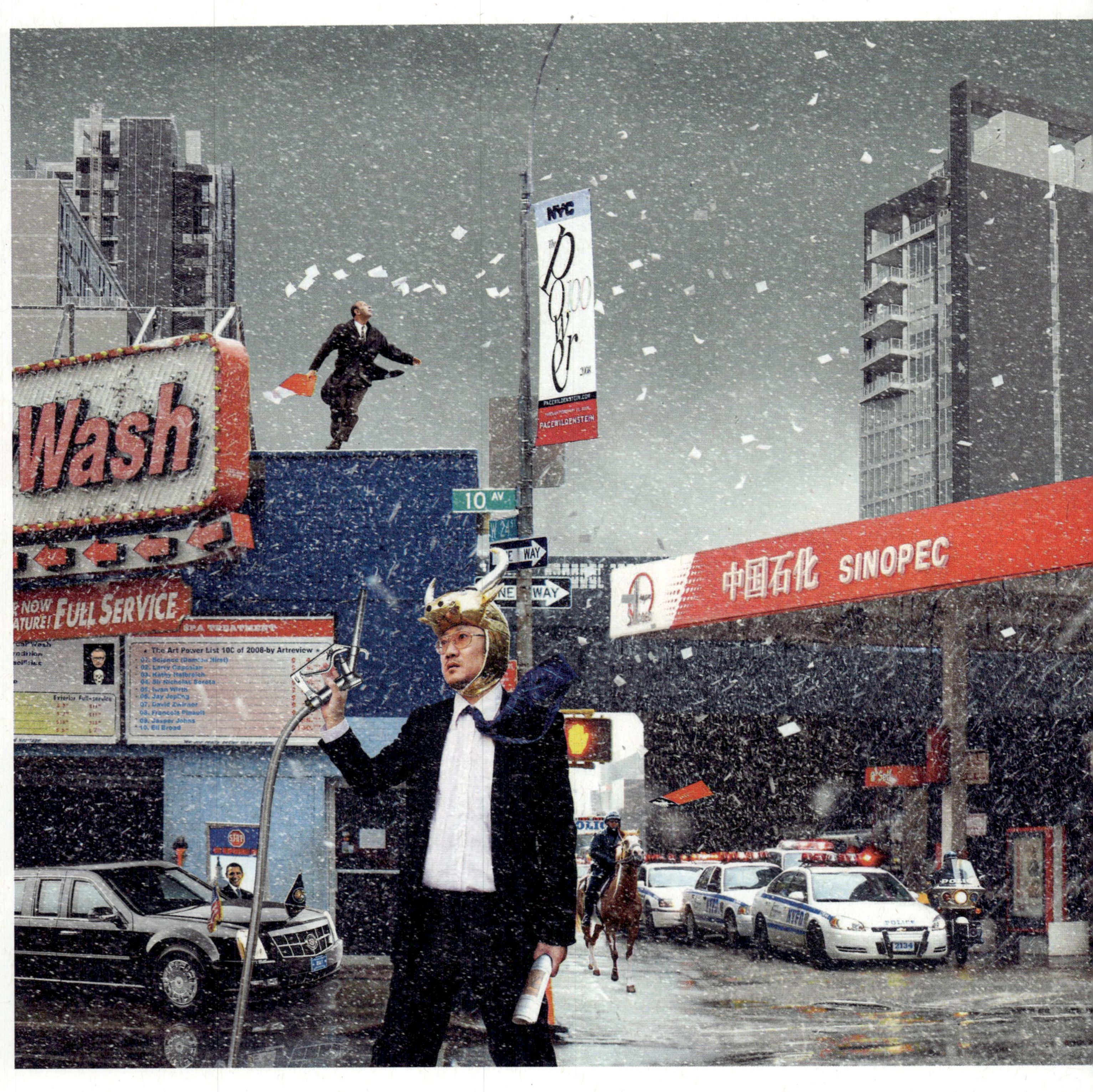
NYC
The Power 100
2008
PACEWILDENSTEIN
Wash
FULL SERVICE
SPA TREATMENT
The Art Power List 100 of 2008-by Artreview
05. Iwan Wirth
06. Jay Jopling
08. Francois Pinault
09. Jasper Johns
10. Eli Broad
10 AV
ONE WAY
中国石化 SINOPEC
NYPD

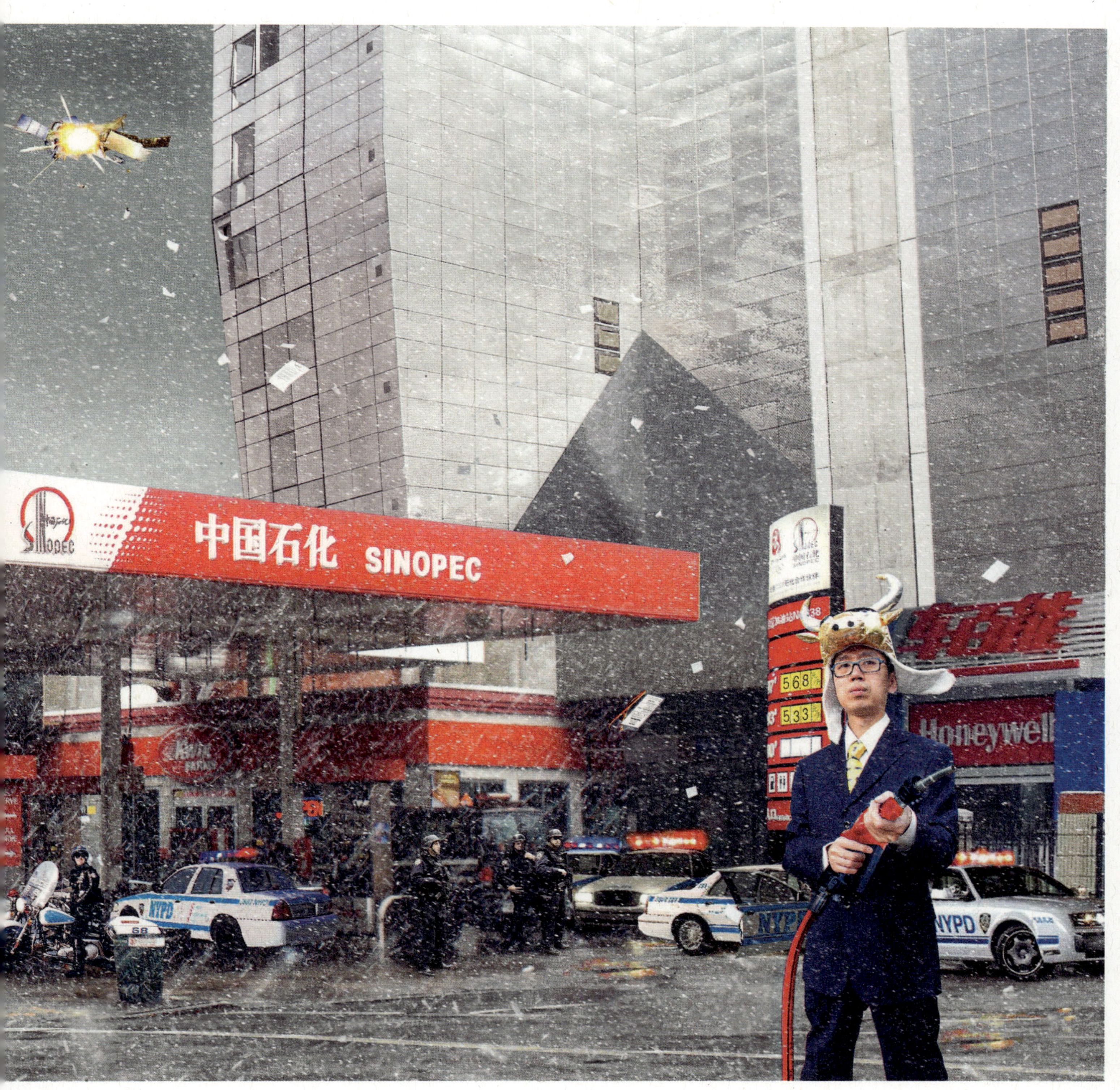
中国石化
SINOPEC
NYPD
Honeywell

NI HAIFENG

Of the Departure and the Arrival, 2005

Glazed porcelain
Variable dimensions

What begins as a simple exchange—objects packed into boxes and sent overseas—unfolds into a complex meditation on identity, labor, and cultural translation. In *Of the Departure and the Arrival*, Ni Haifeng stages an artistic loop between the Dutch city of Delft and the Chinese porcelain capital Jingdezhen, connecting two towns shaped by centuries of global trade. The work was commissioned by the municipality of Delft and involved the public from the outset: residents were invited to contribute personal, everyday items that reflected life in the city. These items—some valuable, others ordinary or obsolete—were then shipped to Jingdezhen, where they were reproduced in blue-and-white porcelain by local artisans.

The process is central to the work. The documentation on video shows the arrival of the shipment in Jingdezhen, the factory workers unpacking and inspecting the contents: tubes of toothpaste, an old glove, a Dutch bean slicer—trying to make sense of these strange forms. As they begin the transformation process, making molds, casting the porcelain, and applying decorative motifs, the objects undergo a quiet transformation from personal items of different values to uniform objects. The work references a long history of mutual imitation and adaptation. Delft's seventeenth-century faience was inspired by Chinese imports, while Chinese manufacturers adapted their wares to suit European tastes in what became known as *chine de commande*. Ni's work reverses this flow, sending contemporary Dutch domestic items to China to be interpreted and returned. What results is a set of objects that are both familiar and strange—recognizable in form but unified through a new material and decorative language.

Paulina Yao notes that the work references both the shared history between Holland and China in relation to the porcelain industry and the relevance of early colonial history to today's economic activity.[7] But *Of the Departure and the Arrival* is also deeply personal. It reveals how cultural meaning is not fixed but remade through labor, touch, exchange, and migration. The remade objects arrive bearing a dual identity: rooted in Delft, but bearing the aesthetic and material traces of Jingdezhen. Their transformation mirrors Ni's own experience as an artist living between China and the Netherlands, caught in what he describes as an "endless process of translation."

What appears at first as a decorative act becomes a study in how individuality—whether of people, cities, or things—is shaped and reshaped in circulation. The work resists any fixed notion of cultural identity, proposing instead that meaning emerges through movement, reinterpretation, and hands-on contact across distance and difference.

7 Haifeng Ni and Pauline J. Yao, eds., *Ni Haifeng: Para-Production* (Hong Kong: Timezone 8, 2009).

Ni Haifeng (b. 1964, Zhoushan, Zhejiang Province) graduated from the Zhejiang Academy of Fine Arts (now China Academy of Art) in 1986 and lives and works in Amsterdam and Beijing. He has held solo exhibitions at GEM Museum of Contemporary Art, The Hague (2003); Museum Het Domein, Sittard (2004); and Stedelijk Museum De Lakenhal, Leiden (2007). His work has been included in major exhibitions such as *China Avantgarde* (Haus der Kulturen der Welt, Berlin, 1993), the Shanghai Biennale (2004); Guangzhou Triennial (2005); and Manifesta 9 (2012), as well as shows at Museum Boijmans Van Beuningen; ZKM | Center for Art and Media, Karlsruhe; BAK Utrecht; Today Art Museum; and UCCA Beijing.

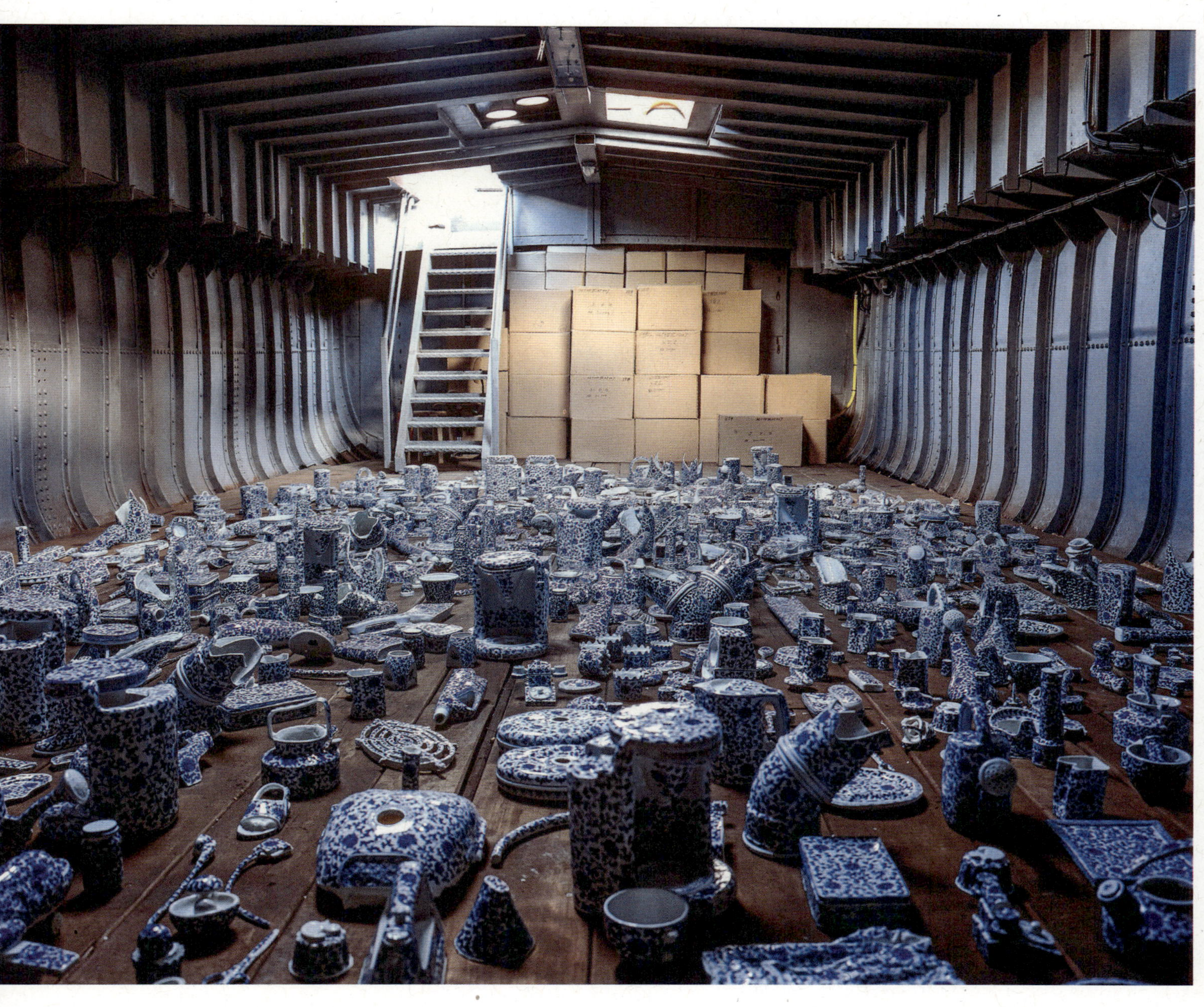

ZHOU TIEHAI

Will/We Must, 1996

single-channel 35mm film transferred to digital video (black-and-white, silent) 9:17 min

Zhou Tiehai's *Will/We Must* is a pointed and playful cinematic satire of the Chinese art world at a pivotal moment in its globalization. Shot on 35mm film in the style of early twentieth-century silent films with inter-titles and expressive acting, it is both slapstick and an allegory of the mechanisms of contemporary art production.

The film is structured into nine episodes, each with a different topic and setting: "The Military Meeting"; "The Cafeteria"; "In the Hospital"; "Art Tour Guide"; "Heartfelt Calls"; "You Betrayed Me"; "You Only Have Traditional Chinese Medicine and Witchcraft"; "The Godfather"; and "The Raft of the Medusa." These fragments act as stand-alone parables, but together they build a sharp critique of the intersecting forces shaping Chinese contemporary art in the 1990s.

In "The Military Meeting," a commanding voice proclaims, "Without your own airport you have nothing of your own"—a hint towards the dependence on international validation and infrastructure. "Heartfelt Calls" shows an artist repeatedly phoning curators, pleading: "I'll take part in any exhibition you have," parading the desperation of artists trying to insert themselves into a global art world. "The Raft of the Medusa," the film's closing chapter, references Géricault's iconic painting to show ten artists on a raft, drifting in place without moving forward or backward.

Yan Xiaoxiao observes that the film offers a concise, direct, and at times humorous analysis of the dynamics between international curators and critics, highlighting their dominant position in shaping discourse, the eagerness of artists to gain visibility, and the persistent gap between local creative context and the framework of Western art history.[8] Zhou's deliberately anachronistic choice of format also underscores the tension between a rapid cultural modernization and the clumsy translation of global art norms into a local practice.

The work skillfully balances wit and melancholy, which at times makes the satire verge on farce. At the same time, it reveals the hardships, uncertainties, and contradictions that accompany artistic practice. By staging the art world as a theatre of cliché, Zhou neither offers solutions nor withdraws in cynicism. Instead, *Will/We must* captures the dilemmas of navigating the unfamiliar terrain of global visibility.

Viewed today, the film retains its relevance. As Zhou later reflected, the environment it depicts may not have changed so much, only the machinery has evolved. Where once the dilemma was how to be seen, now it may be how not to disappear in the churn of fairs, auctions, and trends. But the fundamental questions remain: Is integration the goal? Can resistance take form within the system? Or is the only possible gesture a kind of self-aware participation—one that insists on staging the absurdity while remaining inside it?

8 Liu et al., *The 7th Shenzhen Sculpture Biennale* (see note 4).

Zhou Tiehai (b. 1966, Shanghai), studied at the School of Fine Arts at Shanghai University. He lives and works in Shanghai and has played a key role in shaping the city's art scene, founding West Bund Art & Design and directing the Minsheng Art Museum. His solo exhibitions include: Yuz Museum, Shanghai; MoCA Shanghai; IKON, Birmingham; and Kunsthal Rotterdam. He has shown in major group exhibitions at the Guggenheim Museum, New York; M+, Hong Kong; MAXXI, Rome; Tate Liverpool; Whitney Museum, New York; ZKM | Center for Art and Media, Karlsruhe; Hamburger Bahnhof, Berlin; and the Venice, Gwangju, and Asia Pacific Triennales.

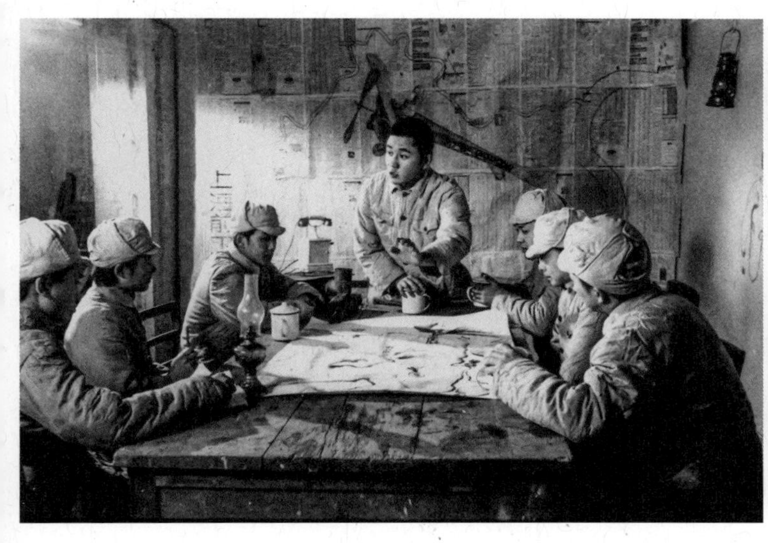

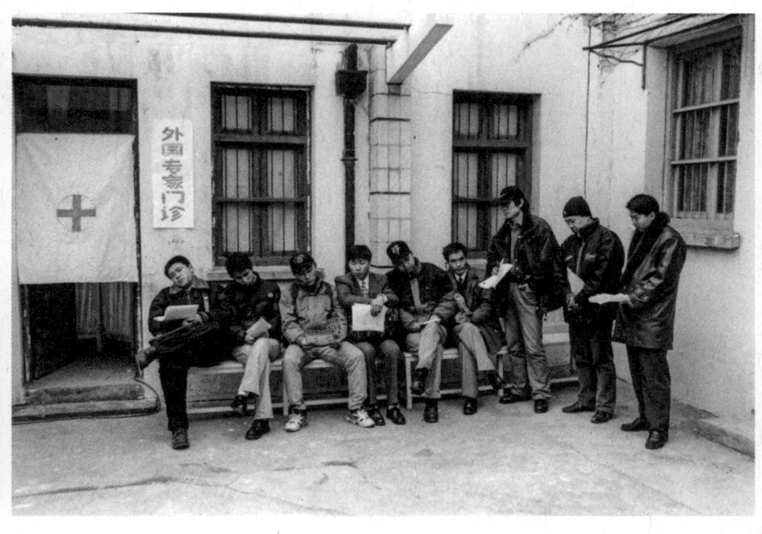
外国专家门诊

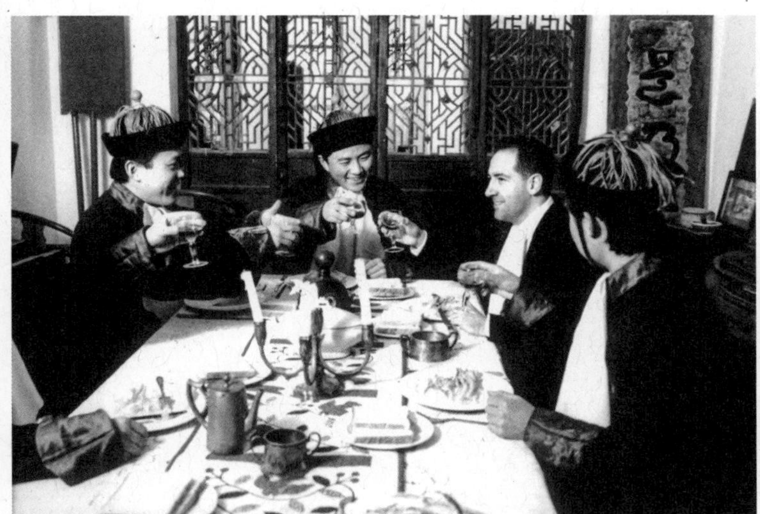

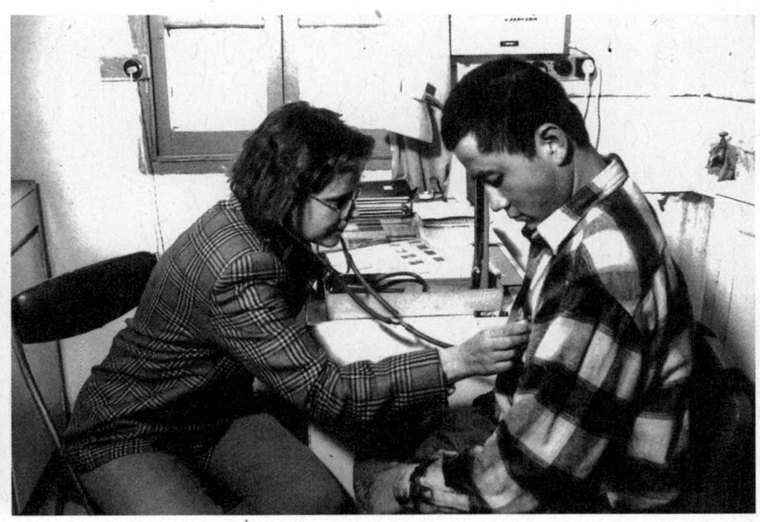

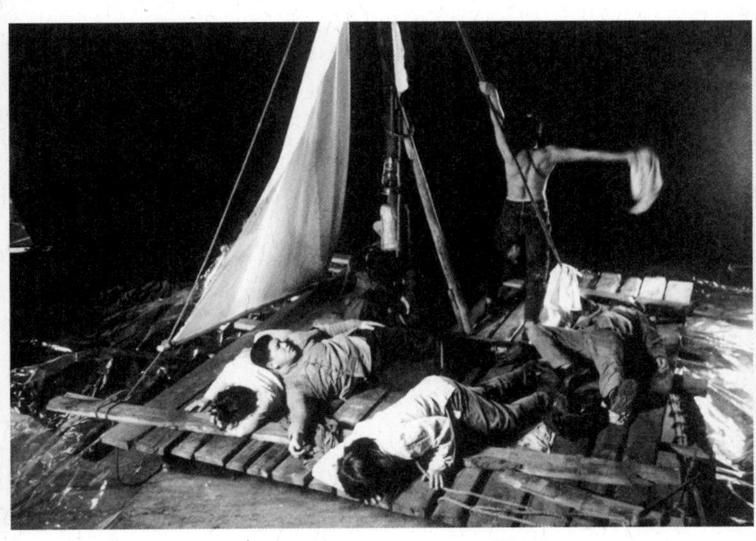

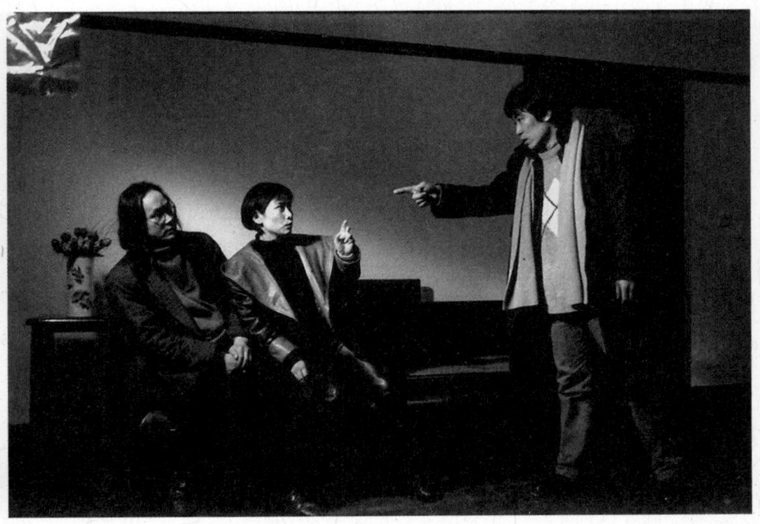

3. INDIVIDUALISM AS RE-ANIMATION OF HUMANISM
个人主义：重新激活人文主义

CAO FEI & OU NING

San Yuan Li, 2003

Video (black-and-white, sound)
39:42 min

A stylized portrait of a village amid the relentless growth of Guangzhou, *San Yuan Li* captures the dissonance between urban sprawl and rural persistence. Directed by Ou Ning and Cao Fei and filmed by twelve artists organized by the U-thèque collective, the work is both a visual poem and a spatial study. San Yuan Li, once a self-contained agrarian village, now sits enveloped by skyscrapers and construction sites, its residents adapting to the city's advance with makeshift coops, rooftop gardens, and rituals of everyday life.

The structure of the film is carried and shaped by the soundtrack composed by Li Chin Sung (Dickson Dee), a legendary musician with decades of engagement in the Chinese music scene. His soundscape ranges from minimalist rhythmic patterns to drum and bass, from sparse piano lines to textured layers of electronic music. Woven into the score are ambient recordings from the city itself: subway announcements, snippets of pop music, aircraft noise, and strains of traditional Chinese melodies. These sonic elements blur the line between score and setting, immersing the viewer in the aural density of San Yuan Li's everyday life.

The work unfolds in six sections: "Introduction," which follows the movement of the city, ending at the San Yuan Li train station; "Village in Silence," focused on architectural details and narrow alleyways with abstracted views upward; "Airplanes," a visual juxtaposition between the shadows of overhead jets and the stillness of chickens and gardens; "Social Life," a glimpse into the lives of well-dressed urban dwellers; "Day after Night," portraying the awakening of the city and its daily rhythms; and "People," featuring quiet portraits of the village residents in groups. Two outtakes included in the presentation reveal the unusual positioning of the cameras and offer a behind-the-scenes look at the collective filming process.

For co-directors Ou Ning and Cao Fei, both based in Guangzhou, *San Yuan Li* marked a pivotal project. Commissioned for the 2003 Venice Biennale, the film was conceived as a local response to the global condition of urbanization. Yet its resonance extends far beyond Guangzhou. It reflects how modernization and expansion have engulfed the village within the city's sprawl, creating a space where individual agency is simultaneously limited and pronounced.

San Yuan Li belongs to a lineage of works that explore individualism not through self-expression, but through re-animating engagement with the ordinary. The life of the villagers in the film becomes a quiet counterpoint to the spectacle of modern progress. In this way film resists sentimentalism yet affirms a form of dignity that lies in adaptation, remaining and continuity. In capturing these scenes with such restraint and lyricism, *San Yuan Li* goes beyond documentation of urban transformation; it reframes it. The viewer is not asked to judge or to mourn, but to observe.

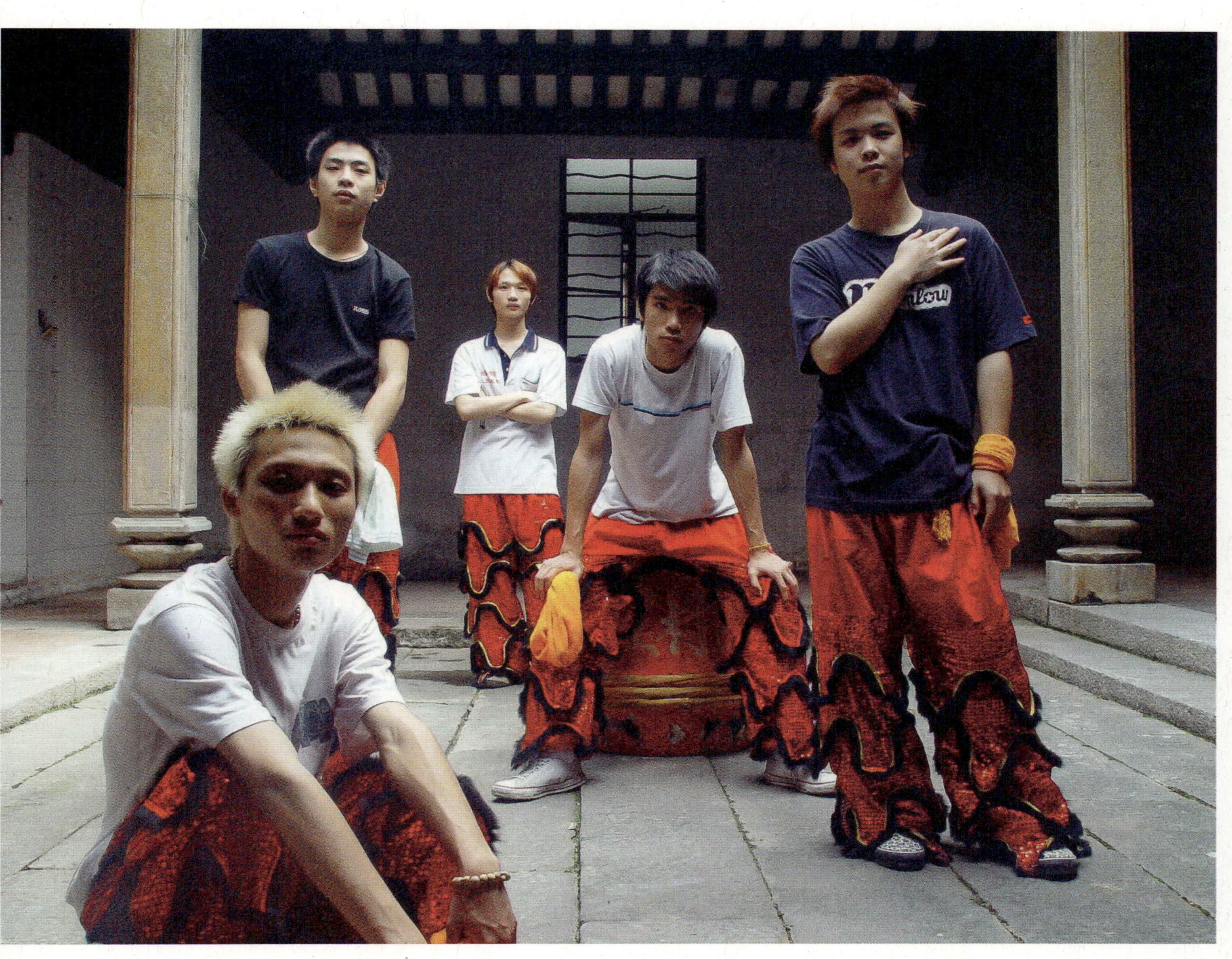

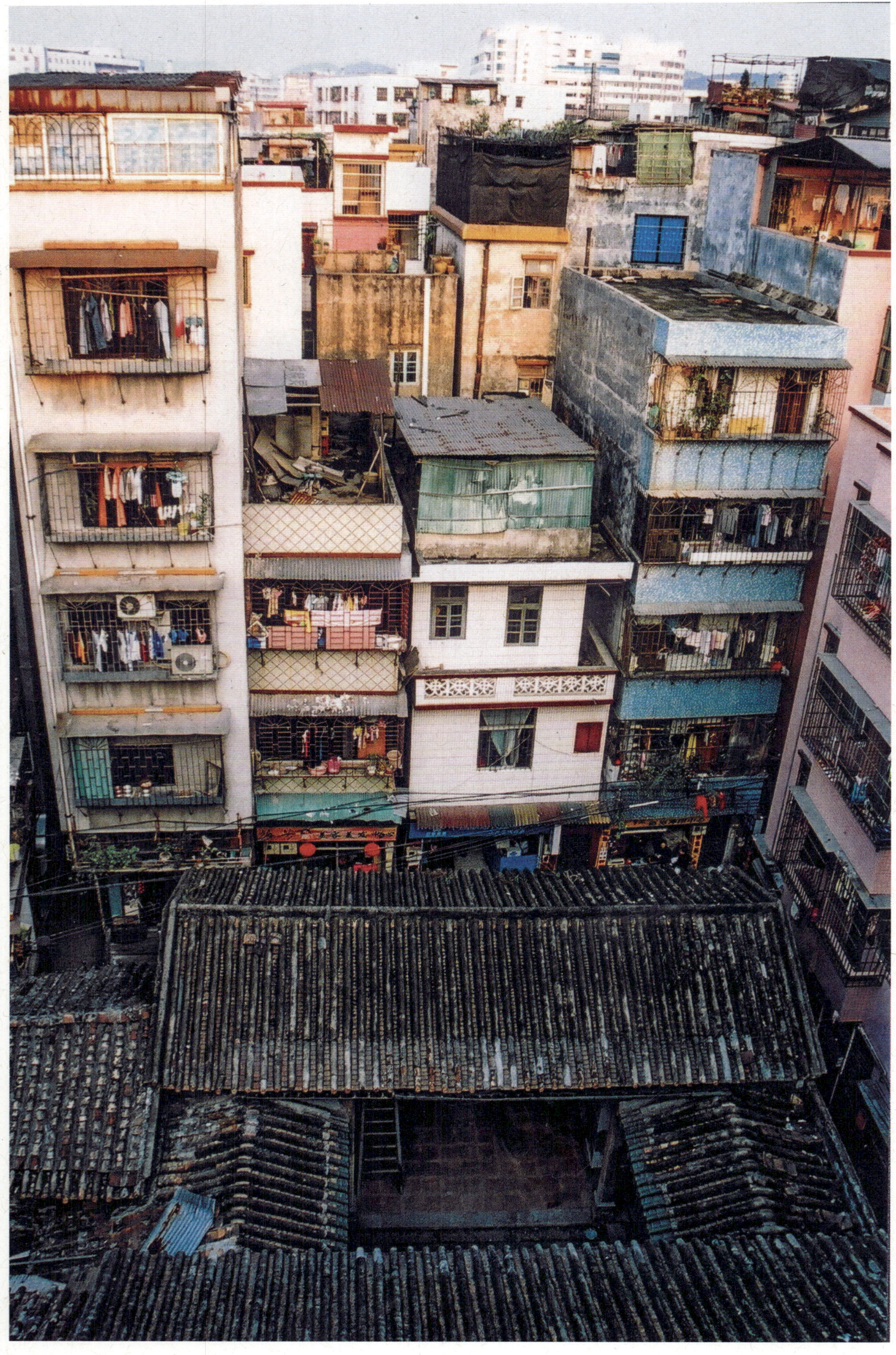

Cao Fei (b. 1978, Guangzhou) lives and works in Beijing. Recent solo exhibitions include UCCA Center for Contemporary Art, Beijing (2021); MAXXI, Rome (2021); Kunsthal Charlottenborg, Copenhagen (2022); Pinacoteca Contemporânea, São Paulo (2023); Lenbachhaus, Munich (2024); SCAD Museum of Art, Savannah (2024); Museum of Art Pudong, Shanghai (2024); Art Gallery of New South Wales, Sydney (2024); and MALBA, Buenos Aires (2024). Her work has also been shown at the Museum of Modern Art (MoMA) and the Guggenheim Museum, New York; Tate Modern, London; Centre Pompidou, Paris; and in numerous international biennales. She received the CCAA Best Young Artist Award (2006) and Best Artist Award (2016), the Deutsche Börse Photography Foundation Prize (2021), and the SCAD deFINE ART Award (2024).

Ou Ning (b. 1969, Zhanjiang, China) is an artist, filmmaker, curator, writer, and activist based in New York. He founded the Bishan Commune (2011–16) and the School of Tillers (2015–16), and published *Utopia in Practice: Bishan Project and Rural Reconstruction* (2020). Earlier publications include *South of Southern* (2014), *The Chinese Thinking* (2012), the journal *Chutzpah!* (2011–14), and *Odyssey: Architecture and Literature* (2009). He founded the touring exhibition *Get It Louder* (2005, 2007, 2010) and curated projects such as sound installations at Battersea Power Station, London (Serpentine Gallery, 2006); the Shenzhen & Hong Kong Bi-City Biennale of Urbanism and Architecture (2009); and the Chengdu Biennale (2011). His films include *Meishi Street* (MoMA, New York, 2006) and *San Yuan Li* (50th Venice Biennale, 2003).

HAN LEI

Kaifeng, Henan Province, 1986
Luochuan, Shaanxi Province VI, 1989

Black-and-white photograph, silver gelatin print (hand enlarged)
60 × 50 cm

Han Lei is one of the most pioneering figures in Chinese documentary photography. Since the mid-1980s, he has regarded reality not as something to represent neutrally, but as a "training ground" for photography—a field in which perception is tested, and the surface of things is gradually stripped away. Over more than a decade, he traveled through rural villages and provincial towns, seeking not to document events or illustrate social critique, but to forge an alternative perception of reality.

Unlike many documentary artists of his generation, Han does not insist on letting the "camera speak." He rejects the idea that objectivity requires erasing the subjectivity of the person behind the lens. His images—of migrant workers, opera performers, and village residents—do not mark a crisis or turning point. Instead, they seem to hold their breath just before something happens or long after it has passed. Han is not interested in the dramatic climax. He delays it, distorts it, and lets it dissolve in order to preserve something more fragile: the texture of time itself.

His photographs often depict moments of pause or ordinary gestures, but they are composed with great care. The result is a subtle disruption of the everyday. Temporality is skewed; meaning is suspended. These choices—capturing subjects in-between, withholding resolution—are not stylistic flourishes. They are part of a broader aesthetic that refuses to reduce life to spectacle or politics to symbolism.

Han deliberately distances himself from art institutions and market trends, not to withdraw, but to protect the autonomy of his practice. He avoids prescribed roles and expectations, choosing instead to observe the world through his own lens, shaped by personal rhythm and judgment. His photographs reflect this stance: they are not made to meet external standards, but to explore reality as he sees it. For Han, individualism is not just a subject—it is the foundation of his artistic method, a way to maintain integrity and independence in how he works and what he shows.

Han Lei (b. 1967, Kaifeng, Henan Province) graduated from the Central Academy of Craft and Design, Beijing (1989), and lives and works in Beijing. His work has been presented in solo exhibitions at m97 Gallery, Shanghai (2010); Taikang Space, Beijing (2010); Iberia Center for Contemporary Art, Beijing (2009); Hanart TZ Gallery, Hong Kong (2007); Art Now Gallery, Beijing (2006); Gallery LOFT, Paris (2006); and Gallery Polaris, Paris (2005). Most recent major group exhibitions include the Lianzhou International Photo Festival (2009, 2007, 2006); *55 Days in Valencia: Chinese Art Meeting* at IVAM, Valencia (2008); the Gwangju Museum of Art, Korea (2007); the Guangzhou Photo Biennial (2005); and the Rome Photography Festival (2005, 2004).

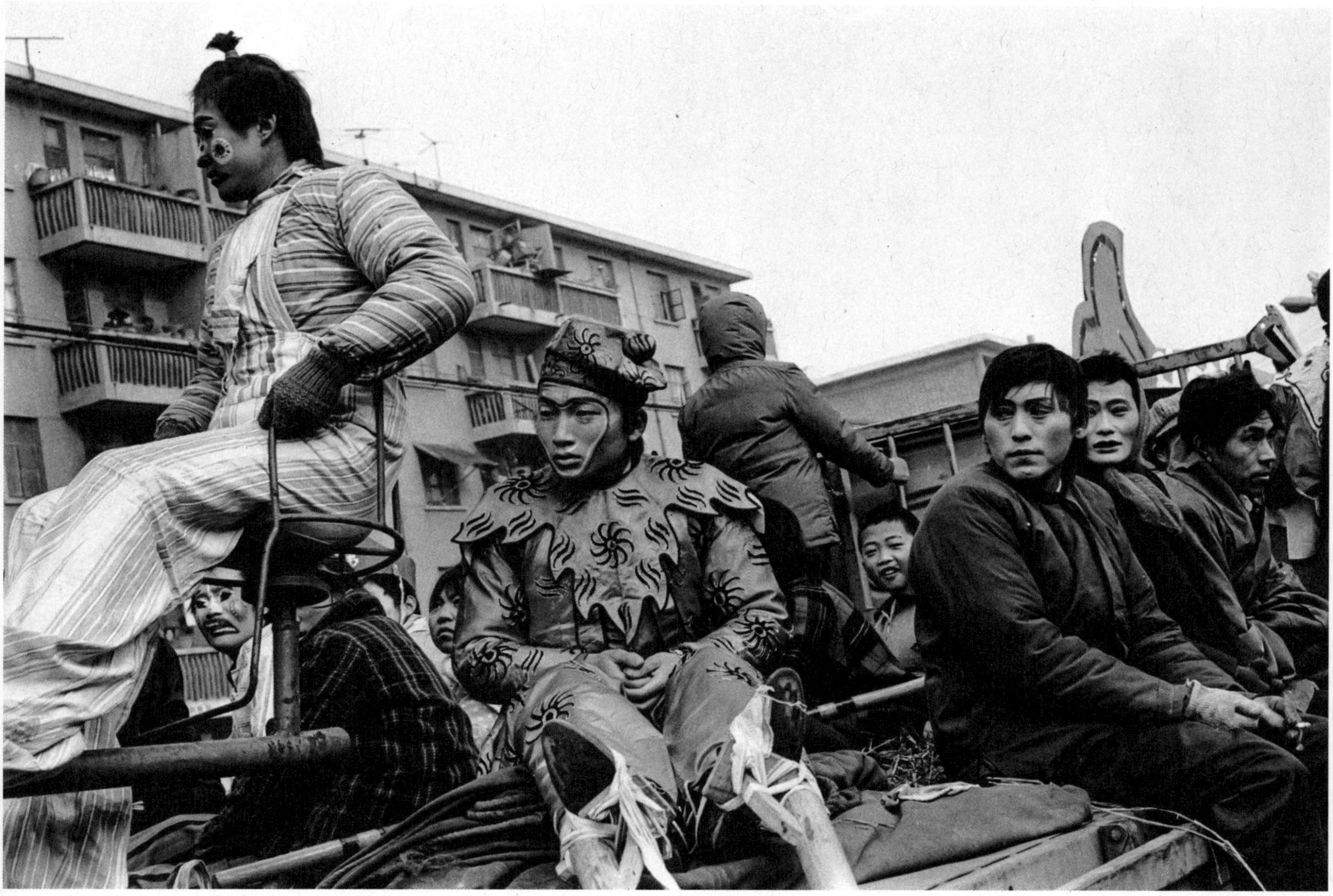

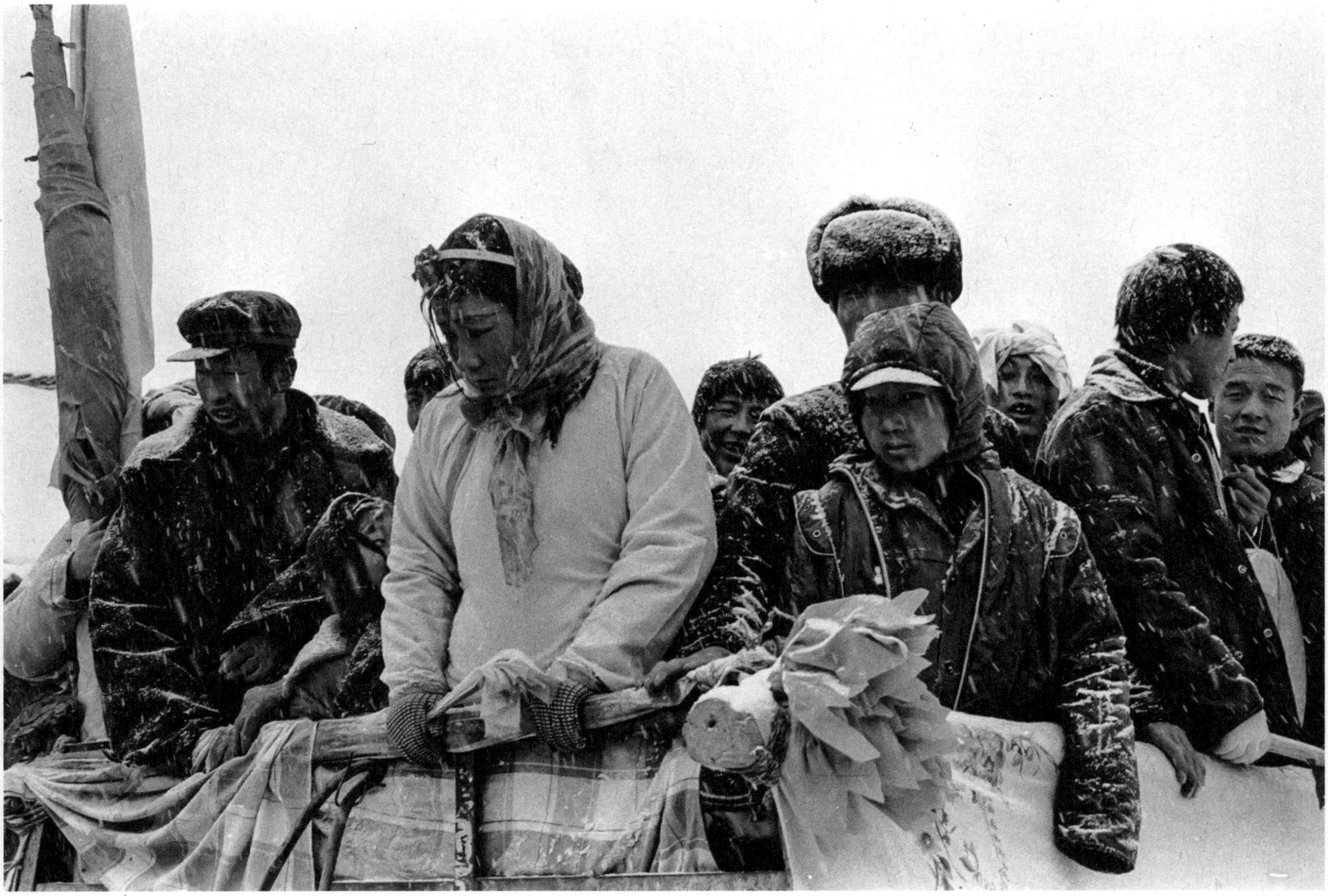

LIVING DANCE STUDIO

Dance with Farm Workers, 2001

Video (color, sound)
57 min

This video documented the rehearsal and performance at Beijing Ocean Art Center
Filmed by Su Ming and Wu Wenguang, edited by Wu Wenguang

Director: Wen Hui
Space Design: Song Dong, Yin Xiuzhen
Music, Sound Production: Wen Bin
Installation: Yin Xiuzhen
Video Installation: Song Dong
Slide Photography: Mao Ran
Initiators: Wen Hui, Song Dong, Yin Xiuzhen, Wu Wenguang

Performers:
Lai Daizhong (27 years old, from Anmin Village, Huilong Town, Wan County, Chongqing, a plasterer in Beijing)
Liang Jicai (28 years old, from Yaba Village, Tonggu Town, Wushan County, Chongqing)
Su Jun (42 years old, from Jinwan Village, Tonggu Township, Wushan County, Chongqing, an electrician in Beijing)
Wan Fangbing (28 years old, from Longqiao Village, Xinying Township, Wushan County, Chongqing, a stevedore in Beijing)
Zhou Zongxuan (52 years old, from Zhuyuan Village, Tonggu Township, Wushan County, Chongqing, a house painter in Beijing)
Liang Keyuan (24 years old, from Baicao Village, Zhonglu Township, Wuxi County, Chongqing, a waterproofer in Beijing)
Huang Tianliang (44 years old, from Wangjiawan Village, Yingzhong Town, Zhongxiang County, Hubei, a carpenter in Beijing)
Zhou Zongde (44 years old, from Zhuyuan Village, Tonggu Township, Wushan County, Chongqing, a handyman in Beijing)
Xiao Yinping (16 years old, from Zhangfeigou, Hebian Town, Daying County, Sichuan)
Wei Zhishan (45 years old, from Maoba Village, Tonggu Township, Wushan County, Chongqing, a handyman in Beijing)
Cheng Yisen (18 years old, from Baima Village, Xinying Township, Wushan County, Chongqing, a handyman in Beijing)
Cheng Yixin (21 years old, from Baima Village, Guanyin Township, Wushan County, Chongqing, a handyman in Beijing)
Tian Benxiong (22 years old, from Wanzhong Road, Longbao District, Wan County, Sichuan, an electrician in Beijing)
Zhang Yuxiang (29 years old, from Pianyan Village, Daping Township, Wushan County, Chongqing, a plasterer in Beijing)
Liang Kezhi (26 years old, from Baicao Village, Zhonglu Township, Wuxi County, Sichuan, a waterproofer in Beijing)
Mei Shaotian (29 years old, from Datang Village, Nongba Town, Yunyang County, Chongqing, a waterproofer in Beijing)
Zhang Shangwen (23 years old, from Xiaoting District, Yichang City, Hubei, a plasterer in Beijing)
Xu Yuanping (39 years old, from Longwan Village, Tonggu Township, Wushan County, Chongqing, a plasterer in Beijing)
Tian Benping (35 years old, from Jinwan Village, Tonggu Township, Wushan County, Chongqing, a bricklayer in Beijing)
Tian Songfa (38 years old, from Jinwan Village, Tonggu Township, Wushan County, Chongqing, a house painter in Beijing)
Yang Yonghua (24 years old, from Dashi Village, Guanwan Town, Wushan County, Chongqing, a house painter in Beijing)
Liang Caishu (35 years old, from Baicao Village, Zhonglu Township, Wushan County, Chongqing, a waterproofer worker in Beijing)
Zhang Xuye (25 years old, from Xiangshu Village, Xinying Township, Wushan County, Chongqing, a house painter in Beijing)
Chen Zhengui (32 years old, from Tiandeng Village, Pingnan Township, Wushan County, Chongqing, a handyman in Beijing)
Su Yong (20 years old, from Qingsong Village, Tonggu Township, Wushan County, Chongqing, an electrician in Beijing)
Liu Rangdeng (25 years old, from Longqiao Village, Xinying Township, Wushan County, Chongqing, a house painter in Beijing)
Tan Qingyun (33 years old, from Baofeng Village, Miaoyu Town, Wushan County, Chongqing, an electrician in Beijing)
Huang Shengke (45 years old, from Tonglin Village, Guandu Town, Wushan County, Chongqing, a house painter in Beijing)
Li Chengshao (34 years old, from Hongliang Village, Miaoyu Town, Wushan County, Chongqing, a plasterer in Beijing)
Tan Daan (24 years old, from Baofeng Village, Miaoyu Town, Wushan County, Chongqing, a welder in Beijing)
Huang Weixin (Freelance performing artist from New York)
Wang Mei (Choreographer, Beijing Song and Dance Ensemble)
Estelle Soep (Theater actor)
Wang Yanan (Performer, Oriental Song and Dance Ensemble)
Feng Dehua (Journalist, writer)
Zheng Fuming (Dancer)
Bi Yan (Performer, Oriental Song and Dance Ensemble)
Alison Friedman (Student, Brown University, USA)
Yuan Qu (Performer, Oriental Song and Dance Ensemble)
Wen Hui (Choreographer)

Production Crew:
Coordinator: Zheng Fuming
Publicity: Wu Kejia
Technical: Su Ming
Stage Manager: Zhang Qiao
Costumes: Zhang Xiaoyan
Production: Living Dance Studio, Ocean Art Center
Performance Date and Venue: August 23, 2001, 8 p.m.; 3rd Floor, Ocean Art Center.

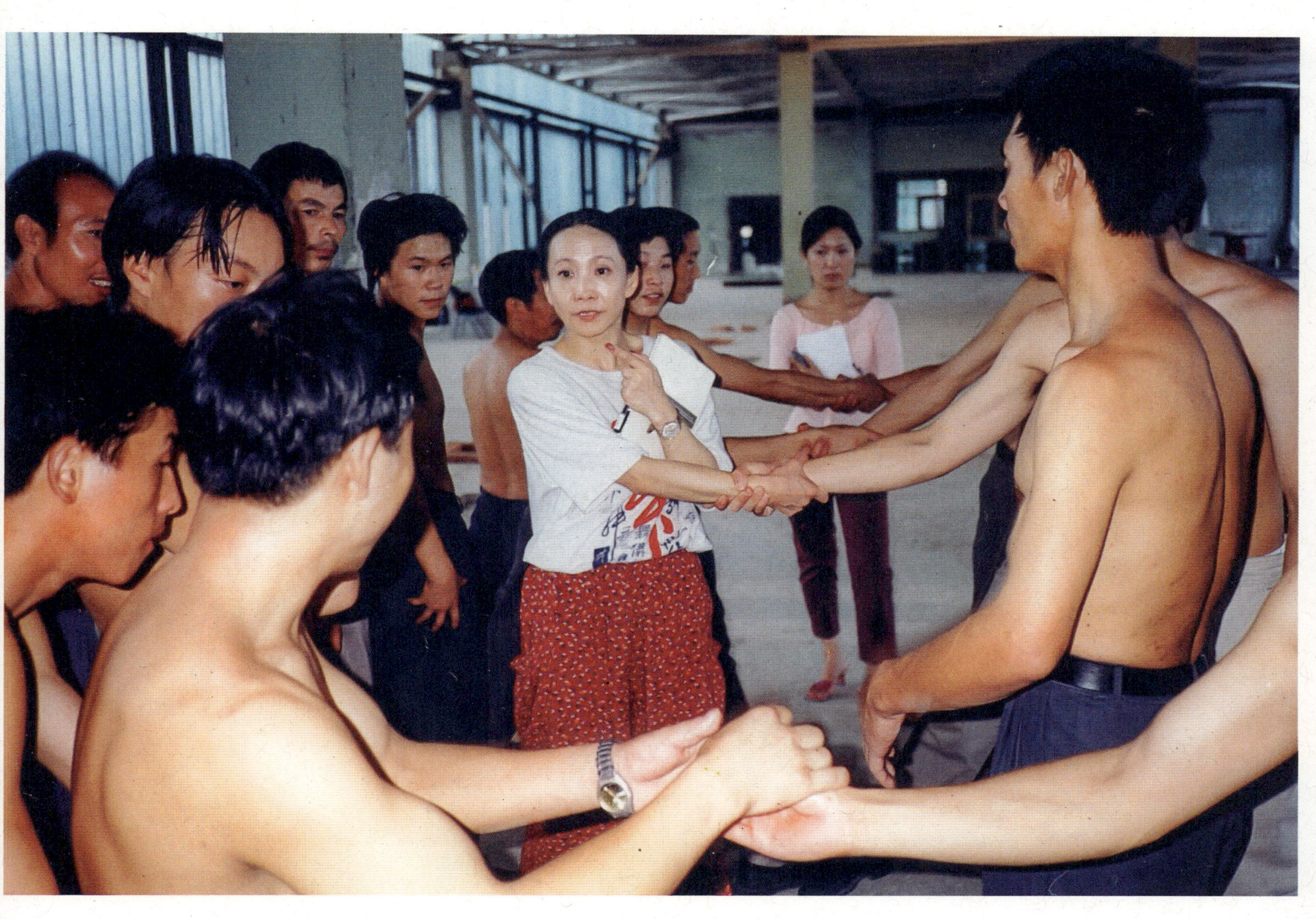

In the summer of 2001, a performance took place in an abandoned textile factory outside Beijing. The venue, like many industrial spaces at the time, was awaiting demolition as the city transformed under the pressures of rapid modernization. It became the temporary stage for *Dance with Farm Workers*, a collaborative project initiated by choreographer Wen Hui, artists Song Dong and Yin Xiuzhen and filmmaker Wu Wenguang.

The work brought together two very different groups: ten professional dancers—some of them foreigners studying in Beijing—and thirty rural migrant laborers, most of them construction workers from Sichuan Province. At first, their roles seemed fixed: dancers as trained performers, farm workers as participants brought in for their physical presence. Some dancers were hesitant to make close contact; the initial rehearsals were marked by social and bodily distance.

But the structure of the work slowly shifted those relationships. Simple physical exercises and shared tasks such as rolling oil drums, singing together, and climbing ladders gave way to unexpected forms of intimacy. A moment in which participants sat face to face and exchanged questions, meant to last 15 minutes, stretched into 45 minutes of open conversation. Slowly, the boundaries between performer and non-performer began to dissolve. The factory floor became a rehearsal space not just for a performance, but for a temporary community.

Living Dance Studio had always used movement to explore everyday life. But *Dance With Farm Workers* went further: it refused spectacle, script, or representation. There was no narrative to deliver, no message to perform. The farm workers were not actors and were not cast in roles. They were participating as themselves—uneasy, curious, quiet, resistant, engaged. Initially, most joined for the modest daily wage of 30 yuan. Later, they found themselves standing at the center of a performance. Not as metaphors for labor or victims of economic displacement, but as people with bodies, presence, and personal agency.

Instead of being staged for a conventional audience, the performance was documented. But the resulting film does not focus on the final presentation, it puts the process in focus: the rehearsals, conversations, and moments of friction and connection.

The empty factory served as a stage with no place to hide which put the interaction itself in the spotlight. At its core, *Dance With Farm Workers* is not about visibility in the usual sense. It does not claim to "give voice" or "raise awareness" in grand terms. Instead, it registers the difficulty of meeting across structural divides. It documents a space in which social hierarchies are not erased but momentarily unsettled through mutual exposure and shared time.

Wen Hui later reflected on the limits of this approach: the lives of the workers did not change as a result of the performance, and public attention soon faded. But the work did leave a mark. It highlighted the contradictions of artistic practice in a transforming society—how art might draw attention to injustice, while remaining part of the systems that enable it. Within this context, the question of individualism takes on a different shape. Here, it is not about asserting selfhood through expressive gesture, nor about heroic opposition. Instead, individualism is found in presence: in being recognized without role or function, without being reduced to a symbol or story. In a performance without plot, without the usual cast protagonists, the participants appear simply as themselves, framed not by artifice, but by the slow unfolding of time spent together.

Wen Hui (b. 1960, Yunnan) is a dancer, choreographer, and documentary filmmaker based in Beijing. She graduated in choreography from Beijing Dance Academy in 1989, later studying modern dance in the United States and Europe, including at Folkwang University and with Pina Bausch's company in Wuppertal. In 1994, together with Wu Wenguang, she co-founded the Living Dance Studio, the first independent dance theater group in China, which has become an important platform for socially engaged dance and performance. Her work has been presented widely at international theaters, museums, and festivals, including Zürcher Theater Spektakel, where *Report on Body* (2004) received the ZKB Prize, and later with *Red* (2013), supported by the Goethe-Institut. In recognition of her contributions, Wen Hui received the Goethe Medal in 2021.

HIROSHI OHASHI (ARTISTIC DIRECTOR), **WANG MOLIN, TONG SZE HONG, ZHAO CHUAN**

Lu Xun 2008, 2008

Video (color, sound)
79 min

Lu Xun 2008 is more than a staging of one of modern Chinese literature's most iconic texts. It is a collective experiment in theater-making, social critique, and artistic collaboration. Developed by the four directors Zhao Chuan (Shanghai), Tong Sze Hong (Hong Kong), Wang Molin (Taipei), and Hiroshi Ohashi (Tokyo), the project marked the 90th anniversary of Lu Xun's *Diary of a Madman* (1918), China's first vernacular fiction and a cornerstone of modern literary consciousness.

Rather than simply re-enacting the story, *Lu Xun 2008* reinserted its themes into contemporary conditions of rapid urbanization, moral ambivalence, and social alienation. The absurdity and darkness of Lu Xun's narrator, who believes those around him are cannibals, became a lens to reflect on present-day anxieties such as corruption, competition, and systemic violence. Moments like the 2008 melamine-tainted milk scandal surfaced as reference points, rendering Lu Xun's critique of "cannibal culture" disturbingly relevant.

Each director emphasized different facets of Lu Xun. Wang Molin described the staging as a "theater of cruelty," conjuring a ghostly world of oppression and revolt through body, image, sound, and poetry. Tong Sze Hong underlined the nihilist undertones in Lu Xun's writings, asking what the author would risk if alive in 2008—whether he would speak out against ideological constraint or remain silent, perhaps in jail. Zhao Chuan framed the text not as a canonically rigid classic but as living electricity on stage: a trigger for collisions between thought, body, and social reality. Hiroshi Ohashi contributed his long-standing improvisational practice, making the play a live confrontation between actors and the present.

At the heart of the project was a rethinking of collective creativity in a time when the value of the collective has been eclipsed by an emphasis on individual expression. The work unfolded through workshops and improvisations where each actor's history shaped the play's evolving form. Individualism surfaced only in the fragile, shared labor of doing theater together: every performer became both subject and mirror, a presence on stage but also a vessel for the social tensions and contradictions of the world beyond it. The documentation of *Lu Xun 2008* thus captures a methodology of interrogating power, resisting the confines of professionalized theater, and reclaiming space for ordinary people to act, think, and transform.

The work toured in 2008 as the *East Asia Four Cities Collaboration* across four cities: Shanghai (ddmwarehouse); Hong Kong (Hong Kong Cultural Centre Theatre); Taipei (Gu Ling Street Avant-garde Theatre); and Tokyo ("Asia Meets Asia," Proto Theatre).

Co-producers: Grass Stage (Shanghai),
Clash Theatre (Hong Kong), Body Phase Studio (Taipei), DA-M Theatre (Tokyo)
Main Actors: Takumi Harada, Lee Chi Man, Cheng Chih Chung, Chen Cheng
Actors: Watan Wuma, Wu Meng, Lu Nian, Hou Qin Hui and others
Improvisation music: Chu Sau Man (Shanghai)
Stage design: Zhao Chuan
Lighting design: Tong Sze Hong
Original wood-cut artist: Zhao Yan Nian
Graphic design: Qu Han
Video editing: Tan Yue Min
Executive producer: Wu Meng, Zang
Ni Bei

Grass Stage (Shanghai) / Zhao Chuan
Founded in 2005 by writer and theater-maker Zhao Chuan, Grass Stage takes its name from rural "grass stage" performances held at weddings, funerals, and festivals. Dedicated to grassroots, community-driven creation, the group organizes workshops, discussions, and productions outside commercial or institutional theater. Their collaborative method, often involving non-professional actors, has resulted in works staged across China, Taiwan, Hong Kong, and South Korea.

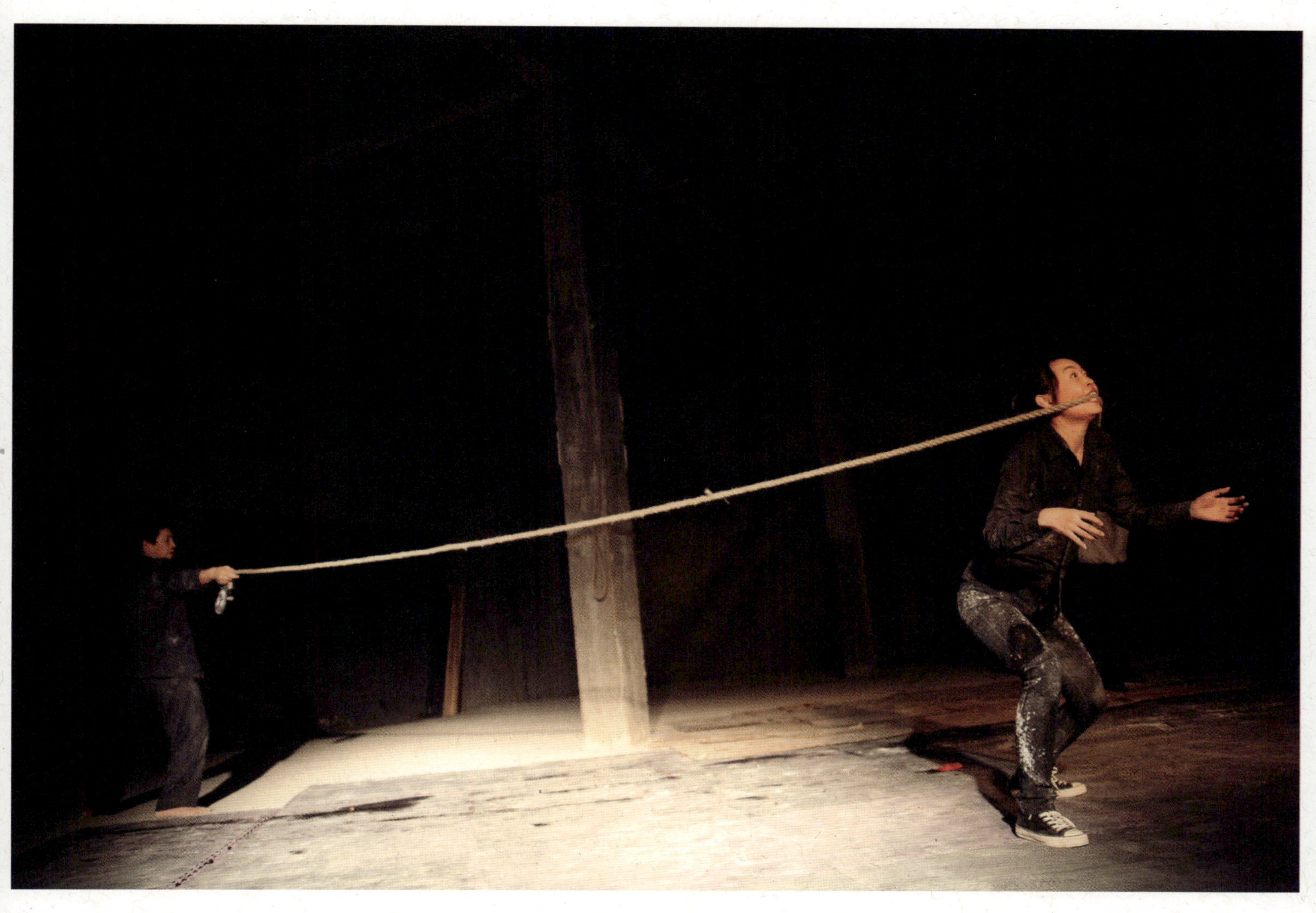

Clash (Hong Kong) / Tong Sze Hong
Clash, founded in 1998 by Tong Sze Hong, is a collective of freelance artists, theater-makers, and social workers. The group engages in street theater, forum theater, contact improvisation, playback, puppet shows, and improvisational performance. Their projects explore social contradictions and welcome "clashes" between formalism and ideology. Tong himself has worked across Asia since the early 1980s, pioneering participatory and movement-based theater in Hong Kong.

Body Phase Studio (Taipei) / Wang Molin
Wang Molin, theater director, critic, and performance artist, established Body Phase Studio in 1991. The studio organized Taiwan's annual international performance art festival and realized large-scale "environmental theater" projects such as *October* (1987). Known for productions that merge performance art with theater, Wang has presented works across Asia and Europe and served as artistic director of Guling Street Avant-garde Theatre (2005–08). His writings on film and theater remain influential in Taiwan.

DA-M Theatre & Proto Theatre (Tokyo) / Hiroshi Ohashi
Hiroshi Ohashi founded Waseda Shin Gekijo in 1978 and later DA-M Theatre in 1986, developing an improvisational and experimental theatrical language. Since 1986, DA-M has been based at Proto Theatre in Tokyo, collaborating across disciplines and borders. Ohashi's projects deconstruct canonical texts and fuse movement, voice, and presence in search of "here-and-now" theater. Since 1997, he has organized the festival *Asia Meets Asia*, which promotes exchange among contemporary Asian theater-makers.

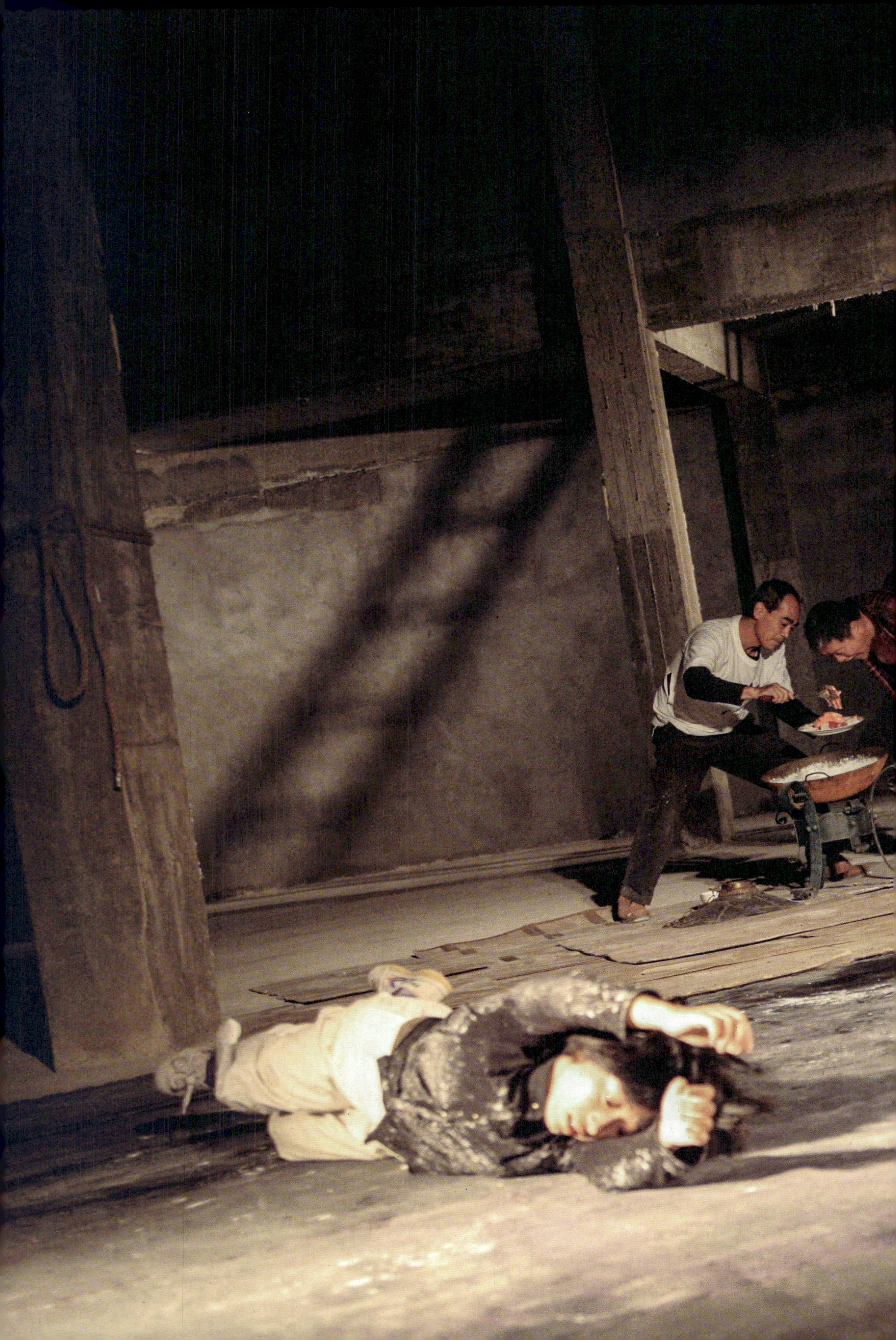

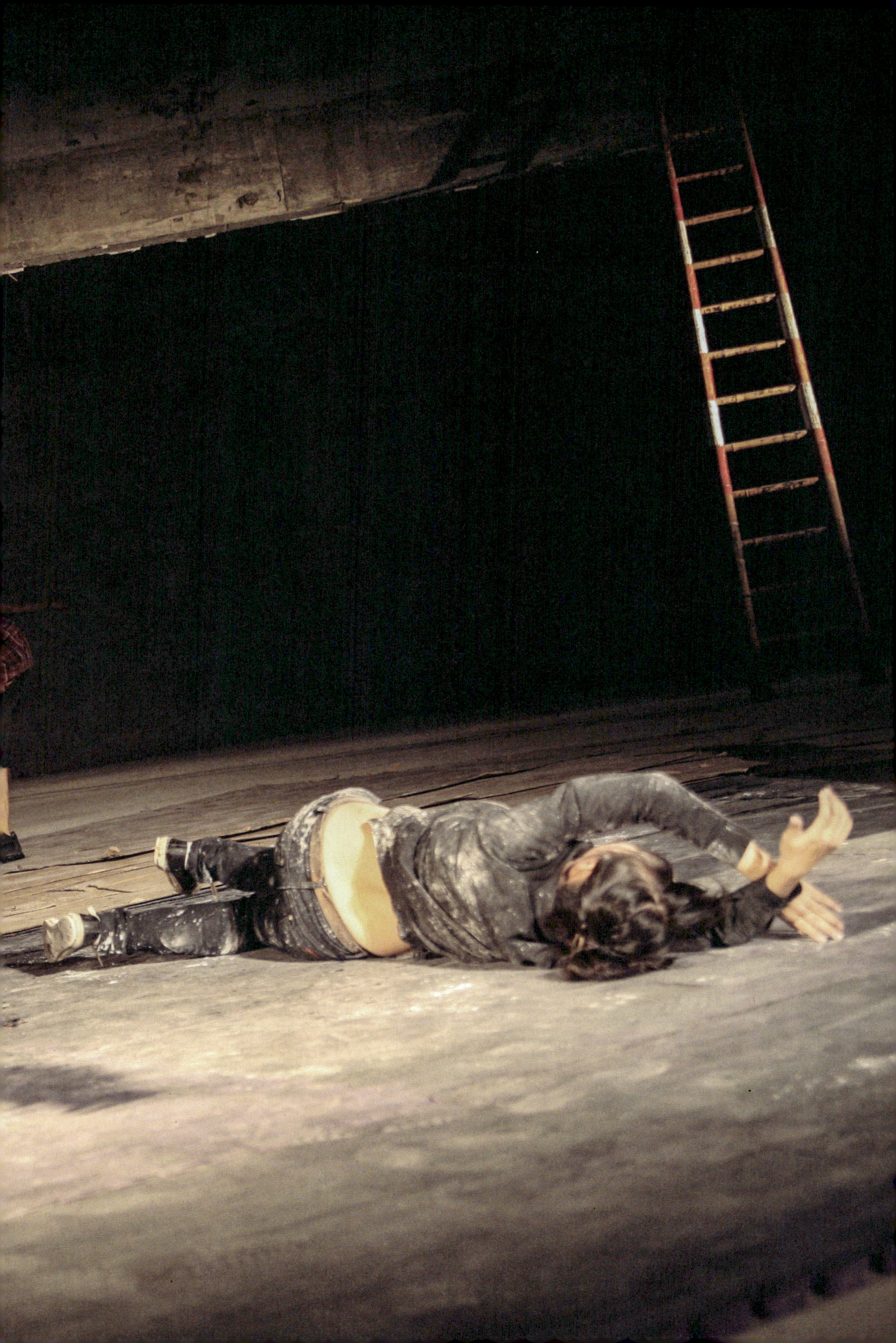

RENT COLLECTION COURTYARD

Rent Collection Courtyard, 2005

Bronze

30 × 15 × 30 cm

During their 2005 visit marking documenta's 50th anniversary, the Sichuan Fine Arts Institute (SFAI) handed over a small bronze sculpture as a gift to a Kassel delegation led by Deputy Mayor Thomas-Erik Junge and Karin Stengel, director of the documenta Archiv. The present referred directly to *Rent Collection Courtyard* (*Shouzuyuan*), a landmark work created in 1965 by SFAI teachers and graduates.

The original *Rent Collection Courtyard* was a site-specific installation of 114 life-size clay figures staged in the former estate of landlord Liu Wencai (1881–1949) in Dayi, Sichuan Province. Commissioned by the provincial Ministry of Culture to depict pre-1949 tenant farmers' exploitation. The artists, including faculty and graduates from the SFAI's sculpture department, worked closely with local folk sculptors, combining direct observation of villagers with artistic research. The result was a monumental ensemble of seven scenes, some such as *Bringing the Rent*, *Asking Too Much*, and *Flames of Anger* referencing reported real events. The work merged Chinese sculptural traditions with Soviet socialist realism and European classicism, involving real tools and agricultural props.

The work's unveiling in Dayi in 1965 drew immense crowds, with visitors traveling long distances, sometimes by foot. This success led to an exhibition of forty figures in Beijing, visited by half a million people in three months. And even before the ensemble was completed, press coverage had already begun, including a short documentary film.

When the Cultural Revolution began in 1966, Jiang Qing, Mao Zedong's wife and head of cultural policy, declared the work a model for all artists. However, it was criticized for lacking positive heroic role models. This requirement prompted altered versions with triumphant endings and numerous of these adaptations toured China, accompanied by illustrated catalogues in many languages, including Western editions. The piece became widely known abroad, notably in Germany where it resonated with the political climate of 1968 marked by student protest movements and anti-imperialist ideas.

Repeated attempts to show the work internationally met obstacles: Harald Szeemann tried to bring it to documenta 5 (1972), and later, with artist Cai Guoqiang, to the Venice Biennale (1999). When the latter failed, Cai created a reinterpretation of the original. The work won the Golden Lion but also stirred debates over copyright, authorship, and artistic freedom in China. Since then, it has inspired numerous reinterpretations by contemporary artists in China and worldwide.

Of the several official versions produced, the only surviving full ensemble is a copper-plated fiberglass traveling version (1974–78) held by the Art Museum of the SFAI in Chongqing. In 2009, this set was presented in the West for the very first time at Schirn Kunsthalle Frankfurt. But whether as an original made of clay, as a traveling edition, as an artistic quotation, or as a present, *Rent Collection Courtyard* remains central in discussions of Mao-era cultural policy, the intertwining of art and ideology, and the enduring impact of Cultural Revolution-era aesthetics on contemporary Chinese practice

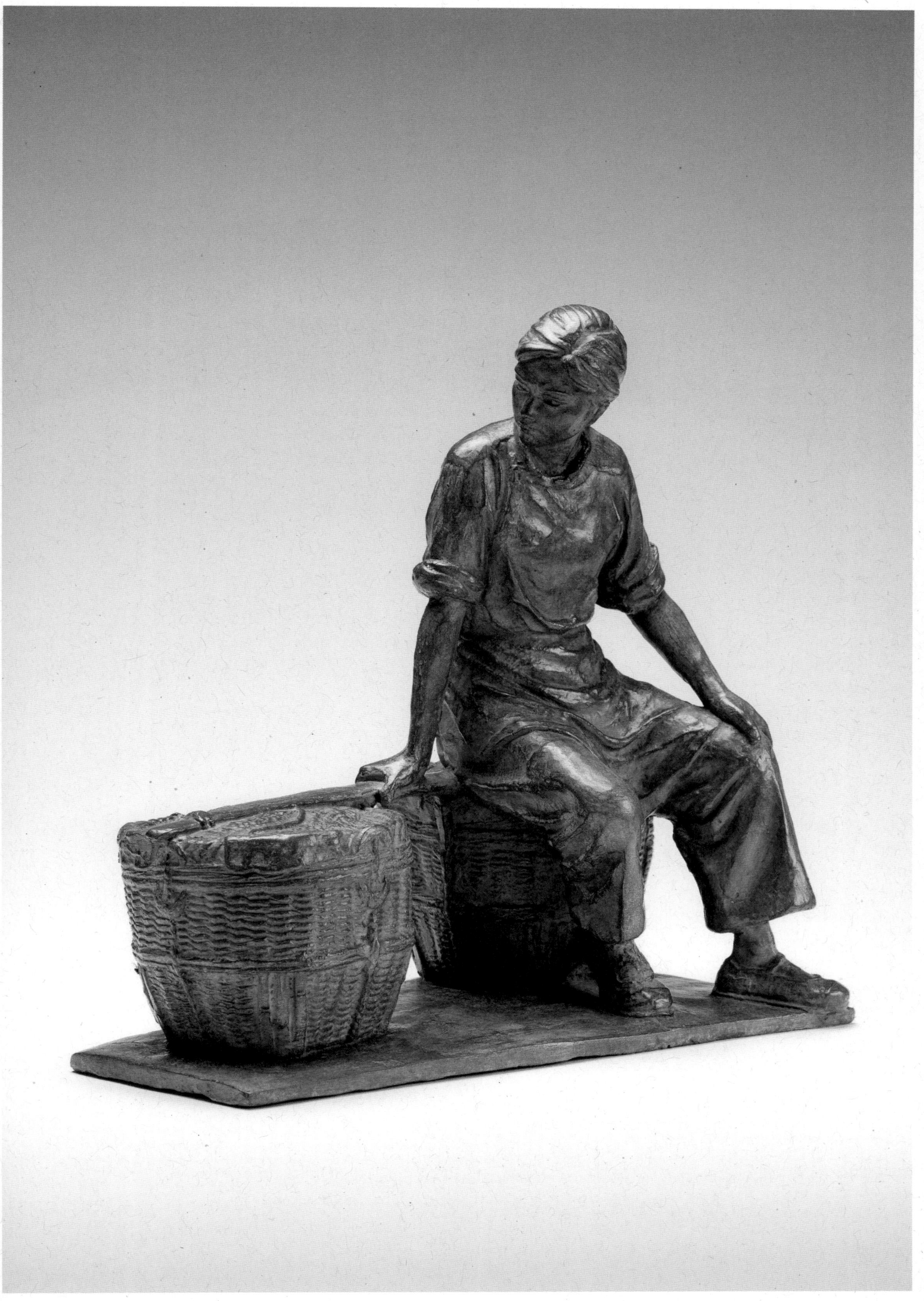

SUI JIANGUO
Kill, 1996
Rubber, nails
65 x 65 x 65 cm

Sui Jianguo's *Kill* marks a pivotal moment in the artist's early sculptural development, capturing a shift from expressive outburst to conceptual restraint. A dense rubber sheet stands rolled upright, its surface punctured by over 100,000 rusted nails. From a distance, the roll appears inert, even soft. Upon closer look it reveals a sharp, bristling structure that simultaneously repels and invites. Its form evokes the appearance of skin or flesh.

Executed in 1996, *Kill* was part of a series of works exploring material endurance and psychological pressure. Though the English title suggests aggression, the original Chinese term "*ji*" refers more precisely to execution by imperial decree, a systematic and remotely executed form of violence. Sui was impressed by the sheer strength of the rubber and its "tolerance" in bearing such a large number of nails without altering its shape.[9] The ability to absorb this intervention without collapse transforms it from passive surface into something active and enduring.

The work's physical density mirrors the psychological weight of its moment. Following the Cultural Revolution, the opening-up reforms, and the trauma of 1989, Chinese society entered a period of intense transformation. For Sui, *Kill* becomes a metaphor: not of resistance as loud defiance, but of compromise and cooperation. "The rubber went from being a passive victim to slowly—with the prick of each nail and the absorption of suffering—turning into an aggressor."[10]

Unlike earlier works—such as *Unborn Bust Portraits* (1989), in which cracked plaster heads barely hold together under gauze bandages—*Kill* suppresses emotional display. The violence here is methodical. Nails are evenly spaced, driven deep, forming an even textured system rather than a visible wound.

And yet, *Kill* is not merely symbolic, its body is literal. The nails suggest crowds, the anonymous many, interchangeable, and sharp. But it is not the masses that are on display, it is their compression. The sculpture holds the tension between control and pain, visibility and containment: both resilient yet vulnerable, pierced and bearing, it offers no catharsis, only presence—an object that asks how much can be endured, and at what cost.

What gives *Kill* its lasting resonance is not its formal innovation alone, but the way it renders the question of survival tactile. The rubber's toughness, the iron's rust, the roll's weight—each element enacts what cannot easily be spoken. The body as part of the sculpture is suggested through impact and accumulation and appears resilient yet vulnerable, both pierced and bearing.

Kill does not present the individual as heroic or defiant. Instead, it shows what it means to endure quietly, under pressure. Each nail carries traces of force, repetition, and time. The sculpture becomes a record of accumulated strain, a body shaped by external pressures and whose strength lies not in resistance, but in lasting.

9 Peggy Wang, "Sui Jianguo: The Matter of Endurance," in *The Future History of Contemporary Chinese Art*, ed. Peggy Wang (Minneapolis: University of Minnesota Press, 2020).
10 Ibid., p. 142.

Sui Jianguo (b. 1956, Qingdao, Shandong Province) earned his BA from Shandong University of Arts in 1984 and MA from the Central Academy of Fine Arts, Beijing, in 1989, where he is now a senior professor. Recent solo exhibitions include TAG Art Museum, Qingdao (2024–25); Pace, Hong Kong (2023); Yimei Art Museum, Beijing (2019); OCAT, Shenzhen (2019); Doris C. Freedman Plaza, Central Park, New York (2014); and the British Museum, London (2012). He has participated in major group shows at LACMA, Los Angeles (2019); Grand Palais, Paris (2017); Foundation Maeght, Nice (2015); and the Shanghai and Guangzhou Biennales.

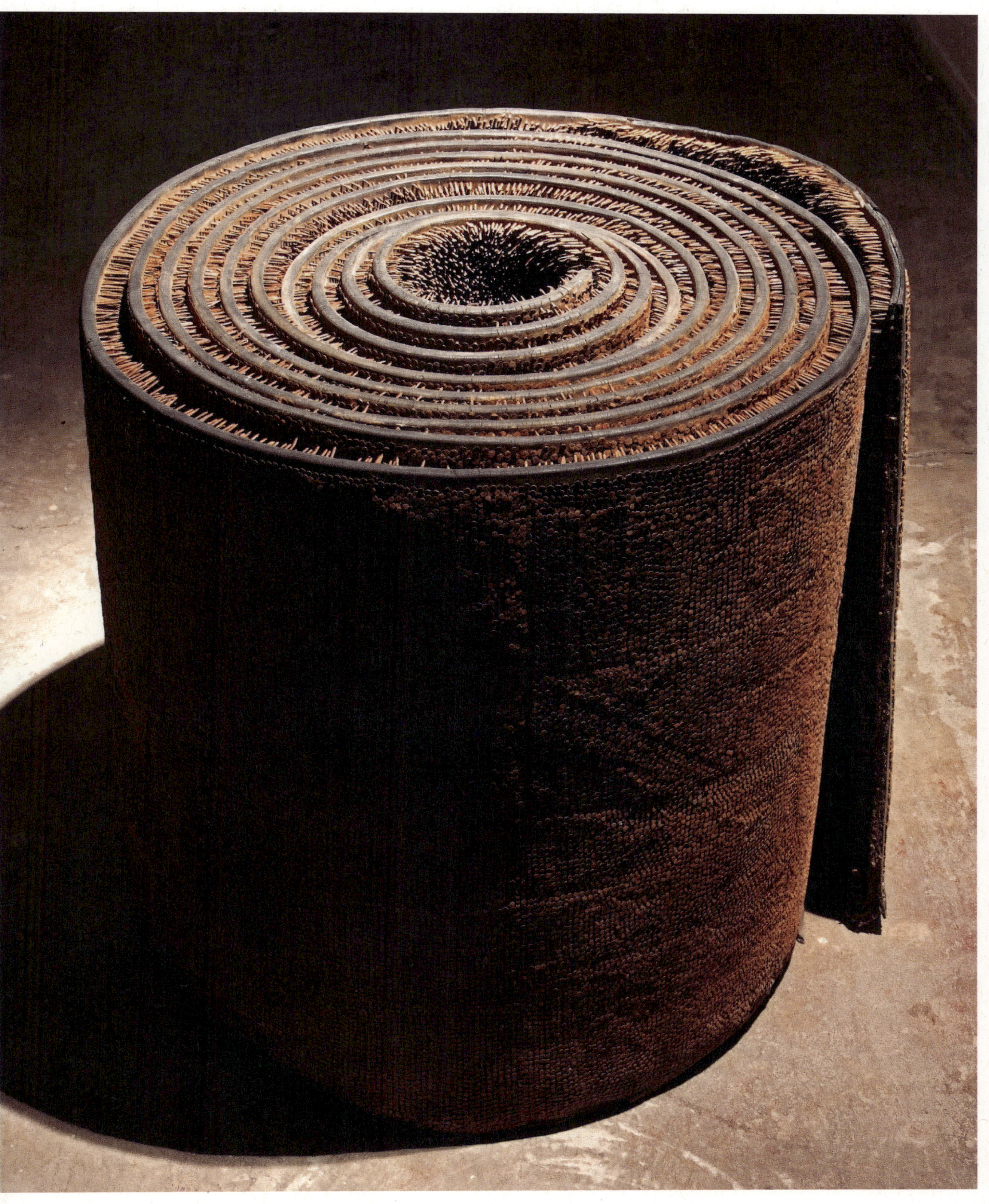

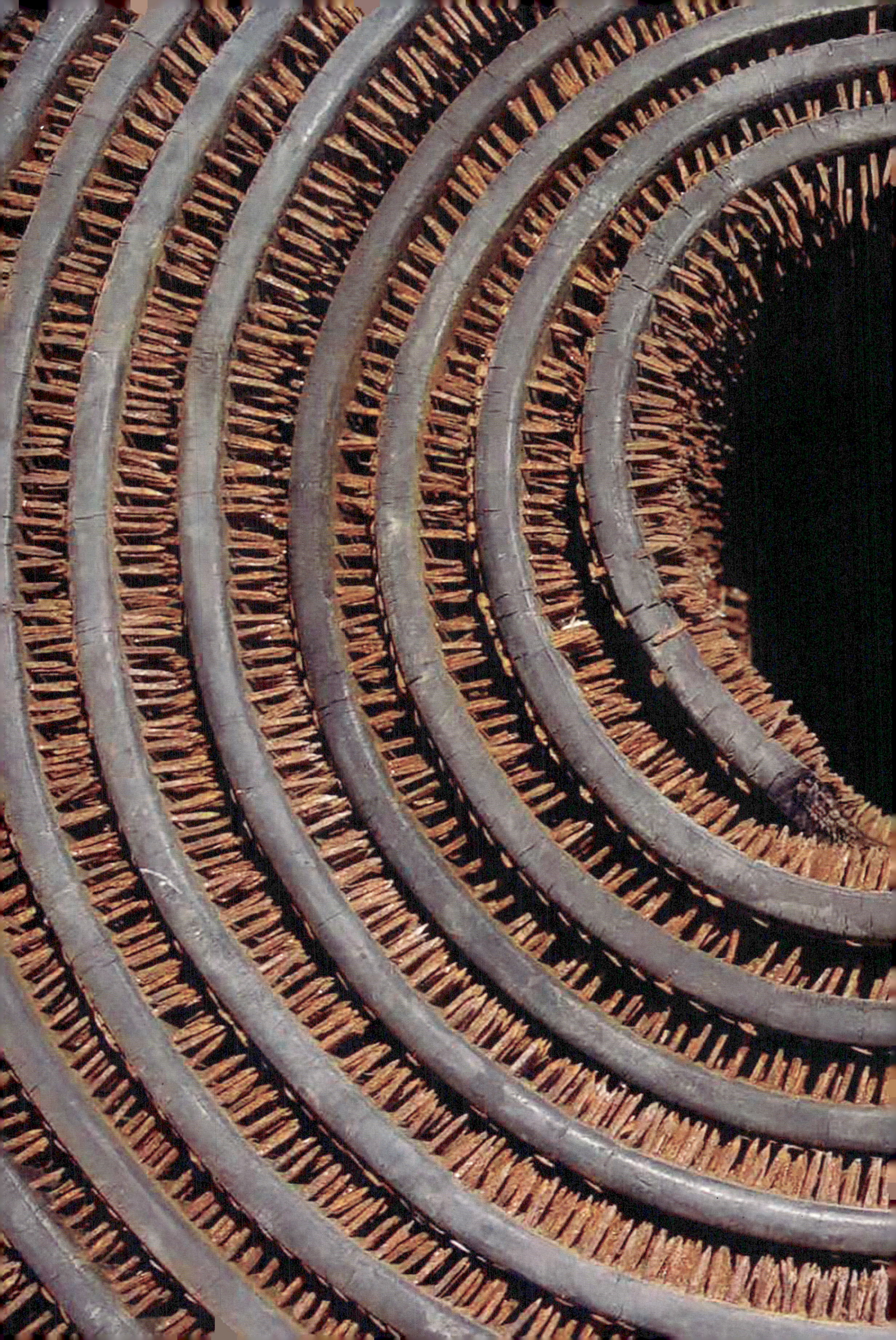

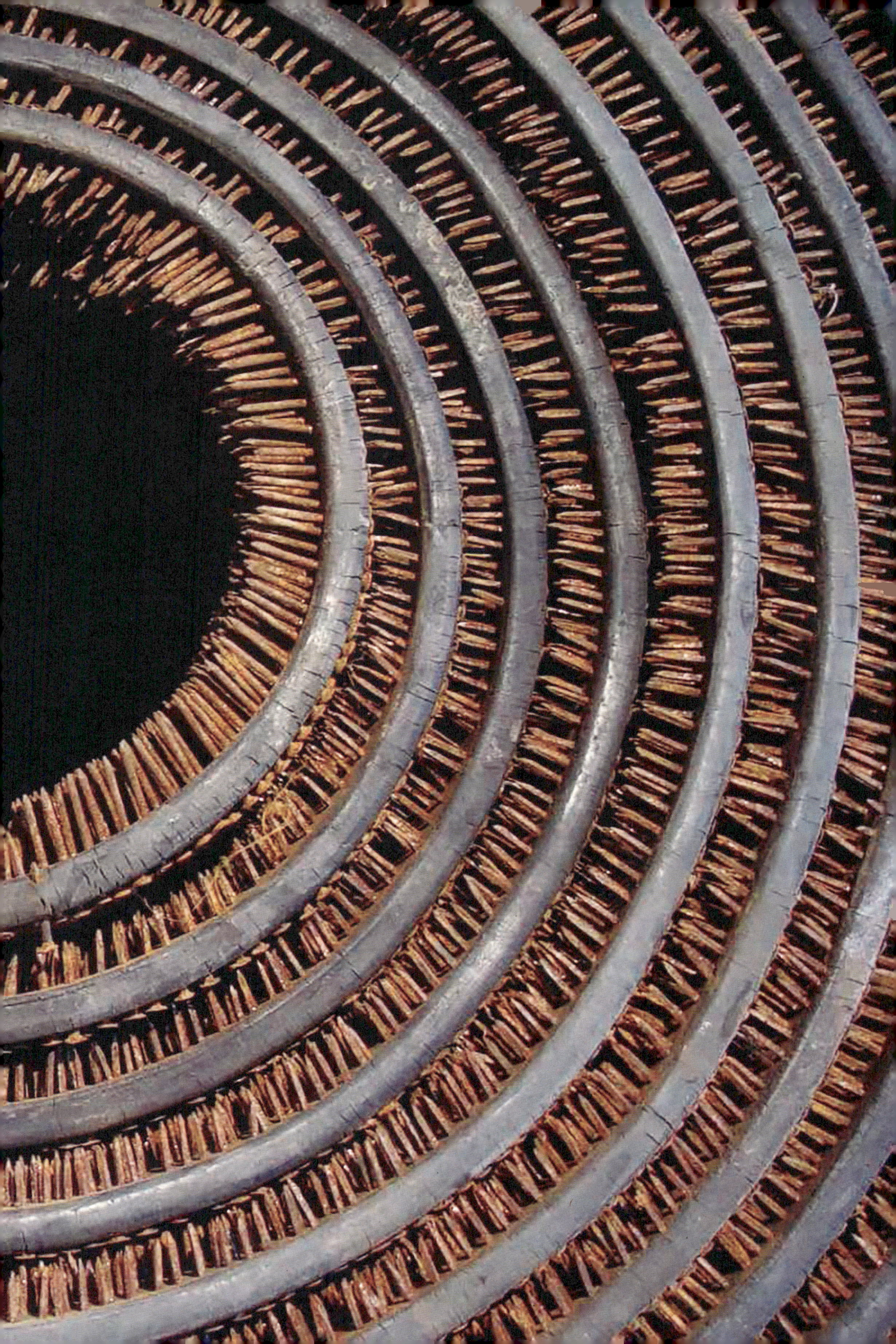

WANG BING

Man with No Name, 2009

Single-channel digital video (color, sound)
92 min

The man appears without introduction; he seems to emerge from the land itself. Without voice-over, music, or explanation, Wang Bing's camera follows his anonymous protagonist with steady persistence: from the basic shelter in which he has spent the night, in the distance, beside him, behind him, close to his hands and face. The result is an unsentimental yet deeply intimate film that documents a year in the life of a man who has removed himself from society but not from human life.

Shot on the outskirts of Beijing, *Man with No Name* tracks the self-contained routines of a man who has built a life on the barest of resources: growing food, collecting water, reusing cast-off materials, tending to his crops and shelter, and sleeping in a rudimentary burrow. He speaks rarely, mostly to himself. Each gesture seems part of a self-developed system of survival whose internal logic remains opaque to the viewer, but consistent within itself. The film unfolds over seasonal cycles, evoking time as physical labor, repetition, and solitude.

Originally conceived as a character study in preparation for Wang's feature *The Ditch* (2010), the film took on a life of its own. As in previous works, Wang's camera does not explain; it accompanies. This refusal to impose narrative or moral interpretation allows the viewer to experience the man's world without filter or reduction. Instead of social critique or psychological probing, *Man with No Name* offers something more difficult: the sustained presence of a human being in motion, persistence, and silence. Yet there is a layer of freedom to be detected, as Elena Pollacchi notes: "The man has taken up the challenge of living alone in a space that, despite its hostile nature, has turned into his shelter."[11] This haunting duality speaks to Wang's broader concern with what remains when systems fail and when community recedes.

While *Man with No Name* may resemble a documentary in form, Wang resists the term. For him, the question is not one of genre, but of attention. He states the most important thing for him is to film people and to understand why and how he films them.[12] In this work, the absence of dialogue and contextual information is not a void: it is a space of radical individualism. Here, the man is not a metaphor or a case study. He is not asked to represent anything other than himself.

Across Wang's body of work, individualism takes shape in quiet resistance: the ability to live, to act, to endure without spectacle. In *Man with No Name*, this resistance is embodied in each small task and daily ritual, filmed not as survival but as life. A man lives, and we watch—not to understand him, but to acknowledge that he exists.

11 Elena Pollacchi, *Wang Bing's Filmmaking of the China Dream: Narratives, Witnesses and Marginal Spaces* (Amsterdam: Amsterdam University Press, 2021) p. 177, www.aup.nl/en/book/9789463721837.
12 Ibid.

Wang Bing (b. 1967, Xi'an, Shaanxi Province) studied photography at the Luxun Academy of Fine Arts (1992) and film at the Beijing Film Academy (1995). His films have been presented at major festivals and institutions worldwide, including Venice, Cannes, Locarno, and the Centre Pompidou, Paris. He won the Golden Leopard at Locarno for *Mrs. Fang* (2017), received the EYE Art & Film Prize in Amsterdam (2017), and the Chanel Next Prize (2021). Recent works include *Jeunesse (Le Printemps)* (2023), premiered at Cannes, and *Man in Black* (2023). He has taught at Le Fresnoy and given masterclasses at the School of Advanced Studies in the Social Sciences, Paris. He lives and works between Paris and China.

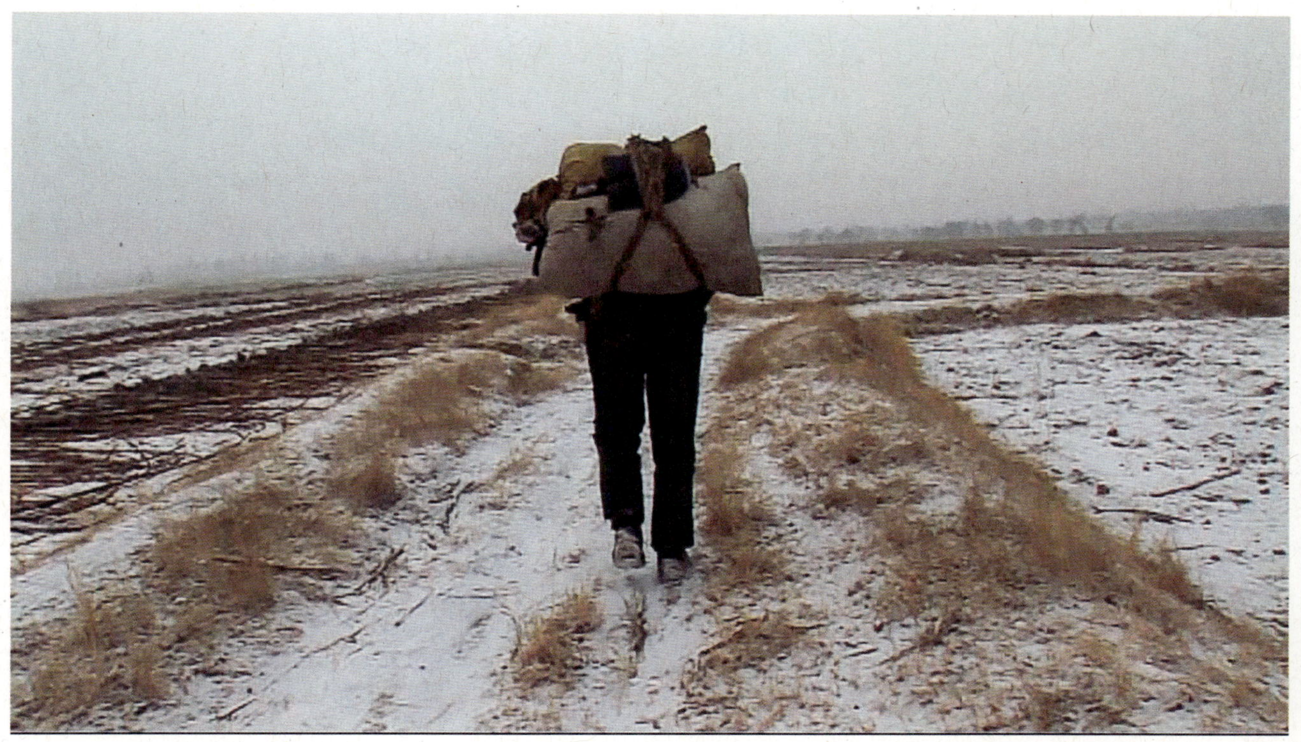

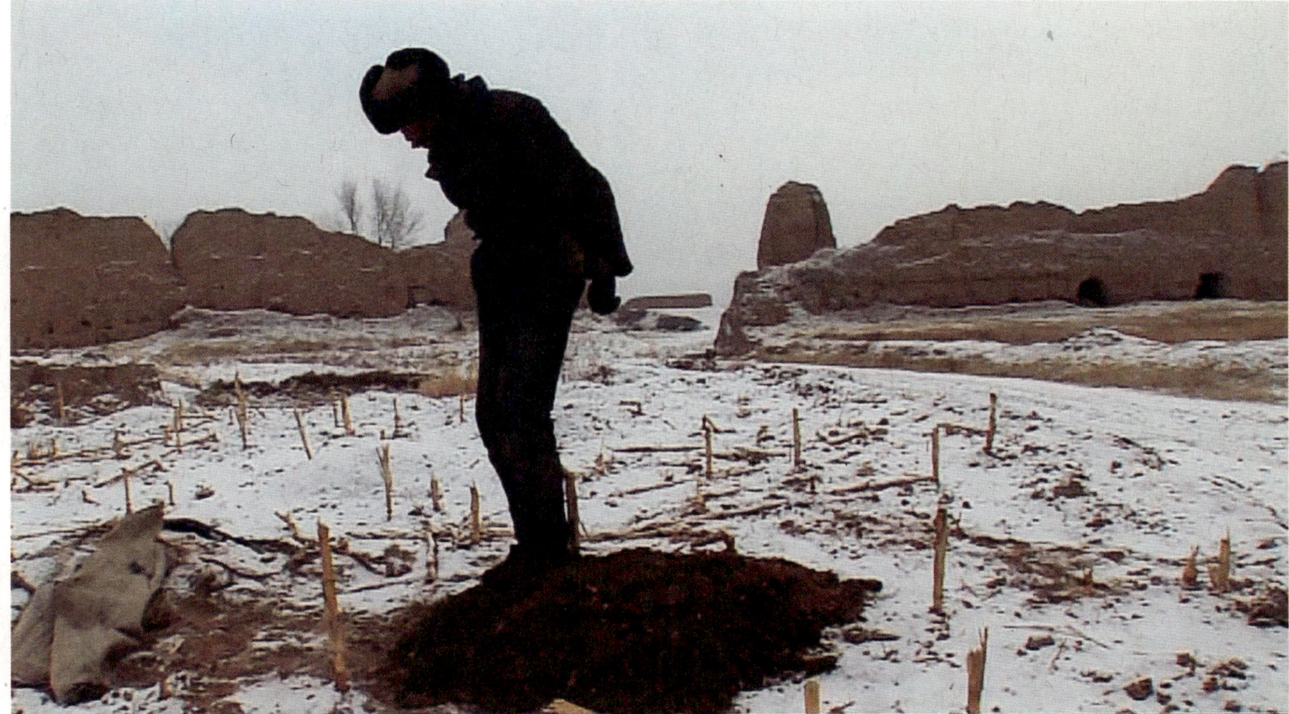

WANG YOUSHEN

Shining · Kassel, 1989–2026

Photographs, glass, light
Variable dimensions

Wang Youshen was among the first group of Chinese artists to enter the global art context, having participated in the 45th Venice Biennale in 1993. Throughout the 1990s, he conducted a series of art experiments centered on media, focusing on local and global contemporary cultural phenomena within the context of globalization. From the 1990s onward, he served as the art editor for *Beijing Youth Daily*, a newspaper under the Beijing Municipal Committee of the Communist Youth League. Through his efforts, Chinese contemporary art gained exposure on this official platform, an extremely rare occurrence at the time. This role also enabled Wang to navigate between the official cultural establishment and Chinese contemporary art—often mistakenly perceived as solely underground or marginal—adopting a stance akin to a double agent. In doing so, he critically examined the profound cultural transformations in China in the 1990s and the emergent sense of cultural urgency experienced by individual artists.

In Wang Youshen's artistic practice, he frequently manipulates conceptual strategies to parody and deconstruct journalism, documentary, and archive, a process intrinsically linked to his work as an art editor. While he often employs photography as a medium, his primary interest lies in the image production process inherent in photographic techniques rather than the images themselves. He has conducted two ongoing distinct series titled *Washing* and *Sun Exposure*, which isolate two eponymous stages from the darkroom film development process. In the *Washing* series, Wang immerses pre-existing photographs in water, allowing the same image to transition from clarity to various states of blurriness depending on the immersion duration. The *Sun Exposure* series operates similarly, mimicking the darkroom process of drying photographs by manipulating pre-existing prints. However, in the latter, the photographs are brought outdoors to dry, thus placing them in a public and everyday context, distinct from the darkroom. This implicitly renders the process of photographic "meaning" formation entirely transparent.

The work created by Wang Youshen for this exhibition belongs to the *Sun Exposure* series. Throughout his artistic career, spanning three to four decades, Wang has maintained a habit of collecting archival materials. A selection of these archives, encompassing both private and public dimensions, is presented in this exhibition. For the exhibiting work, he utilizes photographs he documented of significant moments in Chinese contemporary art, collaging them with sociopolitical news photographs—both global and local—that he collected, as well as photos taken during his personal travels. All these photographs were produced in negative form, essentially reprocessing already completed images and thereby disrupting their stable state. Exhibitions such as the *China/Avant-Garde* exhibition (National Art Museum of China, 1989) or the 45th Venice Biennale, depicted in the photographs, become the subjects of the artist's critique, overt and subtle, of globalized cultural discourse, articulated from a perspective imbued with profound cultural criticism. This critique also constitutes a contemplation and self-reflection on the (creative) individuals' experience within China's process of globalization.

Wang Youshen (b. 1964 in Beijing) lives and works in Beijing. He graduated from the Central Academy of Fine Arts in 1988 and was long affiliated with *Beijing Youth Daily* (1988–2018), where he served as art editor and director. A key participant in the development of Chinese contemporary art, Wang has taken part in landmark exhibitions including *China/Avant-Garde* exhibition (1989), *New Generation Art* (1991), the 45th Venice Biennale (1993), and the 27th São Paulo Biennale (2006). His work has also been shown in major international and domestic institutions, reflecting his ongoing engagement with the intersections of art, media, and daily life.

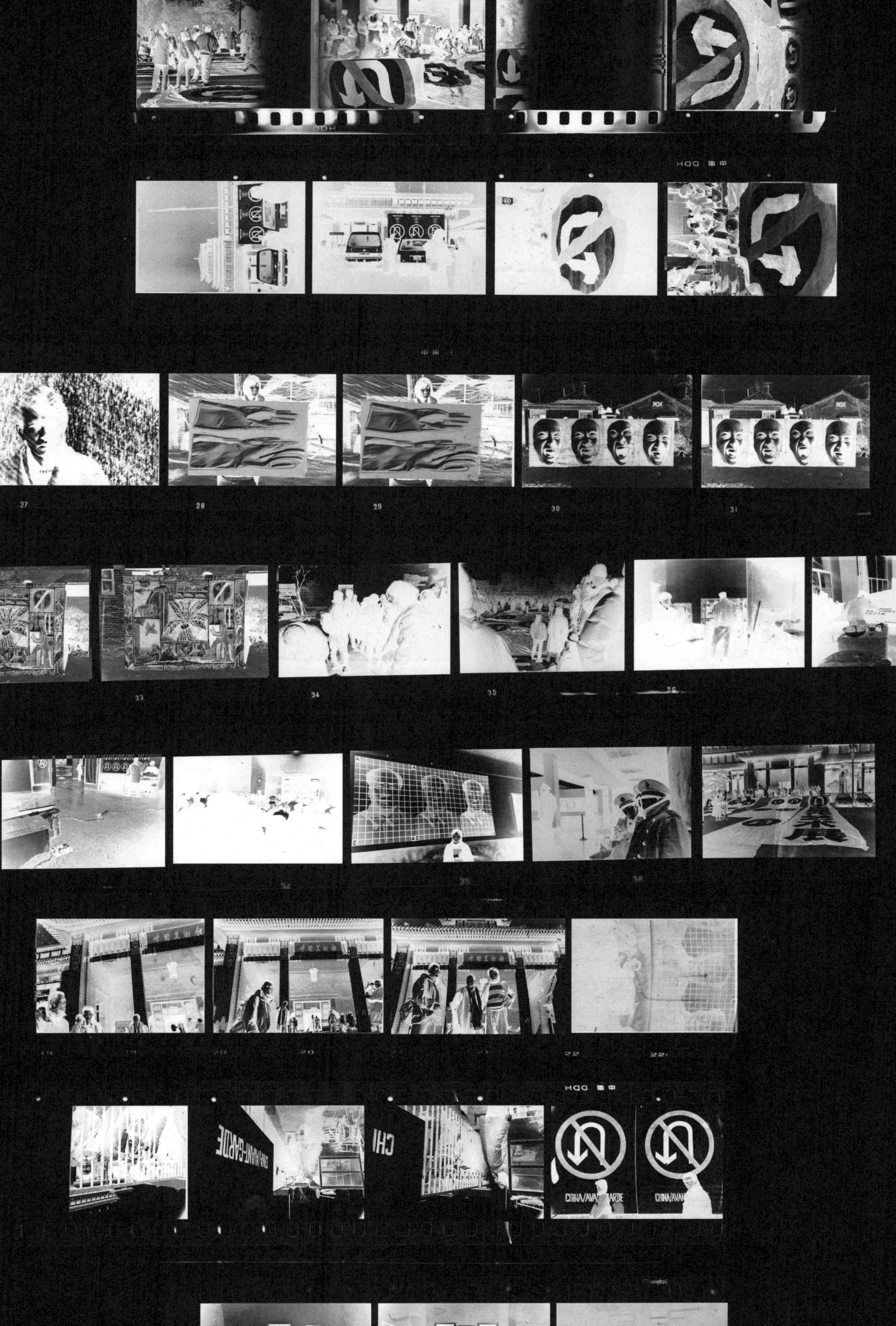

XIAO LU

15 Gunshots...from 1989 to 2003, 2003

C-print, framed gunshot hole
Each 100 x 45 x 30 cm

With *15 Gunshots…from 1989 to 2003*, Xiao Lu returns to a formative moment in both her life and the history of Chinese contemporary art. The work consists of fifteen nearly identical photographic prints. In each image, the artist stands facing the viewer, holding a pistol, her expression composed and unwavering. As the series progresses, her figure gradually fades, with each print more washed out than the last until the final image appears almost entirely white. Every single one of the fifteen photographs has been pierced by a bullet.

The piece responds to the now-iconic event that took place on February 5, 1989, during the opening of the *China/Avant-Garde* exhibition at the National Art Gallery in Beijing. Xiao Lu took part with her work *Dialogue*, an installation composed of two aluminum phone booths connected by a mirror and a dangling red telephone. At the time, Xiao Lu was a young artist trained in oil painting at the Zhejiang Academy of Fine Arts and *Dialogue* was her graduation project. During the opening, she spontaneously fired two shots into the installation. The reaction was immediate and chaotic. The exhibition was temporarily shut down, Xiao Lu and fellow artist Tang Song were arrested, and the incident was widely reported. Critics interpreted it as an act of terrorism or sabotage, though Xiao herself later described it as deeply personal. In the years following, Tang Song became her partner, which led to the widespread assumption that it was a collaborative work. Fifteen years later, Xiao Lu created *15 Gunshots* as an objection to this assumption. With the assistance of fellow artist Li Songsong, she created a photograph of herself in the same pose. The image was printed fifteen times, one for each year that had passed since *Dialogue*, and each was shot with a live bullet at a shooting range near Beijing. The result is a series of controlled and private gestures that revisits a lifetime act between private life, love and social/political circumstances, rather than a milestone political gesture. The work marks the eruption of feelings long repressed, a way to confront the psychological aftermath of an abusive relationship. The performance altered the course of her life, drawing public attention while also subjecting her to interrogation and suspicion.

While *Dialogue* was sudden and unpredictable, *15 Gunshots* reflects over time. The work does not reenact the original event but re-examines its impact. The gradual disappearance of her figure in the prints tells of this transformation and each bullet becomes a marker of endurance, a signal of continuity and change. The once impulsive act is now repetitive and reflective and thereby becomes a way of reclaiming agency. *15 Gunshots* points to the endurance of selfhood through time, loss, and confrontation. In place of spectacle, the work signals persistence and the gesture of shooting, repeated with precision and intention, becomes a method of survival, self-confrontation and reinvention.

Xiao Lu (b. 1962 in Hangzhou) graduated from the Zhejiang Academy of Fine Arts in 1988 and lives between Beijing and London. Her work has been shown in major group exhibitions at MoMA, New York (*Collection 1970s–Present*, 2019–2020); Tate Modern (*Performer and Participant*, 2018–2019); Guggenheim Museum (*Art and China After 1989*, 2017–2018); and the National Gallery of Victoria (*China – The Past is Present*, 2022). Recent solo exhibitions include *Junk* at Passage Gallery, Sydney (2024) and *Skew* at 10 Chancery Lane Gallery, Hong Kong (2019). Her work is held in the collections of MoMA, Tate, NGV, and Taikang Art Museum.

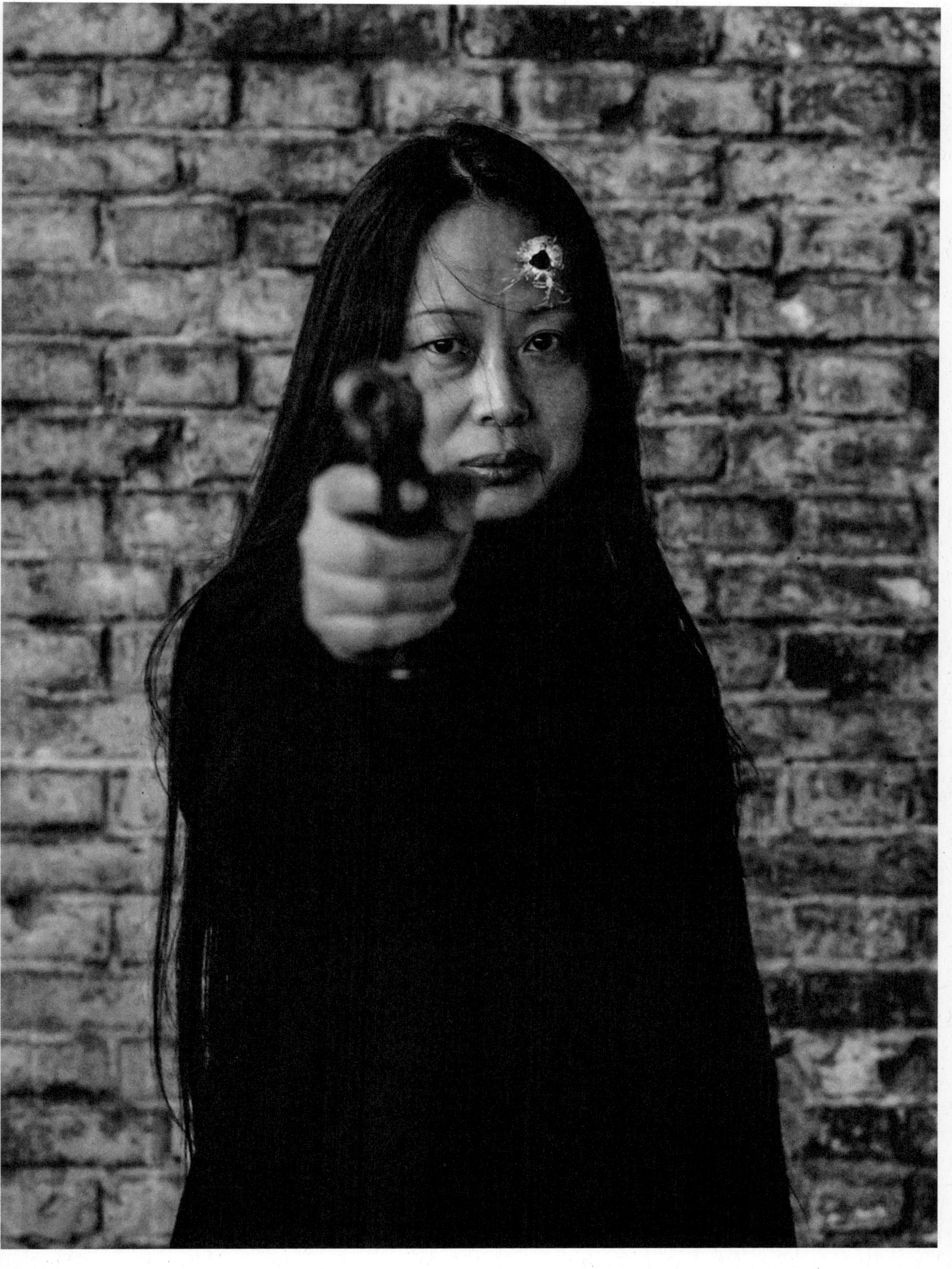

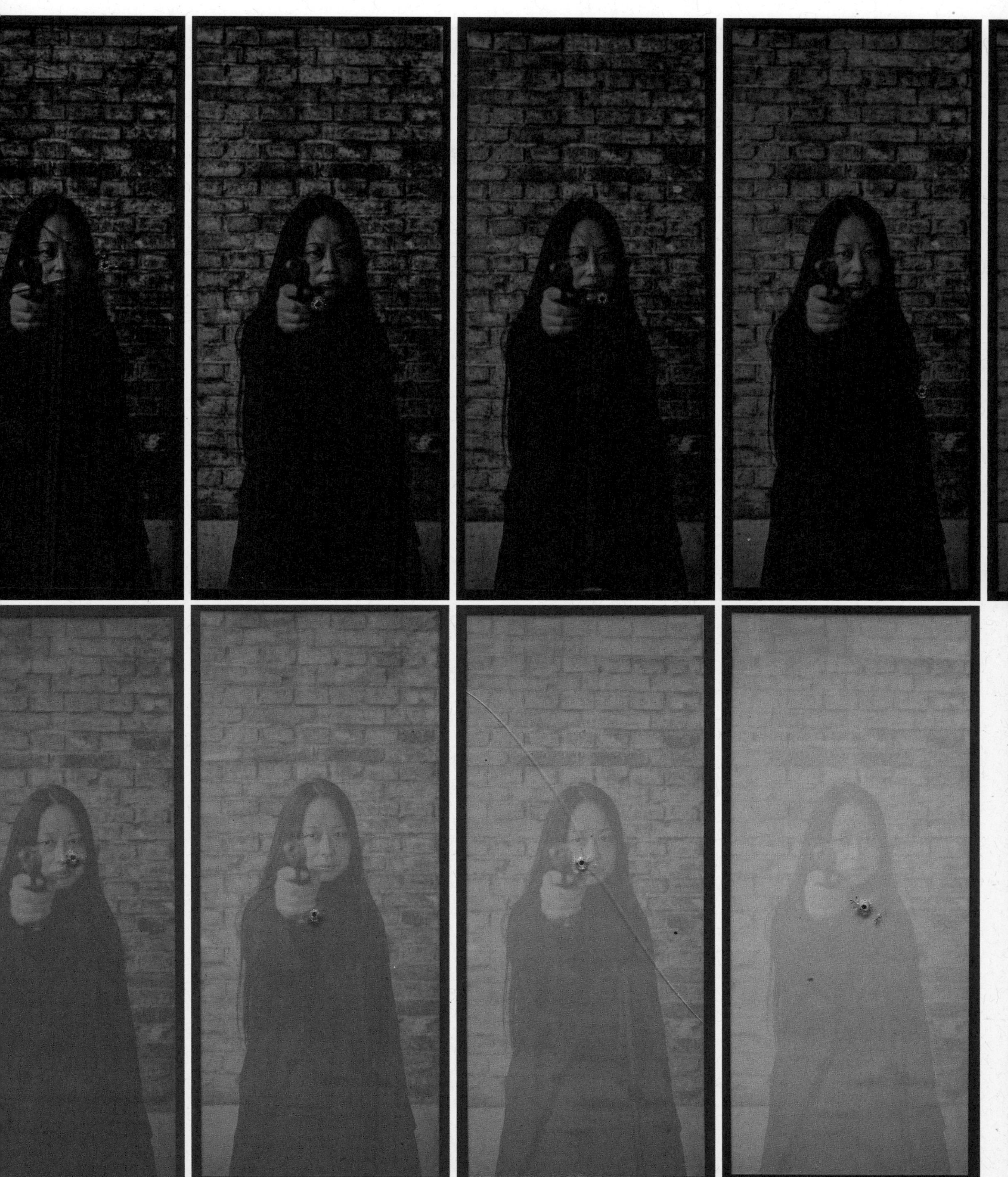

ZHAO YINOU
75.2007, 2007
Oil on canvas
100 × 70 cm

Zhao Yinou's *Rehabilitation Project* (2005–09) began with a refusal—not just of artistic trends or institutional frameworks, but of the distance they create. After stepping away from the expectations of Beijing's art scene and the techniques she had mastered during her academic training, Zhao sought a more immediate, less mediated way of working. Her paintings turned toward encounters that bypass explanation: moments where roles, identities, and art itself are temporarily suspended.

The works *4.2006* and *75.2007* reflect this approach. Made during her regular visits to a psychiatric hospital in Beijing, the paintings capture fleeting impressions from short, unstructured sessions with patients. They are not portraits in any traditional sense. Rather, they document Zhao's attempt to relate—to see and be present—without the usual scaffolding of language or narrative. In this pared-back environment, stripped of symbolic weight or professional distance, she pursued a different kind of artistic attention—one rooted in proximity, not commentary.

In *4.2006* a large group is gathered at a table, eating. Their features blur into one another, none distinct enough to be isolated from the rest. A barred window behind them quietly signals the institutional setting, but the painting's focus is elsewhere: on shared rhythm, the mundane repetition of everyday acts, the dissolution of self into a collective routine. What appears anonymous is, in Zhao's eyes, a scene of intimacy—one where individual presence is not declared, but embedded in a subtle, fragile dynamic.

In *75.2007* by contrast, the scene tightens. A single figure sits on a bed, body and bedframe almost indistinguishable, as if the person and their surroundings have fused through time or habit. The rapid, economical brushstrokes leave traces of their urgency; the painting is as much about the act of seeing as about the subject seen. This moment of solitude—constrained but calm—suggests a kind of selfhood outside of performance: not expressive, not shaped for recognition, but quietly existing.

Zhao's practice rejects the idea that individualism must be loud or resolved. Her works do not claim to "speak for" her subjects, nor do they try to redeem or explain them. Instead, they model another way of being singular: by paying attention to what is overlooked, by remaining open to discomfort and stillness, and by insisting on an artistic process that does not reduce people to symbols. In doing so, Zhao carves out space for a form of individualism that is neither heroic nor isolated, but located in the fragile and fleeting encounters between selves.

Zhao Yinou, born in 1972, lives and works in Beijing. Among her latest solo exhibitions are *GHOST RAISING* (2022) and *DYS-TOPIANS* (2022) at HdM Gallery, and ASIA NOW in Paris (2022). She has also shown her work in *Being of Evils*, Hive Center, Beijing (2020); *Psychicalreality*, Space Station, Beijing (2019); *Prisonnier*, Vanities, Paris (2019); *HAPPY PEOPLE...*, Inside-Out Art Museum, Beijing (2019); *HER KIND·CHUANG*, Zhuzhong Art Museum, Beijing (2018); *The Pleasures of Adventures*, N3 Gallery, Beijing (2016); and *OPEN TO YOU*, Busan (2014). Additionally, Zhao's work has appeared in group exhibitions such as *Beijing Contemporary* (2023), *ART021* (2022), and *When All At Once I Turn My Head...* at Nanjing University Art Museum (2023).

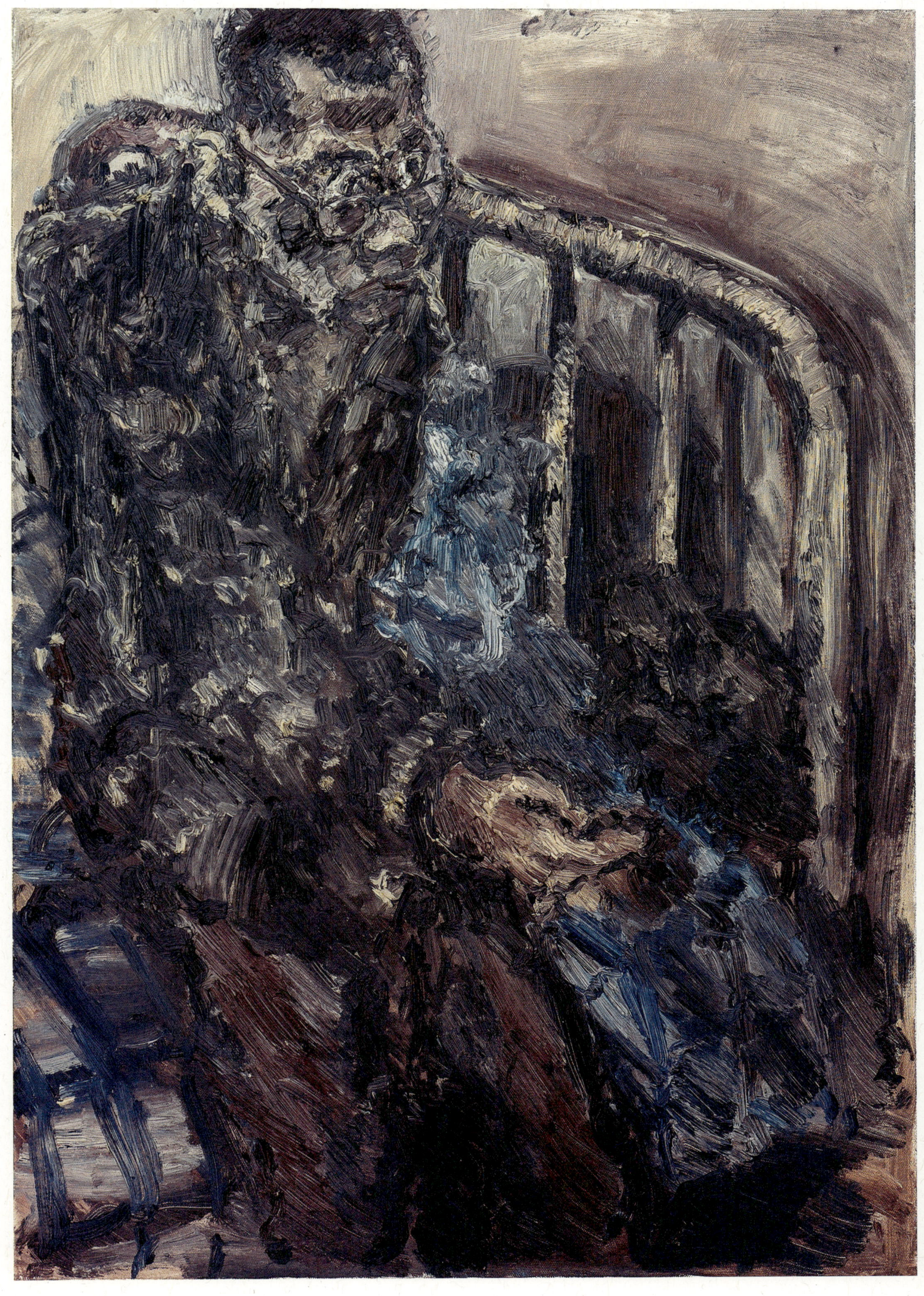

ZHENG GUOGU

Me and My Teacher, 1993

Chromogenic print
180 x 270 cm

In *Me and My Teacher*, Zheng Guogu presents an unexpected portrait of intimacy, vulnerability, and attention. The photograph shows the artist squatting next to a shirtless, disheveled young man. Both are laughing and appear at ease in the middle of a street in Zheng's hometown of Yangjiang. The man beside him is a local vagabond with a mental illness. For a year, Zheng followed him through the city—observing, listening, and gradually forming a relationship that blurred the lines between documentation, friendship, and artistic inquiry.

Zheng's photographic gesture is simple but layered. At a moment when contemporary Chinese art was turning toward international discourse and global visibility, the artist chose instead a quiet, local observation away from spectacle. *Me and My Teacher* is less a portrait of a subject than a study of a dynamic. The artist does not assume the role of interpreter, but of student. "He has a lot of knowledge that I will never, ever have,"[13] Zheng later reflected. "The inspiration he gave me was beyond my entire education—more than Duchamp, Beuys, or Warhol."[14]

This reversal, in which the marginal figure becomes the source of insight, is central to the work. The man, living outside of social convention, seemingly immune to shame, sickness, or judgment, is not portrayed as an object of pity or moral reflection but as someone who moves through the world with radical freedom. Zheng saw in him a form of embodied knowledge that resists codification: not something to be studied, but something to be felt—what he described as an "untouchable" heat.[15]

In its large scale and clarity, the photography cannot be clearly categorized as documentary or fictional: a staged or curated encounter that resists being fully decoded. There is no clear narrative, no revelation, just a fleeting moment of shared laughter between two young men. One is a trained artist; the other lives on the street. The image does not resolve this difference but temporarily suspends it.

This early work marks a turning point in Zheng's practice, not only in his engagement with photography but also in its quiet claim that insight, whether philosophical, emotional or aesthetic, can emerge from beyond the boundaries of education or status. *Me and My Teacher* is both a tribute to individual difference and a reflection on the ethics of attention. It raises questions about who gets to speak, who is heard, and who is recognized as a source of knowledge.

Rather than portraying the other as spectacle or object, Zheng constructs a relationship that unsettles familiar binaries such as artist and subject, sane and mad, cultured and marginal. What at first glance appears to be a simple street scene unfolds into a layered meditation on perception, care, and what it means to learn from someone without asking them to change.

13 Jérôme Sans, ed., *China Talks: Interviews with 32 Contemporary Artists* (Hong Kong: Timezone 8, 2009), p. 195.

14 Hili Perlson, "Artnet Asks: Zheng Guogu Where Does Spirituality Stop and Humor Start?," *Artnet*, March 25, 2015, https://news.artnet.com/market/artnet-asks-zheng-guogu-280454.

15 Ibid.

Zheng Guogu (b. 1970, Yangjiang) graduated from the Guangzhou Academy of Fine Arts in 1992 and lives and works in Yangjiang. Solo exhibitions include *Zheng Guogu: Visionary Transformation*, MoMA PS1, New York (2019) and OCAT Xi'an, Shanghai. His work has been presented in *Art and China after 1989: Theater of the World* (Guggenheim Museum, New York; Guggenheim Bilbao; SFMOMA, San Francisco, 2017–18); the Shanghai Biennale (2014); the Lyon Biennale (2009); documenta 12 (2007), the Asia Pacific Triennial (2018); and the Gwangju Biennale (2002). Additional exhibitions have taken place at M+, Hong Kong; Tate Liverpool; Walker Art Center, Minneapolis; Hamburger Bahnhof, Berlin; Mori Art Museum, Tokyo; and UCCA Beijing. In 2002, he co-founded the Yangjiang Group, and in 2006 received the Chinese Contemporary Art Awards (CCAA) in the category "Best Artist."

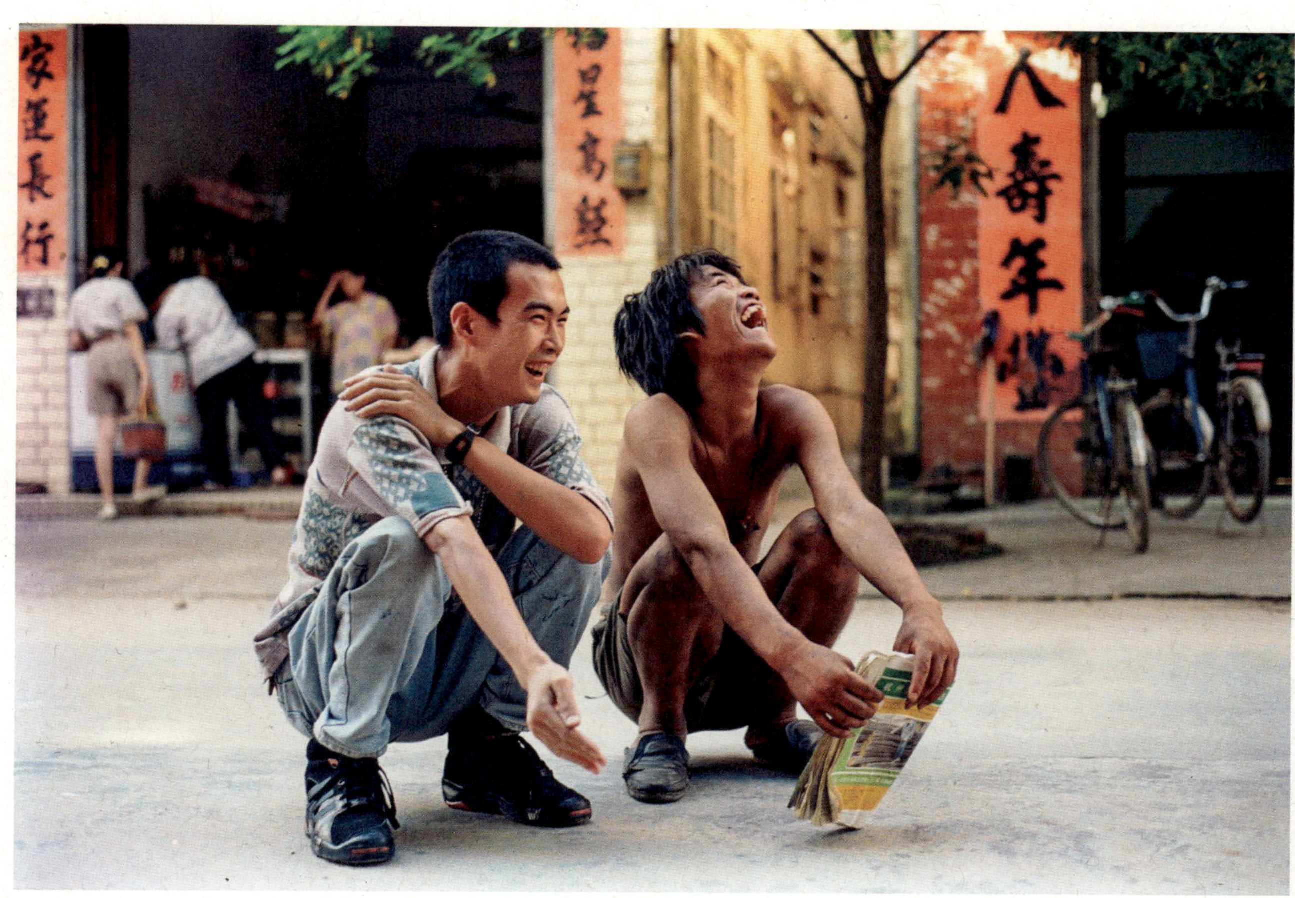

4. INDIVIDUALISM AS INTERROGATION OF THE MASS
个人主义：对大众的质询

WANG TUO

The Second Interrogation, 2022–2023

Video installation (color, sound, 4K)
Part One: Two-channel video, 24:28 min
Part Two: Single-channel video, 30 min

Wang Tuo's *The Second Interrogation* is a fiction rooted in the real mechanics of censorship, control, and artistic survival. Set in the tense space between state surveillance and creative expression, the two-part video installation enacts a speculative role reversal: the artist becomes the censor; the censor becomes the artist.

The work builds on Wang's earlier piece *Interrogation* (2017), which emerged from conversations with a friend who had become a commissioner for discipline inspection for the government. This work traced the psychological skillset required to extract confessions: emotional manipulation, ideological finesse, and total control. With *The Second Interrogation*, Wang expands these themes into a storyline, driven by dialogue, performance, and historical references.

At the center of the narrative is the infamous 1989 *China/Avant-Garde* exhibition and the so-called "Seven Sins" performances that were censored by authorities just months before the student democracy movement erupted in Tiananmen Square. The memory of that moment, when radical art and protest briefly aligned, becomes the pivot point of *The Second Interrogation*. It tells the story of an artist preparing a tribute to the "Seven Sins." A cultural censor, initially tasked with overseeing the work, gradually becomes immersed. Their roles begin to blur, and the artist starts to surveil the ideological undercurrents of the art world, while the censor absorbs the ambiguity and potential of art itself. By the end, both roles have reversed, and it is the censor who completes the work, recasting both its historical and contemporary meaning.

In his work, Wang references Ingmar Bergman's *Persona* (1966) as a recurring template which infuses the film with a psychological tint. Beneath the political narrative lies a deeper meditation on subjectivity in conditions of control. The figures in Wang's work represent more than opposing forces; each of them inhabits each other's logics, gradually intervening one into the other.

The Second Interrogation explores how systems of power are internalized. It carefully stretches how ideology lives not only in institutions, but in speech patterns, relationships, and doubts. This way, the film does not offer a stable moral position but instead constructs a hall of mirrors in which art, surveillance, and belief reflect and distort one another. In this unstable space, the idea of the individual is never singular. Wang proposes a more troubling image: subjectivity as something porous, malleable, and conditioned by forces that exceed personal will.

Wang Tuo, (b. 1984 in Changchun), lives and works in Beijing. Wang first studied biology at Northeast Normal University, Changchun. Turning to art, he completed an MA in Painting at Tsinghua University, Beijing in 2012, and then an MFA in Painting from Boston University in 2014. Recent solo exhibitions include K21, Düsseldorf (2024); UCCA, Beijing (2023); and Present Company, New York (2017). His work has also been shown at M+, Hong Kong (2023); Queensland Art Gallery, Brisbane (2022); MMCA, Seoul (2022); and Power Station of Art, Shanghai (2021). Wang was the recipient of the Sigg Prize 2023 from the M+ in Hong Kong and the K21 Global Art Award from K21 Düsseldorf in 2024.

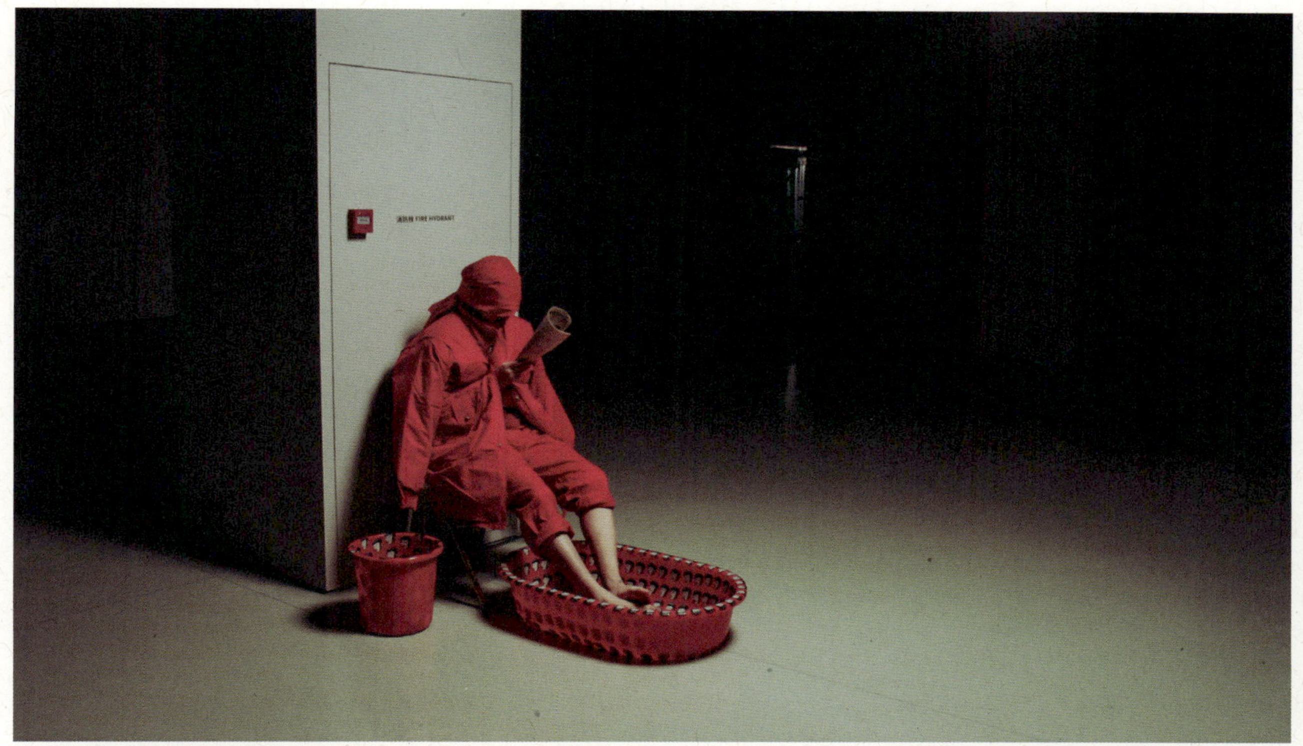

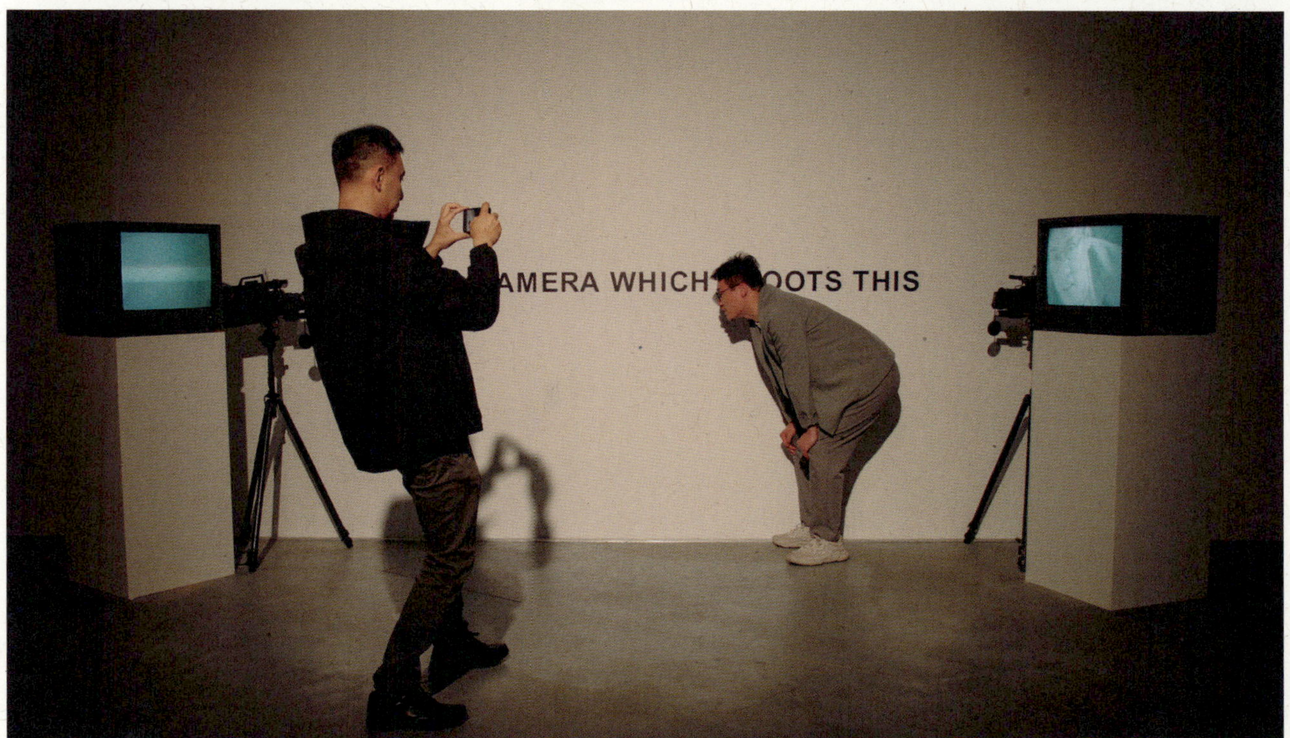
AMERA WHICH
OOTS THIS

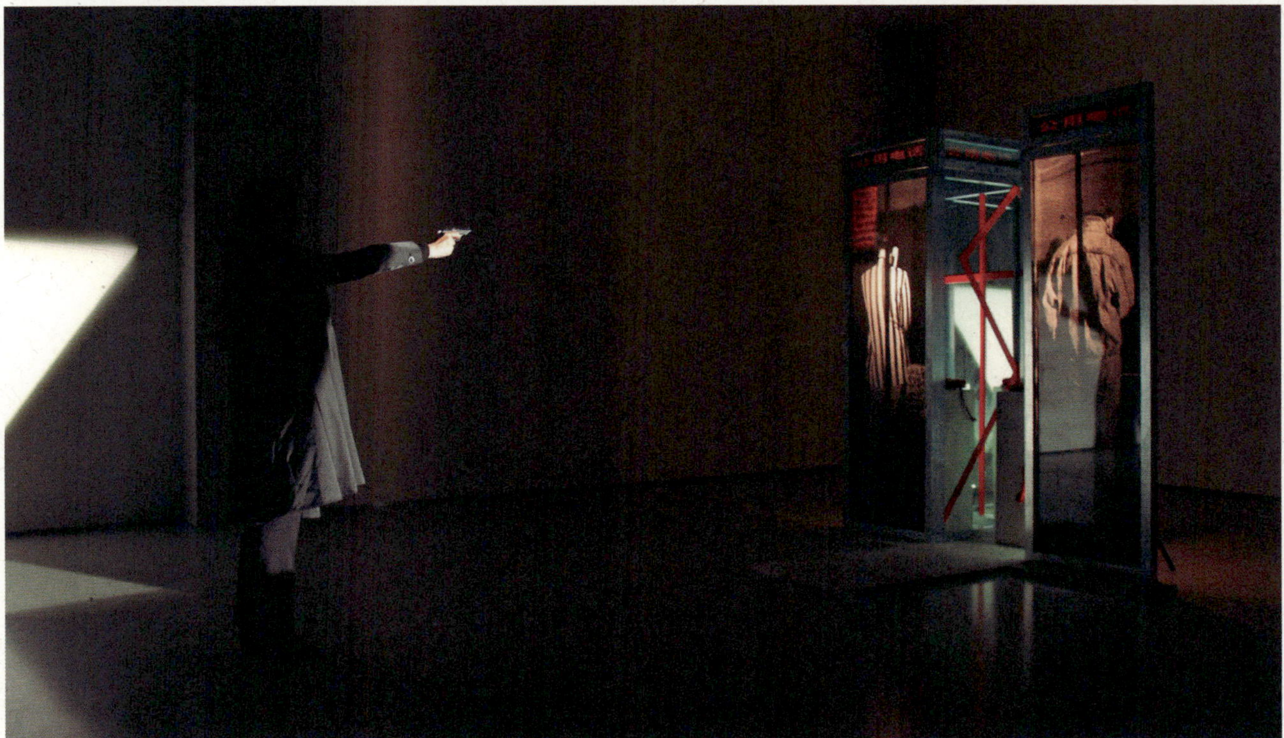

ARCHIVE

ON THE ARCHIVE OF “INDIVIDUALISM” IN CHINESE CONTEMPORARY ART

SU WEI

ON THE ARCHIVE OF "INDIVIDUALISM" IN CHINESE CONTEMPORARY ART

SU WEI

In the past decade, archiving has emerged as a key practice within the Chinese art world. This is not solely the work of researchers; museums, both state-run and private, along with art academies, commercial galleries, and art foundations, have all contributed to a widespread movement of self-documentation.

Archives create a tangible link to history. When the narrative of that history is still very much open to interpretation—and deeply relevant to the current predicaments of contemporary art in China—the archive itself becomes instrumental for the understanding of China's ongoing history and the position of art practitioners within it. This "archive fever" stems from a renewed urgency to define a local subjectivity, which has come to the fore after Chinese contemporary art's direct encounter with globalization at its zenith. This urgency is multifaceted. Firstly, in the past decade, dialogue between China and the world has shrunk dramatically; and for a long time, various internal and external pressures have positioned Chinese contemporary art outside the broader discourses of "Asia" and, to some extent, of the "Global South." Against this backdrop, the cultural identity forged by the "China narrative" has produced achievements almost inseparable from a narrow, nationalist sentiment. Secondly, on a cultural-political level, Chinese contemporary art has long sought to establish a dialogue with Western Europe and North America, but this dialogue has rarely been conducted on an equal footing, nor has it often achieved genuine intellectual depth. Thirdly, as commercialization and institutionalization have reached a crucial juncture, art practitioners have developed a profound desire for a history of artistic independence. Whilst they understand that autonomy and interdependence are two sides of the same coin, they are eager to revisit past efforts that brought art closer to an ideal of independence. Archives offer a path toward answering these questions and achieving a fuller self-understanding.

The practice of archiving also raises questions of historical ethics. What makes a good archive, or good archiving? When we use archives to restore the complex folds of history, what tensions arise with established narratives? For instance, could we present archives from the Cultural Revolution—political edicts, "red, bright, and shining" (红光亮) propaganda images, and scenes of brutal armed struggle—on a gallery wall without any contextual scaffolding? While the Cultural Revolution is sometimes celebrated outside of China as the pinnacle of Mao Zedong Thought, for most cultural workers within the country, its catastrophic absurdity far outweighs any conceptual value it might retain today. Such starkly contrasting interpretations of history, shaped by context, also characterize the study of Chinese contemporary art. The way researchers frame the problem of subjectivity, and how they identify and critique the methods of historical narration, often determines the very archives they choose to examine, as well as the methods they employ.

The historical materials in this exhibition are not organized chronologically. Instead, they are woven into thematic sections that plumb specific questions. Guided by "individualism" as a central

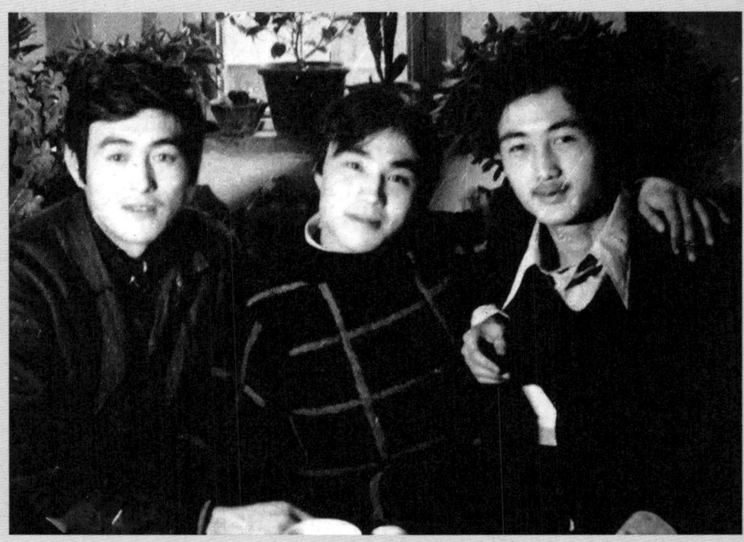

1. Group of poets (from left to right: Mang Ke, Yan Li, Zhao Guoqiang), courtesy of Yan Li. Image copyright obtained with the help of Cheng Xi

theme, we have selected not only an extensive range of archives related to artistic practice but have also incorporated relevant cultural and social documents. This approach presents the audience with a multi-dimensional historical landscape where "individualism" intersects with complex intellectual discourses, negotiates with shifting political contexts and social dynamics, and ultimately gives rise to alternative artworks and visionary individual practices.

We wish to extend our gratitude to those who provided these materials: the artist Wang Youshen; poet and curator Cheng Xi; curator and artist Andreas Schmid; BizArt Art Center and its co-founder Davide Quadrio; and the artists Wang Luyan and Zhuang Hui. These individuals, long committed to collecting and preserving archives, have recently gained significant recognition. They include artists who witnessed history firsthand, founders who built pioneering institutions where none existed, and foreign art workers who were present for key moments. They are practitioners who, with a deep sense of empathy, began collecting the work of their friends and documenting exhibitions early on. Their archival efforts, though sometimes appearing fragmented, are increasingly valuable to researchers for their intimate and unique perspectives.

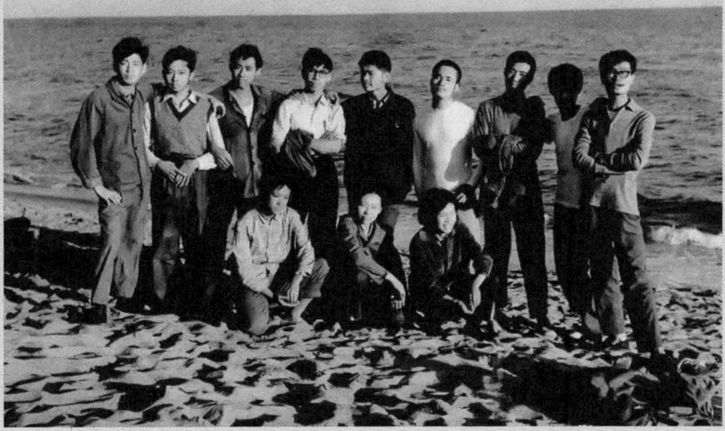

2. Members of the No Name Group (from left in the back row: Shi Xixi, Wei Hai, Zhang Wei, Ma Kelu, Shao Xiaogang, Yang Yushu, Zhao Wenliang, Zhao Rugang, Shi Zhenyu; front row from left: Zheng Ziyan, Wang Aihe, Li Shan), unknown photographer, courtesy of Yang Yushu. Image copyright obtained with the help of Xing Yao and Cheng Xi

1. PRECURSORS AND NEW BEGINNINGS

The archival presentation of the exhibition begins in the period just before the recognized start of Chinese contemporary art. During the 1970s, a few underground painting societies and poetry clubs began to form in cities like Beijing and Shanghai. Their members were often the children of the political elite, drawn to the forbidden allure of Western modern culture and personal free expression. Beijing's "Sun Column" (太阳纵队) and the "No Name Group" (无名画会) were two key examples. Given their family connections, their secret meetings were less about direct political rebellion than about finding alternative modes of living and creating, beyond the strictures of daily life and the monolithic "red, bright, and shining" aesthetic that was predominant.

In these clandestine gatherings, they wrote poetry, painted, listened to Western classical music, and debated art. Just a month before the end of the Cultural Revolution, the daughter of the persecuted historian Wu Han (1909–1969) wrote a poem filled with self-mockery and bitterness. A young poet painstakingly copied out Nietzsche's *Thus Spoke Zarathustra* by hand. The first exhibition of the No Name Group was held in secret at artist Zhang Wei's Beijing home on the last day of 1971. It would be five years before they could show their work publicly, an opportunity made possible only when an enlightened cultural official, who had been imprisoned during the Cultural Revolution, was reinstated and sought them out (figs. 1–5).

After the Cultural Revolution ended in 1976, exhibitions commemorating Mao Zedong's death continued across the country. Mao's influence was still potently felt, and his successor upheld

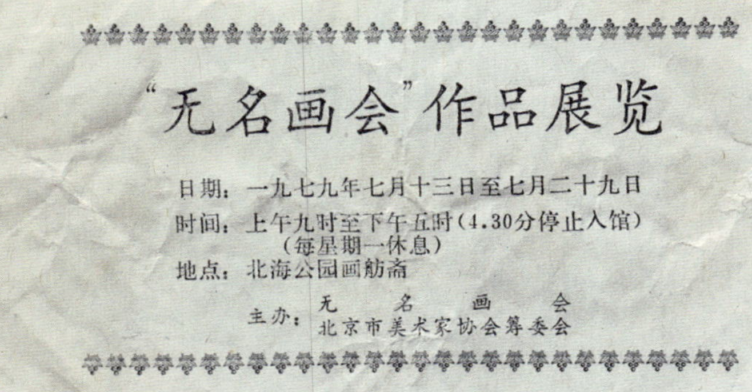

“无名画会”作品展览

日期：一九七九年七月十三日至七月二十九日
时间：上午九时至下午五时（4.30分停止入馆）
（每星期一休息）
地点：北海公园画舫斋
主办：无名画会
北京市美术家协会筹委会

3. Invitation for the first No Name Group exhibition, courtesy of Wang Youshen

his legacy with the “Two Whatevers” (两个凡是) policy. This began to change in 1978 with a nationwide debate sparked by the article “Practice is the Sole Criterion for Testing Truth.” Deng Xiaoping (1904–1997) seized on this moment to introduce his famous call to “emancipate the mind and seek truth from facts” (解放思想，实事求是), urging China to abandon the ultra-leftist politics of the Mao era. His pragmatic focus on economic recovery set the nation on the path to modernization. In December 1979, the policy of Reform and Opening Up (改革开放) was formally adopted. The art world’s response was swift. In early 1979, the *New Spring Painting Exhibition* in Beijing received a strong endorsement from Jiang Feng (1910–1982), chairman of the China Artists’ Association. This paved the way for a wave of officially supported exhibitions by both professional and amateur artists

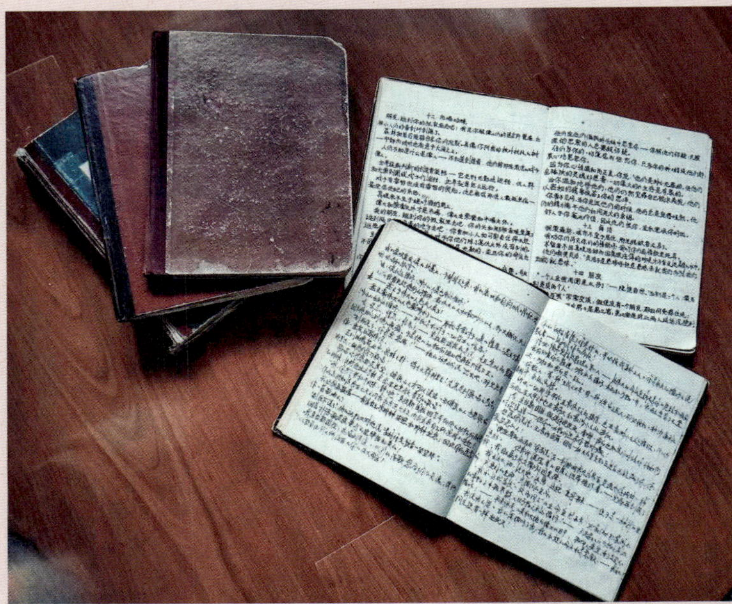

4. Hand transcript of Friedrich Nietzsche’s *Thus Spoke Zarathustra*, Photo: Zhou Ti, courtesy of Zhou Ti; Image copyright obtained with the help of Cheng Xi

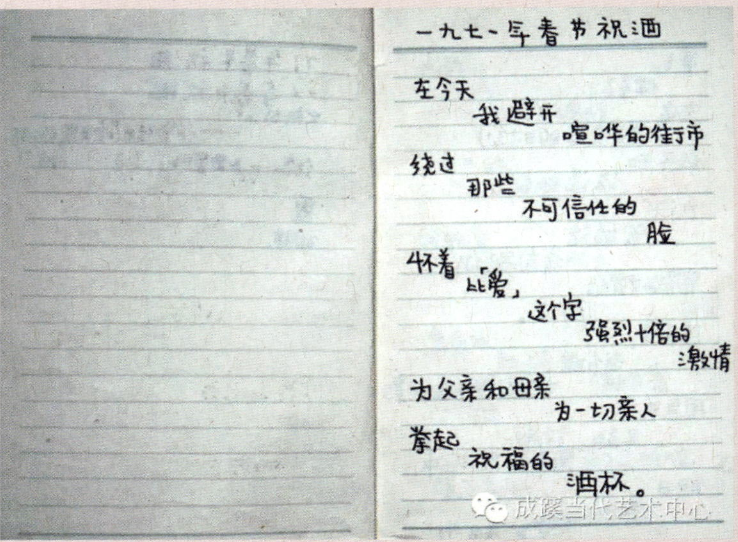

一九七一年春节祝酒

在今天
我避开
喧哗的街市
绕过
那些
不可信任的
脸
怀着
「爱」
这个字
强烈十倍的
激情
为父亲和母亲
为一切亲人
举起
祝福的
酒杯。

5. A handwritten Spring festival toast poem of 1971 by Zhang Liaoliao, courtesy of Zhang Liaoliao, Image copyright obtained with the help of Cheng Xi.

nationwide. The art world began to normalize, and emboldened by a new climate of “freedom of expression” and “modernization,” individual creativity returned to the fore.

While Deng pushed for economic reform, he remained cautious about political change, prioritizing the stability of the Communist Party rule. His successor, Hu Yaobang (1915–1989), a key proponent of the “truth” debate mentioned above, became a popular figure for his sympathy towards students during the 1989 demonstrations. His sudden death just before the Tiananmen Square protests became a catalyst, as students used private memorials for

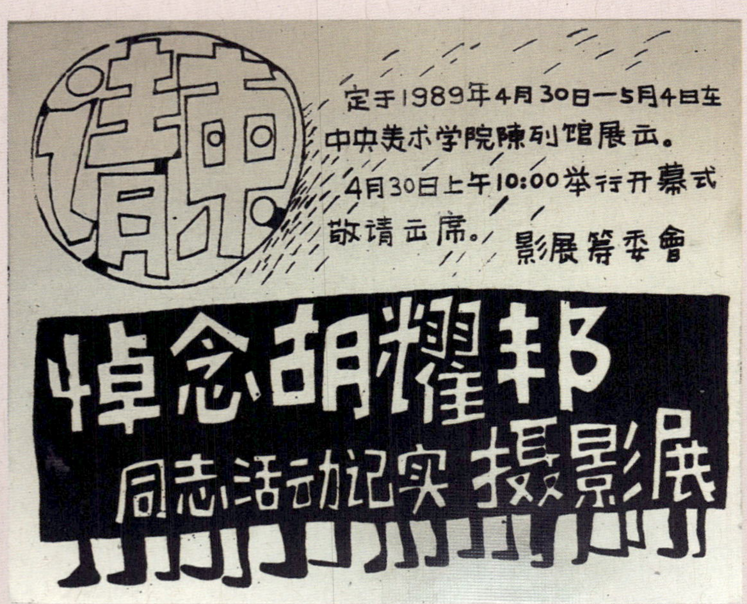

6. *In Memory of Hu Yaobang* photography exhibition, Courtesy of Wang Youshen

7. *Black Cover Book*, 1994, *White Cover Book*, 1995, and *Grey Cover Book*, 1997. Editors: Zeng Xiaojun, Ai Weiwei, Xu Bing (*Black Cover Book*); Zeng Xiaojun, Ai Weiwei (*White* and *Grey Cover Book*). Courtesy of Zhuang Hui.

him to subtly communicate their desires for democracy and free expression (fig. 6).

In the early 1990s, the political atmosphere remained tense. Then, in 1992, Deng Xiaoping's Southern Tour speeches (南巡讲话) reignited the engine of reform, propelling China into an era of accelerated economic growth and toward a new commercial society. Cultural workers began to move past the immediate trauma of politics. In an environment with almost no arts infrastructure, they relied on self-organization and a certain "roguish," troublemaking spirit (流氓主义精神) to exhibit their work and generate discourse. They created underground publications like the *Black Cover*, *Gray Cover*, and *White Cover Books*, initiated by figures such as Ai Weiwei (1957–) and Feng Boyi (1960–), which documented conceptual proposals and critical discussions (fig. 7). They mounted shows in unconventional venues—the basement of a collectivist apartment building, for instance, or along railway tracks for an exhibition entitled *Traces of Existence* (生存痕迹). They formed communities in the Yuanmingyuan Painters' Village and the East Village in Beijing. They sold works at the International Art Palace (国际艺苑), a gallery with a complex and shifting ownership structure, and participated in exhibitions at the few official venues that would have them, always aware that their shows could be shut down any moment. In 1993, the *China Avantgarde* art exhibition at Haus der Kulturen der Welt (HKW) in Berlin, along with several other international shows, thrust Chinese art onto the global stage and created a new sense of urgency at home.

2. NAVIGATING AND PARTICIPATING IN NEW LANDSCAPE

In 1985, the American artist Robert Rauschenberg visited Beijing. At the time, artist-led groups were forming across China, many of whom would later participate in the "Zhuhai Conference" (珠海会议) that helped launch the '85 New Wave ('85美术新潮) movement. At the time, Chinese artists were voraciously consuming Western modernist art and theory, and some were already critically reflecting on its influence. Rauschenberg, a world-renowned artist who had moved beyond modernism, was a figure of immense interest among Chinese art practitioners. The day after his Beijing exhibition opened, he visited a smaller show in a diplomatic apartment building. There, Zhang Wei of the No Name Group critiqued his work, prompting Rauschenberg's now-famous retort: "Artists don't criticize artists." A photograph captured the moment: Rauschenberg stands before an abstract painting, looking at the camera, while the silhouette of artist Wang Luyan of the New Measurement Group (新刻度小组) occupies the foreground. Their gazes seem to cross but never connect—a fitting metaphor for the complex, often misaligned relationship between

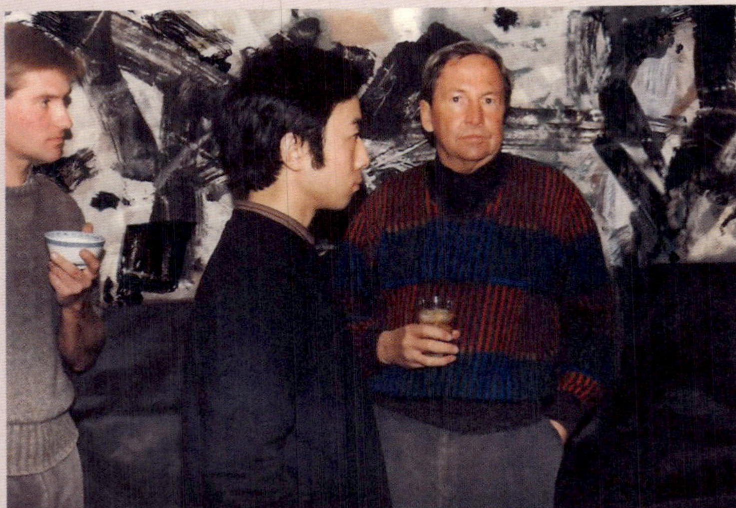

8. "Robert Rauschenberg's Glance," courtesy of Wang Luyan

Chinese artists and the Western-dominated global art system (fig. 8).

In the early 1990s, despite restrictive household registration (*hu kou*) policies, artists began to adopt a transient, roguish, footloose and precarious existence. They flocked to Beijing from across the country, forming communities in the East Village (东村) and Yuanmingyuan Painters Village (圆明园画家村). This self-imposed marginalization was no less a statement of artistic independence (fig. 9). Following the political disillusionment of 1989, a curious pragmatism emerged among some cultural figures, who began to move fluidly between official and private platforms. On May 1, 1993, the state television program *Oriental Horizon* (东方时空) premiered, shifting the focus of news coverage from state events to the lives of ordinary people. Its

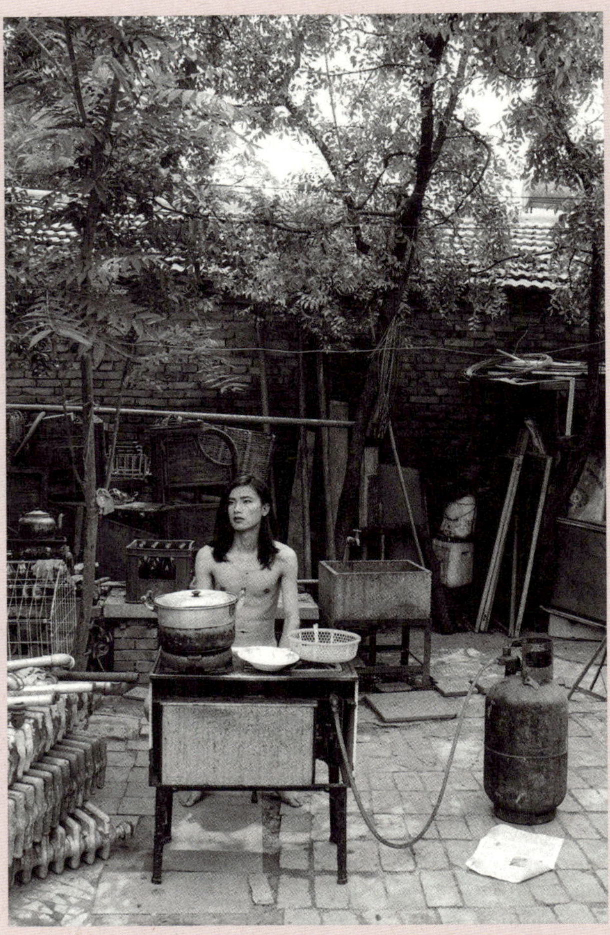

9. Performance artist Ma Liuming in East Village, Beijing, 1993, courtesy of the artist

flexible production model empowered independent filmmakers like Jiang Yue (1962–), who brought his documentary sensibility to broadcast news. Starting with *The Three Heroes of the East* (东方三侠), a short film about three elderly swimmers in Beijing, Jiang and his collaborators created a series of works that found extraordinary moments in everyday life, influencing the documentary aesthetic of a new generation of Chinese filmmakers, including the Sixth Generation directors (fig. 10).

Deng Xiaoping's 1992 "Southern Tour" catalyzed another profound social shift. As the market economy accelerated, a consumer culture began to take shape, with public ownership eroded and social hierarchies redrawn. In the art world, that same year, several Chinese artists were invited to the exhibition *Begegnung mit den Anderen: Zeitgenössische Außereuropäische Kunst aus Afrika, Asien und Lateinamerika* (Encounter the Others: Contemporary Non-European Art from Africa, Asia, and Latin America) in Kassel and the nearby town Hann. Münden, Germany. The curator, Professor Hamdi el Attar from

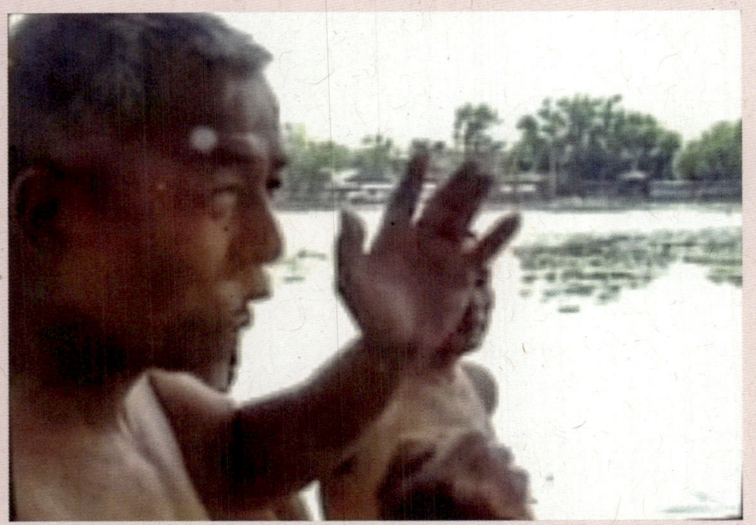

10. The Three Heroes of the East (东方三侠), a short film about three elderly swimmers in Beijing, Oriental Horizon, 1993, courtesy of Jiang Yue

Kassel University wrote in his foreword the following remarks: "*Überlegungen wie die, ob die europäische Kunstauffassung auf andere Kontinente überhaupt übertragbar ist, stehen im Vordergrund der Untersuchungen*" (Considerations such as whether the European conception of art is transferable to other continents at all are at the forefront of the investigations) (fig. 11). This was followed in 1993 by several major international exhibitions, including the *China Avantgarde* exhibition at HKW in Berlin, which suddenly situated Chinese art within a global framework (fig. 12). The chief curator, Hans van Dijk (1946–2002), grappled with how to present a national "avant-garde" without resorting to exoticist platitudes. The Chinese curators and dealers involved, however, were more concerned about sales. For them, the market was now seen as a new

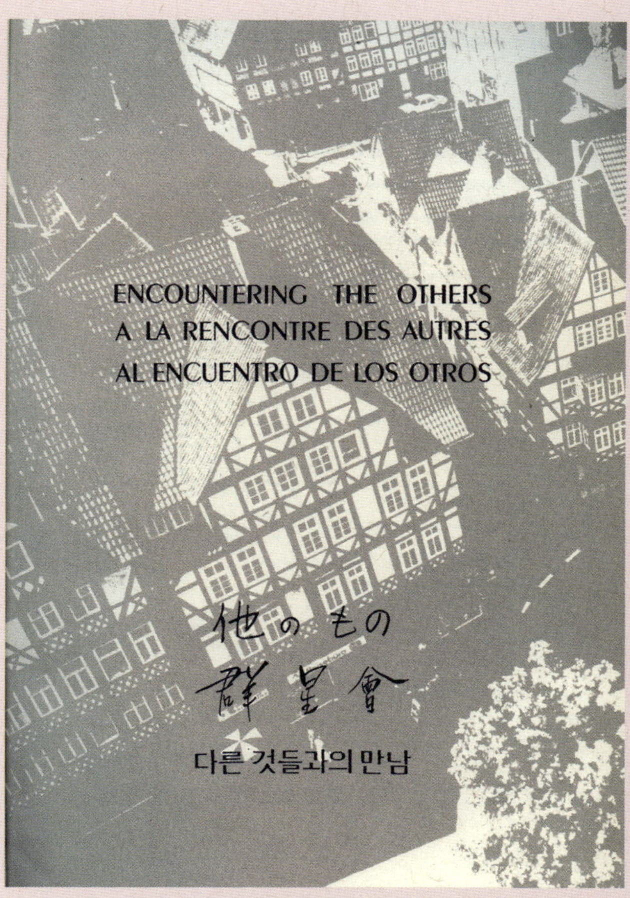

11. Catalogue of the exhibition *Begegnung mit den Anderen: Zeitgenössische Außereuropäische Kunst aus Afrika, Asien und Lateinamerika*, Kassel and Hann. Münden 1992, p. 3

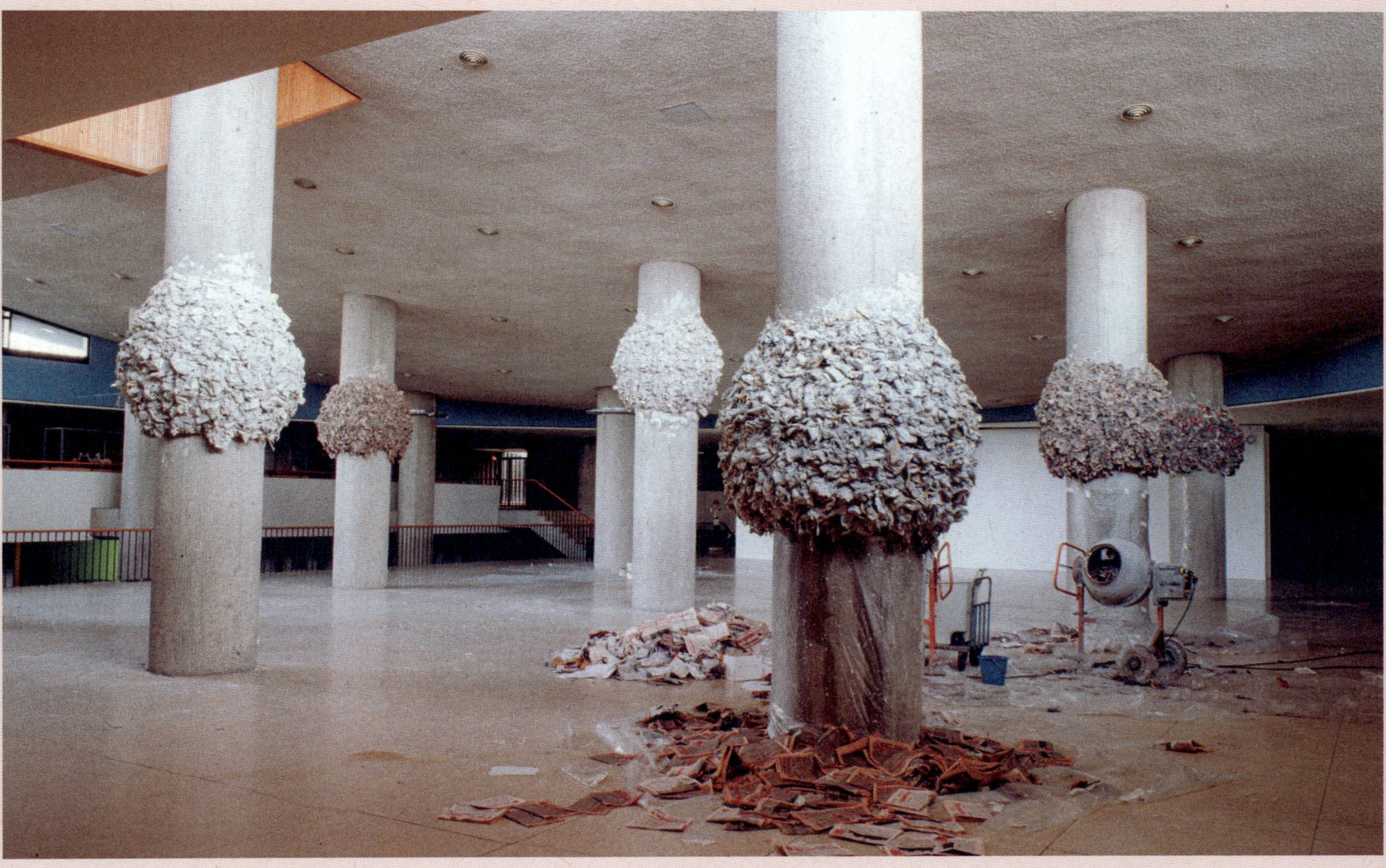

12. Installation of the *China Avantgarde* exhibition at Haus der Kulturen der Welt, Berlin, 1993, courtesy of Andreas Schmid

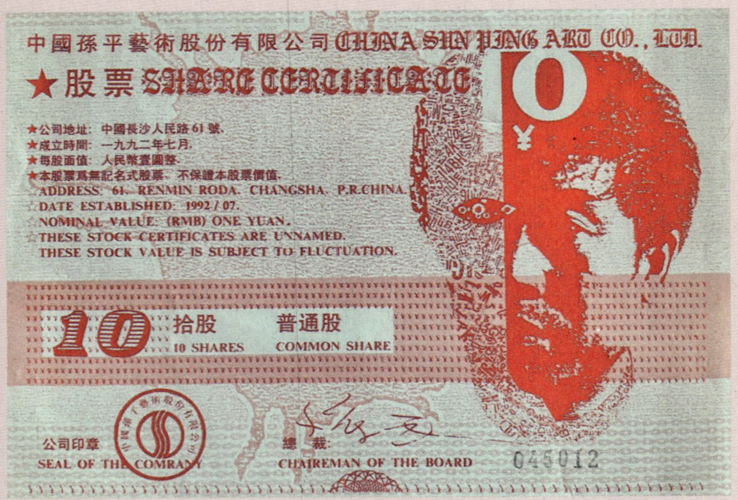

13. Stock issued by artist Sun Ping, 1992, courtesy of Wang Youshen

and liberating force, a way to gain recognition (a form of validation many accepted with self-deprecating irony) and circumvent the official state system. In 1992, the curator-businessman Lü Peng had already organized the Guangzhou Biennale: the first 1990's Biennale & Art Fair (The Oil Painting Section). Positioning the commercial market as a driver for Chinese contemporary art, the exhibition was funded by private businesses and state-affiliated investors and featured a juried competition. The winning works were sold in their entirety to a Shenzhen-based company. The event also served as the platform for artist Sun Ping (1953–) to formally issue a stock he had created (fig. 13).

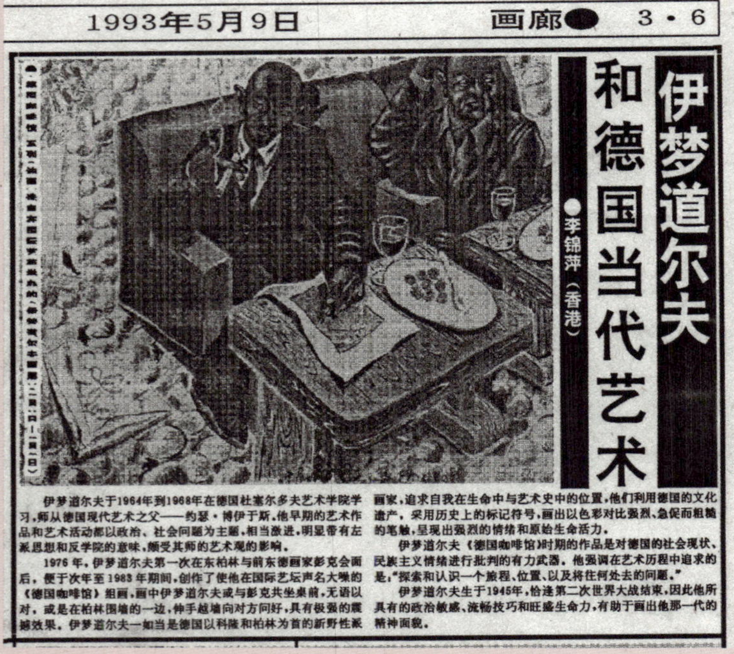
1993年5月9日 画廊 3·6

伊梦道尔夫和德国当代艺术

●李锦萍（香港）

伊梦道尔夫于1964年到1968年在德国杜塞尔多夫艺术学院学习，师从德国现代艺术之父——约瑟·博伊于斯，他早期的艺术作品和艺术活动都以政治、社会问题为主题，相当激进，明显带有左派思想和反学院的意味，颇受其师的艺术观的影响。

1976年，伊梦道尔夫第一次在东柏林与前东德画家彭克会面后，便于次年至1983年期间，创作了使他在国际艺坛声名大噪的《德国咖啡馆》组画，画中伊梦道尔夫或与彭克共坐桌前，无语以对，或是在柏林围墙的一边，伸手越墙向对方问好，具有极强的震撼效果。伊梦道尔夫一如当是德国以科隆和柏林为首的新野性派画家，追求自我在生命中与艺术史中的位置，他们利用德国的文化遗产，采用历史上的标记符号，画出以色彩对比强烈、急促而粗犷的笔触，呈现出强烈的情绪和原始生命活力。

伊梦道尔夫《德国咖啡馆》时期的作品是对德国的社会现状、民族主义情绪进行批判的有力武器。他强调在艺术历程中追求的是："探索和认识一个旅程、位置、以及将往何处去的问题。"

伊梦道尔夫生于1945年，恰逢第二次世界大战结束，因此他所具有的政治敏感、流畅技巧和旺盛生命力，有助于画出他那一代的精神面貌。

15. Report on the solo exhibition of Jörg Immendorff at the International Art Palace gallery (国际艺苑), Beijing Youth Newspaper, 1993, courtesy of Wang Youshen

(1994)中国当代艺术家工作计划(1994)中国当代艺术家工作计划(1994)中国
1994) CHINESE CONTEMPORARY ARTISTS' AGENDA(1994) CHI

14. Chinese Contemporary Artists' Agenda, 1994, courtesy of Wang Youshen

Throughout this period, artists sustained their practices through self-organization and a tenacious spirit. A new kind of individual consciousness took hold, one that steered away from grand concepts toward the textures of private life. Their existence was a hybrid of underground activity and semi-official engagement. They published zines like the *Black Cover, Gray Cover,* and *White Cover Books* (黑皮书, 灰皮书, 白皮书) mentioned earlier, *Wild* (野生) and *Chinese Contemporary Artists' Agenda (1994)* (中国当代艺术家工作计划) (fig. 14). They sold paintings in commercial institutions like the International Art Palace gallery (国际艺苑画廊)—an entity initially spearheaded by cultural bureaucrats and subject to complex shifts in ownership (fig. 15). They organized exhibitions like *Corruptionist* (偏执) in semi-private spaces such as the basements of ordinary residential buildings (fig. 16), and, inspired by the format of documenta in Kassel, they spontaneously mounted their own "documenta" exhibitions (fig. 17). Through the mediation and curation of certain critics holding official posts, they also participated in exhibitions at the few official institutions that were open to them on a limited basis, though these shows often faced the risk of being

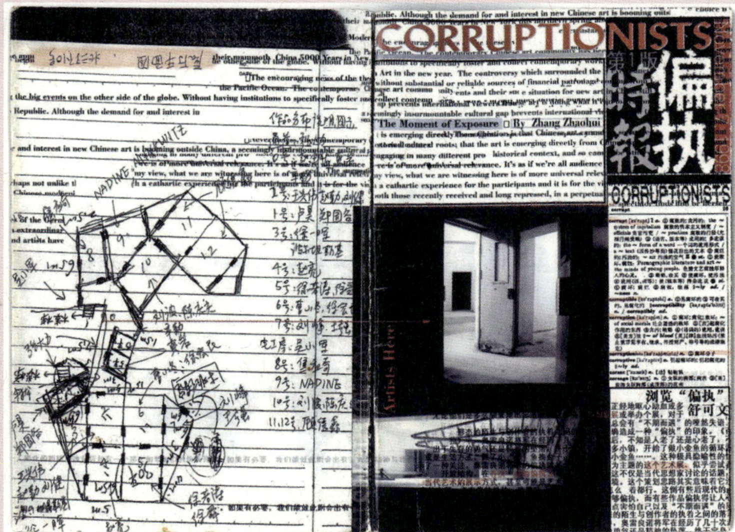

16. Catalogue of the *Corruptionists* exhibition, Beijing, 1998, courtesy of Su Wei

shut down. Entering the new millennium, the rise of China's real estate industry provided a new platform for contemporary art. Many exhibitions were held in property developers' sales offices, and by around 2008, a wave of private museums had also emerged, fueled by the real estate sector. Indeed, until 2020, the real estate industry remained a primary driver of the marketization and institutionalization of contemporary art. Individual artists, to varying degrees, were all participants in this evolving landscape.

Underpinned by an ethos of self-organization and a roguish spirit, individual artists navigated the spaces between the market, state will, private commercial activities, and loose-knit art communities.

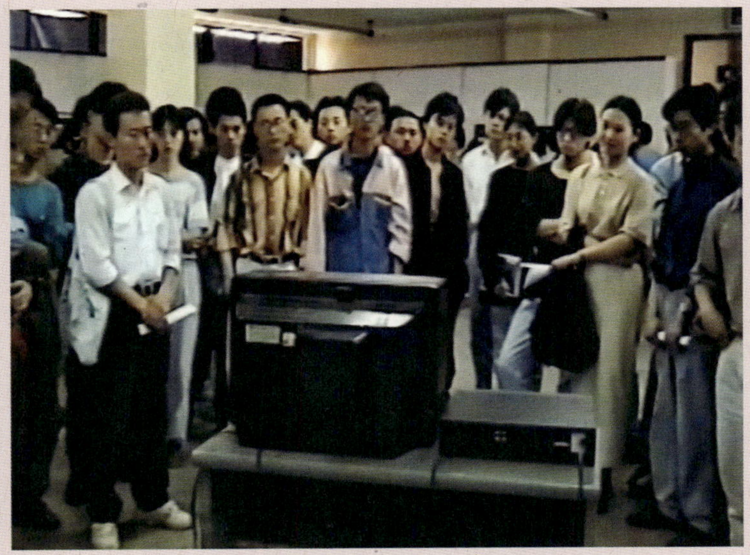

17. A Chinese "documenta": 3rd Modern Chinese Art Research Documents Exhibition (中国当代艺术研究文献（资料）展第三回展), Shanghai, unknown filmmaker, 1994, courtesy of Zhuang Hui

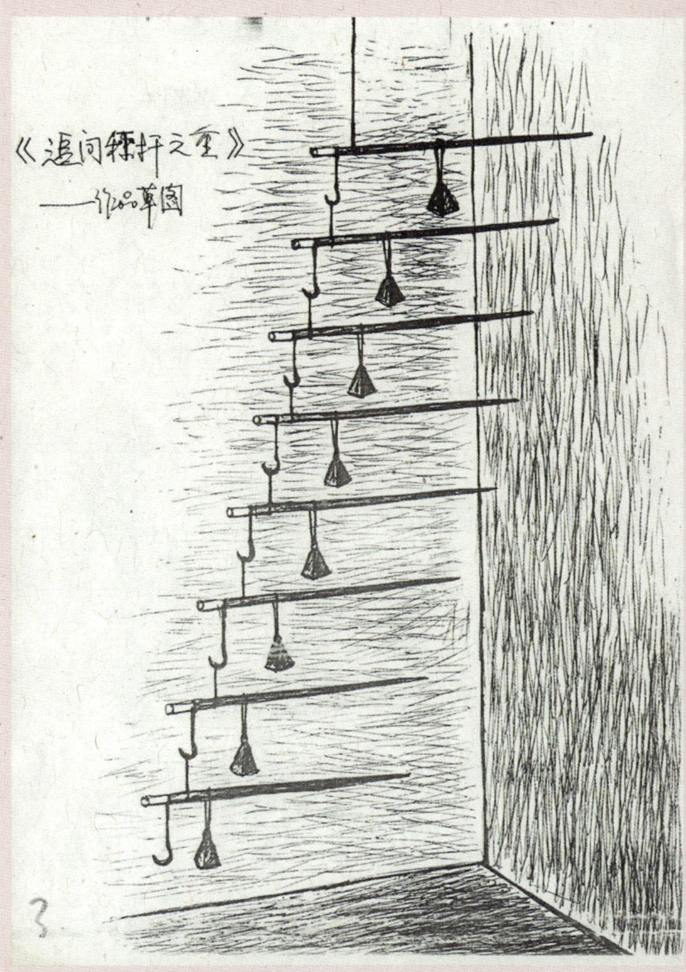

18. Datong Dazhang's "Mail Art", 1996–97, courtesy of Wen Pulin Archive of Chinese Avant-Garde Art, Beijing

This defined the artistic practices of the 1990s, which were characterized by a radical experimentalism and a potent sense of subjectivity. Many artists who had begun working in the late 1980s with rigorous, clinical forms, everyday and private expressions, and diverse media reached their most intense phase of practice in the 1990s.

A few artists, however, were acutely conscious of the problems posed by globalization and commercialization. Figures like Datong Dazhang confronted this irresistible trend with a stance of mockery and critique. In 1993, he completed a series of works in the form of mail art, sending conceptual proposals to people in China's art field. This practice continued until 1997, at which point he officially declared that any recipient was free to realize the work and thus become its author. By critiquing the mechanisms of exhibition and circulation through the postal system, and by resisting commercialization through the renunciation of authorship, Dazhang's practice carved out a distinct individual path (fig. 18).

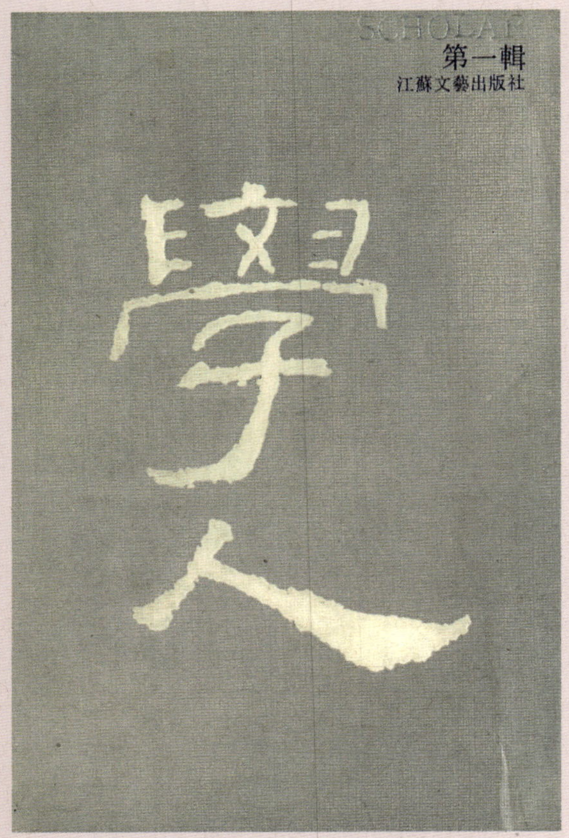

19. *The Scholar*, 1991, Jiangsu Literature and Art Publishing House, courtesy of Su Wei

3. INTELLECTUAL CURRENTS AND DEBATES

While the first half of the 1980s was defined by an enlightenment-era search for creative identity, the second half initiated a critical shift and a linguistic turn that would shape the entire 1990s. In the field of contemporary poetry, the "Third Generation" rose in opposition to the established Misty School (朦胧诗派). In film, the Sixth Generation directors turned their cameras to the lives of ordinary people. In art, practitioners grew wary of direct political commentary and grand modernist aesthetics, shifting toward more conceptual approaches. Many artists of the 90s were dissatisfied with the international reception of Political Pop and Cynical Realism, which they felt reduced their work to a cultural spectacle. For them, the imperative was to experiment relentlessly, pushing art into new conceptual and geopolitical territory.

Yet, as more conceptual and media-based practices flourished, a fundamental issue remained: art in China could not simply discard the legacy of socialist culture. This legacy continued to resonate, and any creative individual had to be understood in relation to it, a problem the art world would only begin to seriously address around 2010.

Before the reassessment of the socialist legacy became a matter of urgency, China's contemporary intellectual circles had already begun to act. They hoped to prevent intellectual work from devolving into mere political commentary. Even with the political trauma of 1989 that lingered, they were willing to rethink the role of the intellectual and began to construct an academic framework for contemporary Chinese thought and culture. The 1991 launch of the journal *The Scholar* (学人), with financial support from Japanese intellectual and business circles, was a manifestation of this new tendency. Published by Jiangsu Literature and Art Publishing House, the journal featured the early academic writings of many scholars who are now pivotal in the fields of Chinese intellectual history, history, and social philosophy. In the harsh political atmosphere of the time, this decade-long journal attempted to professionalize knowledge production, guiding the public intellectuals of the 1980s toward the role of specialized scholars. While *The Scholar* may not have explicitly embodied the call to reassess the socialist legacy, it profoundly influenced the construction of China's genealogy of knowledge production, a genealogy in which that legacy is inherently embedded (fig. 19).

The suppression of the humanistic spirit by mainstream socialist culture is a well-known fact; it was typically dismissed as either bourgeois discourse or a product of Soviet revisionism. Consequently, the revival of the humanistic spirit remained a crucial topic throughout the 1980s and 1990s. This concept is naturally connected to the evolutionary path of individualism in New China. In the early 1980s, the still deeply entangled intellectual and political circles in China launched a major debate on "humanism and alienation," attempting to vindicate for the "humanism" that had been suppressed between 1949 and 1979. The definitive intellectual debate on the "humanistic spirit" occurred between 1993 and 1995 (especially in 1994), as reflected in a series of discussions published in the journal *Dushu* (读书,

"Reading"). The literary world's "dispute of the two Wangs" (Wang Meng and Wang Binbin) and the "resonance of the two Zhangs" (Zhang Chengzhi and Zhang Wei) brought this great debate to a climax. Broadly speaking, one side of the argument inherited the position of the 1980s elite intellectuals, rejecting what they saw as the moral degradation and loss of humanistic spirit brought about by the market-driven mass culture of the 1990s. The other side accused the former of cultural despotism and hypocritical moralism. In the wake of the debate, some intellectuals moved beyond its binary opposition, choosing instead to directly confront the complex realities of China's societal shift from public to private and the intricate discursive field of its cultural world, insisting on combining the practice of social critique with that of cultural theory.

In the art world, the "humanistic spirit" was not directly invoked. Some artists still adhered to the idea of art as a spiritual high ground for humanity, a belief that supported practices transcending China's social reality, even as their own social status remained ambiguous. For others, as mentioned earlier, the focus was on ordinary people and marginalized groups; they strove to transform this concern for the anonymous individual, imbued with a sense of moral universalism, into alternative artistic creations and more precise critiques of artistic concepts. The position of the many artists engaged in conceptual and multimedia practices was more subtle: they concealed any explicit interest in the humanistic spirit in their work, approaching it instead from the more secular perspectives of the art industry, commerce, or daily life. This stance seemed to align with the opposing side in the "humanistic spirit" debate, yet it also highlighted the creative individual's effort to forge a parallel path distinct from the trajectory of cultural and intellectual thought. Regardless, across these different artistic communities, the "humanistic spirit" was thoroughly liberated from its previous state of suppression, allowing individualism to manifest in varied forms across different artistic philosophies.

The socialist cultural legacy ultimately found expression in another debate of the 1990s: the famous and far-reaching dispute between New Left and liberal intellectuals. The polemic was sparked in 1997 by the scholar Wang Hui's article "Contemporary China's Thought-Situation and the Question of Modernity" (当代中国的思想状况与现代性问题), published in the journal *Tianya* (天涯). To this day, how to define the two sides of the debate remains highly contested. The meanings of "left" and "right" in China's socialist market economy system not only differ from their Western counterparts, but the theoretical tools and positions of the two camps often overlap. In broad strokes, the New Left focused more on the legacy and reinterpretation of indigenous socialism under new social conditions, prioritizing social distributive fairness and justice over privatization, the capitalist free market, and Western modern governance systems based on individual freedom. The liberals, many of whom were trained in universities or research institutions in the West, particularly the United States, advocated for a social order based on a free market and modern rule of law, emphasizing the primacy of individual political rights.

In reality, the debate was truly about the direction and principles of China's reforms: how to understand and act upon the relationships between public and private, the collective and the individual, and China and the West in the post-Mao era. Scholars from different camps also engaged in sustained exploration of issues such as the paradoxes of modernity, social fairness, economic ethics, nationalism, and globalization. However, they also discovered that China's mode of political operation might not lead to any of the developmental paths they envisioned—a point made increasingly evident by the resurgence of extreme nationalism and political conservatism in China today.

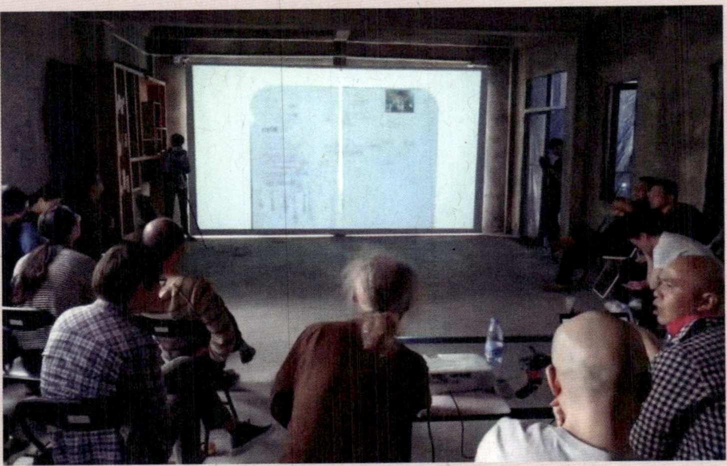

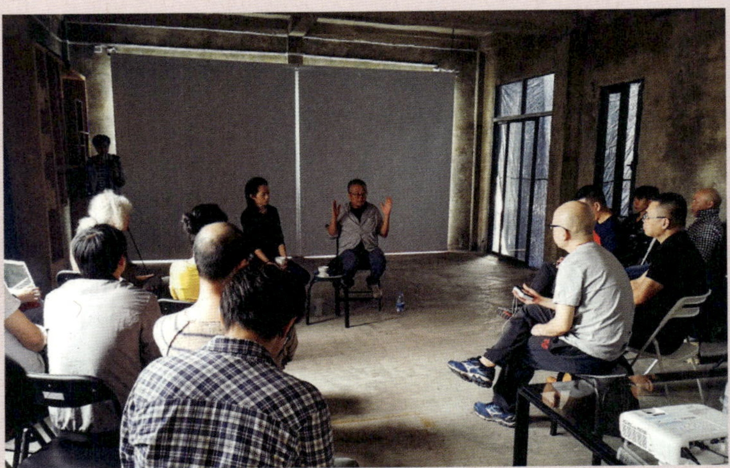

20. "Individual as Society," 2017, courtesy of Man Yu

4. A RETURN TO THE COLLECTIVE

The archival material in this exhibition centers on the evolution of individualism in China from the 1980s through the 2000s. But we are also interested in the subtle shift that has occurred in the last ten years, a shift captured by archives still in formation. The globalist art that defined the first decade or so of the twenty-first century is no longer the premise for these "archives." With the wane of the feverish consumption by the West and the art market, Chinese contemporary art has arrived at a pivotal historical moment of self-confrontation and self-reckoning. This moment brings into focus "China's Conundrum"—an issue that was continuously deferred amidst the nation's comprehensive economic development and modernization.

In the past, artistic individualism was sustained by institutional support, the benefits of modernization, and savvy global strategies. But in an era of de-globalization and resurgent political conservatism at home, Chinese artists are returning to more fundamental questions: How do we live with others? How can we forge solidarity to resist the erosion of individual rights and free expression? How can art find a new relevance not through professionalized production, but through the practice of relating to others? These questions are both political and a direct challenge to the established norms of the art world. In response, some Chinese artists are turning from the "individual" to the "community." They use the community as a space to test and even dissolve the established legitimacy of contemporary art, creating an alternative practice of individualism. Their efforts resonate with a growing call to rebuild civil society—a contemporary echo of the 1980s democratic aspirations, now reimagined as a more localized, tangible form of freedom.

This notion of "community" in China refers not to mass political movements but to small-scale, tangible social formations. The goal is not national change but individual care and empowerment, achieved by exploring new ways of living together. Within these communities, Chinese artists must engage in deep self-reflection, critiquing their own individualistic habits within a context of shared emotion and everyday ethics. We see the project "Individual as Society," initiated by Man Yu (1977–) among others in 2017, as one such living archive. It challenges the premise that individual suffering is solely the result of an unequal social structure. Instead, it brings together psychoanalysts, artists, and "nameless" individuals—those who feel marginalized or struggle to define themselves—to reflect on their own subjective difficulties (fig. 20). Through fieldwork, social action, and discussion, they explore fundamental human predicaments as they manifest in contemporary China, and the suffering that arises from them. This suffering took on absurd and cruel forms during the COVID-19 pandemic from 2020 to 2023, reviving traumatic memories and deep anxieties about the present.

READER

THE ECONOMY OF RISING CHINA AND ITS CONTRADICTIONS

WANG HUI 汪晖

STATE-SOCIETY RELATIONS AND THE DISCOURSES AND ACTIVITIES OF A MOVEMENT

DINGXIN ZHAO 赵鼎新

DILEMMAS OF TWENTY-FIRST CENTURY GLOBALIZATION: EXPLANATIONS AND SOLUTIONS, WITH A CRITIQUE OF THOMAS PIKETTY'S TWENTY-FIRST CENTURY CAPITALISM

QIN HUI 秦晖

THE NEW ERA AND ITS INTELLECTUAL ELITE

XUDONG ZHANG 张旭东

ON INDIVIDUALISM IN THE NEW CULTURE MOVEMENT

YANG GUOQIANG 杨国强

ON THE ISSUE OF THE INTEGRATION OF LITERATURE UNDER SOCIALIST IDEOLOGY

HONG ZICHENG 洪子诚

THE DIARY OF HOPE (PARTS 3 & 4)

WANG WEI 王炜

THE ECONOMY OF RISING CHINA AND ITS CONTRADICTIONS[1]

WANG HUI 汪晖

The development of China's economy has defied many predictions—since 1989, China's collapse has been predicted many times, but China has not collapsed. Instead, the theories of collapse have collapsed. For this reason, people have started to seek an explanation for why China not only has not collapsed but has continued to develop. In the process of reform and opening, there have been many debates in favor of and against reform, and these debates have often touched on how to evaluate questions related to the socialist era and the era of reform. More and more people believe that no matter how we evaluate the achievements and difficulties of the socialist period and the period of reform and opening, China's economy has been built on the foundation of these two traditions. At the same time, the ongoing worldwide financial crisis and the contradictions accumulated over a long period also signal that China cannot and should not simply return to the past developmental model, whether we mean by that the traditional planned economy model, or the developmentalist model whose only goal was GDP growth. We need to find a new way to think about China's experience over the past sixty years.

INDEPENDENT SOVEREIGN CHARACTER AND ITS POLITICAL MEANING

In discussions of the China model, many scholars emphasize the stability of China's development, arguing that there has been no great crisis. This is incorrect. In the thirty years of reform and opening, China's biggest crisis was that of 1989. China survived this great crisis, but traces of the unfortunate outcome can still be found in different areas. That crisis also had an international aspect, although it was political instead of economic.[2] China's crisis can be seen as the prelude to the crises of the Soviet Union and Eastern Europe. Like China, these countries were also socialist countries led by Communist parties, so why did China not fall as they did? What were the features that maintained China's stability and fueled China's rapid growth? After thirty years of reform, how have the conditions that made that possible changed? If we want to discuss the Chinese path or China's uniqueness, this is the first question that we have to answer.

The collapse of the Soviet Union and Eastern Europe had complex and deep historical causes, including the opposition between bureaucratism and the masses, the authoritarian politics of the Cold War era, and the difficulties in the people's livelihood caused by a shortage economy, among others. By way of comparison, the capacity of self-renewal of the Chinese system has proved to be much stronger. Even after the conflicts of the Cultural Revolution, in which high-level state and Party officials were sent by Mao Zedong to work and live at the base level of society, the state displayed a responsiveness to the needs of base-level society when these same officials resumed power in the late 1970s. This was not the case in the Soviet Union and Eastern Europe. But I will not engage in a detailed discussion of the ins and outs of these questions here. My main point is to stress the difference between the Chinese system and those of the Soviet Union and Eastern Europe, which is that China independently and autonomously sought out its line of social development, and on this basis created its unique sovereign position.

After World War II, the system of national sovereignty was affirmed, but in fact, in the world at that time, very few countries possessed genuine sovereignty. This was true not only of countries in the Soviet bloc, but also those in the Western Alliance. During the period of the First Five Year Plan (1953–57), China's industrial development, postwar reconstruction and international status all received immense help from the Soviet Union, and in a certain sense China may be said to have been in a dependent relationship with the USSR.

Nonetheless, just as China's revolutionary process had its own unique path, China eventually also sought out its own unique developmental path. From the mid-1950s, China actively supported the non-aligned movement, and later also developed open disputes with the Soviet Union, not only on political issues, but on economic and military issues, and gradually broke away from what some scholars called its "lineage relationship" with the USSR, establishing its own independent position in the socialist system and in the world.

Despite the division of the Taiwan Straits, the Chinese nation's political character is sovereign and highly independent and autonomous, and the national economic and industrial systems shaped under the leadership of this political character are also highly independent and autonomous. Without this autonomy as a precondition, it is very hard to imagine China's path of opening and reform, and it is also very hard to imagine China's post-1989 fate. At the outset of the process of reform and opening, China already had an independent and autonomous national economic system, which was a precondition for reform. China's reform has its own internal logic; it is an autonomous reform, a dynamic—not passive—reform, which is completely different from the various "Color Revolutions" of Eastern Europe and the Middle East and their complex backgrounds.

China's development is not only different from the dependent economies of Latin America, it is also different from the East Asian model as represented by the experiences of Japan, South Korea, and Taiwan (even if in terms of the role played by the state, of government industrial policy, and on certain developmental strategies there are similarities and interactions). But from a political perspective, the precondition of China's reform was autonomy, while to a large degree the development of those countries can be considered dependent (the difference with Latin America is that the dependent relationships of the Cold War became the political precondition for development).

This relatively independent and complete sovereign nature was created through the practice of a political party, and this is an outstanding feature of twentieth-century politics. No matter how many errors of theory or practice the Chinese Communist Party (CCP) has committed, its anti-imperialism and its later debate with the Soviet Union were the basic elements culminating in China's sovereignty, and on these questions one cannot make a limited judgement based on minor details. As a result of its open debate with the Communist Party of the Soviet Union, China first shook off the lineage relationship between the two parties and subsequently shook off the lineage relationship between the two countries, thus becoming a new, independent model.

In the realms of economics, politics, and culture, China's explorations of the path of socialism and her experiences with reform produced all sorts of errors, problems, and even tragic results, but during the 1950s, 1960s, and 1970s, the Chinese government and political party continually adjusted its policies. These adjustments were not directed by outside forces, but for the most part were self-adjustments based on problems encountered in the course of practice. As a mechanism by which a political party corrects its path, theoretical debates —and especially open theoretical debates—played an important role in the process of self-adjustment and self-reform in which the party and nation were engaged. Because of the lack of a democratic mechanism within the CCP, line struggles often can turn into power struggles fueled by ruthless attacks, but such factors should not obscure the historical importance of debates over line or theory.

From this perspective, we need to rethink certain habitual interpretations of the reform era, for example, the idea that the reform did not possess a preconceived model or strategy, that we "crossed the river by feeling the stones." This is obviously correct, but in fact the lack of a preconceived model is the special characteristic of the entire Chinese revolution, and Mao Zedong said something to this effect in "On Contradiction." What do we rely on when we do not have a model? We rely on theoretical debate, on political struggle, on social practice. On what we call "from practice to practice."

Today, debates about what path of development to follow are no longer limited, as they were in the past, to inner-party debates, but the importance of theoretical debates to the adjustments of the policy line remains very important. If there had not been the criticism of and resistance to the GDP-driven pure developmentalism[3] from within and outside of the establishment in the 1990s, the exploration of the new scientific development model[4] would never have made it onto the agenda.

In the 1990s, following the change in China's political structure, debates in Chinese intellectual circles partially came to replace the function of what heretofore had been inner-party debates on line, and had important impacts on adjustments of national policy on the three rural issues of the 1990s, on medical reforms after 2003, on state enterprise reform and labor rights in 2005, and on theory, propaganda, and social movements related to environmental protection.

These days people often speak of democracy as a correcting mechanism, but in fact theoretical debates or debates on party line are also correcting mechanisms, correcting mechanisms for the CCP. Because of the lack of democratic mechanisms within in CCP, in the history of the twentieth century, debates over the party line often produced violence and authoritarianism, and we should think long and hard about this, but criticism of the violence that characterized inner-party struggle should not lead us to negate theoretical struggle or struggle over the party line, because in fact these latter serve as the mechanism allowing us to shake off authoritarianism and find the path of self-correction. The slogan "practice is the sole test of truth" asserted the absolute importance of practice, but this fundamental question is itself theoretical, and we can only understand the importance of this slogan by grasping the importance of theoretical debate.

THE ROLE OF THE STATE

Another crucial element in understanding reform era China is how to understand the nature of the Chinese state and its transformation. As many historians have demonstrated, East Asia has a rich and ancient tradition of states and state relations. For example, Giovanni Arrighi (1937–2009) argued in his recent book, *Adam Smith in Beijing*, that:

> "In the context of nation-states and interstate systems, the national economy was not the invention of the West [...] Throughout the entire eighteenth century, the world's most important national market was not in Europe but rather was China."

He further analyses the reasons for the development of the contemporary Chinese economy, and especially its attractiveness to outside capital, and argues that:

> "The principal attractiveness of the PRC for foreign capital is not its rich resources of cheap labor [...] but instead is high quality of that labor in terms of health, education and self-management ability, coupled with the rapid expansion of the productive capacity of China's domestic economy."

In his understanding, Adam Smith was not a leader in the creation of the market order, but was rather a thinker with penetrating ideas about the nature of state regulation of the market. Generally following this line of analysis, the Beijing University economist Yao Yang (b. 1964), in a summary of the conditions behind China's economic development, argued that a neutral government or a neutral state constituted the preconditions for the success of China's reforms.

State capacity is an important question in the context of reform. I have two observations to supplement what Arrighi and Yao Yang have said. Arrighi's viewpoint is built on a narrative in which Chinese and Asian national markets have a long tradition, yet in the absence of the Chinese revolution and its reorganization of social relationships, it is difficult to imagine that the traditional "national market" would automatically transform into a new national market. Late Qing efforts to build military strength and a commercial system through state strength, and unstinting land reform efforts after the 1911 Revolution created a national market unlike that of traditional times, newly configured domestically and in relations with foreign countries.

In criticizing Sun Yat-sen's "Plan for National Development," Lenin pointed out that land revolution and a new national program with socialist or popular welfare overtones would fulfill the prerequisites for the development of agricultural capitalism. In discussing the nature of the modern Chinese state, we cannot abstract it from the preconditions of the land relations brought about by the Chinese Revolution and the change in the status of the peasantry. For example, people criticize the experiment of the Great Leap Forward, but rarely note that this same experiment was the result of the ongoing changes in land relations in modern China. On the one hand, the small peasant economy of lineages and families came to an end, and on the other, family property, lineage, and territorial relations were reorganized into a new set of social relations. Village reforms were reforms of the commune system, but at the same time were also constructed on the basis of the social relations created by this experiment. Early village reforms were carried out at the initiative of the state, a reform movement involving many efforts to manage and adjust the prices of rural commodities. This reform movement in fact inherited many elements, and the development from township industry to township enterprises unfolded according to a logic that was not that of neoliberalism[5].

As for Yao Yang's argument that the history of the modern revolution and socialism produced a neutral government, the precondition for this was actually not neutrality. China's socialist practice devoted itself to the creation of a state that would represent the universal interests of the majority of the people, and the precondition for this was a rupture with the notion that the state or the government would be linked to special interests. From a theoretical perspective, this socialist state practice was produced through an early revision of Marxist theory, and texts like Mao Zedong's "On the Ten Great Relationships" and "On the Correct Handling of Contradictions among the People" are the basis of this new state theory. Because a socialist state takes the representation of the interests of the majority as its mission, then under market conditions it is freer than other forms of state from connections with interest groups. Only in this sense can we describe it as a neutral state.

This was a key element in the success of the early reforms. At least in the early period of reform, the legitimacy of the program came precisely from the fact that interests represented by the socialist state were universal. Had there not been the checks and balances of socialist strength within the state, within the party, and within all social fields, the state would have rapidly been monopolized by interest groups. In the mid-1980s there were calls for privatization, but against strong resistance from both within the establishment and without, the idea of first establishing the market mechanism prevailed. This was the key to China's resisting the Russian-style shock treatment.

In other words, social capital accumulated during the socialist period constituted a brake on social policy at this key moment of transformation. Even in this sense, it is difficult for us to define these critical forces as opposed to the revolution.

Actually, in the ideological debates that erupted in the 1990s, we can find a similar phenomenon. The critique of developmentalism finally stimulated the emergence of ideas related to scientific development or other kinds of development. Chinese society's universal condemnation of and resistance to corruption was also a force pushing for reform of the system. The neutrality of the state emerged out of the mutual interaction among the above-mentioned non-neutral forces.

In the era of globalization, the nature of the state is changing in domestic terms. To simply describe China as an "extremely sovereign state" too often conflates the positive side and the negative side. Unlike Russia, China's reforms did not go through the "shock treatment," and the state's ability to guide the economy remains quite strong. China's financial system is relatively stable, because China did not completely take the neoliberal path; China's land has not been privatized (even if land can readily change hands to meet the demands of the market), which not only provided the basis for the preservation of the low-cost nature of China's rural society, but also made possible national organizations using land resources to initiate and push forward land certificates.[6]

These topics all are related to state capacity and its meaning. The Chinese state should take up its responsibilities, for example by actively resolving the rural crisis, rebuilding the social security system, protecting the environment, increasing investment in education, and reforming the educational system. On these fronts, the Chinese government must transform its posture from that of a developmental government to that of a social welfare government, a transformation that will also force the Chinese economy away from an over-reliance on exports and toward an economy driven by internal demand.

Whether these positive social policies can be carried out will not be decided solely by the will of the state. After thirty years of reform and the efforts of those pushing for market reforms, state organs are deeply implicated in market activities to the point that it is no longer appropriate to describe the various bureaus and ministries of the state as "neutral." The state does not stand alone, but is embedded in the social structure and in relation to interest groups. The question of corruption today is not solely a question of the corruption of individual officials, but is also connected to social policies, economic policies and the question of special interests.

For example, the development of the high-carbon industry and energy projects has frequently been dominated, or even monopolized, by certain interest groups. Efforts to contain such groups through public policy include public discussions, social protection movements, and different traditions from within the state and the party. At the end of the 1990s, for example, the great discussion of the "three rural issues" prompted an adjustment of national rural policy; in 2003, the SARS crisis produced a great discussion of the health-care system and led to changes; in 2005, the debate over the reform of the state enterprise system and a large-scale workers' movement led to a series of related policies; calls from within the state system demanding an end to corruption and strict party discipline provided impetus for the anti-corruption movements.[7] But domestic and international interest relationships have penetrated state mechanisms to an unprecedented degree, to the point that even the process of law-making, the question of how to ensure that the state and its public policies represent broad interests and not the interests of minority interest groups, has already become a pressing problem.

THE PARADOX OF THE STATICIZATION OF THE PARTY

A discussion of the state has a direct bearing on the question of the development of democratic mechanisms. Discussions of the question of the Chinese state must confront a basic paradox: on the one hand, in comparison with the governments of many other states, Chinese government capacity is widely acknowledged, as is evidenced by the mobilization of aid in the wake of the Wenchuan earthquake that occurred in May 2008, by the rapid fashioning of market-saving plans after the financial crisis, by the successful staging of the 2008 Olympics, and by the efficiency of various local governments in terms of organizational development and crisis resolution—all of these signal the outstanding advantages of Chinese state capacity.

Yet on the other hand, even if public opinion surveys show that the people are broadly satisfied with government performance, still, in some regions and at some periods, contradictions between the officials and the people are very acute, and the policy implementation ability of various levels of government as well as their level of honesty are often subject to doubt. The most crucial question is that these kinds of contradictions often trigger a crisis of legitimacy. By contrast, in some countries, even if state capacity is weak and the government ineffectual, the economy lagging and social policies not implicated, there still does not exist a systemic political crisis. This question is intimately related to democracy as a source for political legitimacy.

In the 1980s, the question of democracy seemed fairly straightforward. Having gone through twenty years of democratic mobilization, on the one hand, democracy still was the most important source of political legitimacy; on the other, simply importing Western democratic methods in the Asian region in the 1980s and 1990s seemed less attractive. After the crisis of the new democracies and the fading of the "Color Revolutions," the democratic movements in Eastern Europe, the Middle East, and other regions fell into decline after 1989. At the same time, in Western and Third World democracies (such as India), the emptiness of democracy was becoming a universal crisis. The crisis of democracy is intimately linked to the conditions of marketization and globalization:

1. The major form of political democracy in the postwar period was either the multi-party or bi-party parliamentary system, but under conditions of marketization, political parties progressively lost the ability they once had in the earlier period to represent the people, and in order to get votes, the political values of the political parties became ever more ambiguous, which led to the eclipse of representative democracy in all but name.

2. The relationship between democracy and the state under conditions of globalization also faced a challenge: because economic relations increasingly transcended the realm of the traditional national economy, thus escaping the control of the state, all states had to shape their political arrangements in conformity with the demands of the international system.

3. Following the conversion of political parties into interest groups, or even the emergence of oligopolies, formal democracies progressively became political structures disconnected from the base levels in their societies, so that the demands of those dispossessed groups were unable to be represented in the political realm, which led these groups to employ non-governmental means of protection (such as the rise of "Mao Zedong" in India).[8] Under these conditions, not only formal democracy, but at times even the state itself came to be hollowed out in many places.

4. Because the electoral process relied on large amounts of money and financial strength, in different democratic counties there existed both legal and illegal forms of electoral corruption, which damaged public faith in elections. By this I do not mean that the value of democracy has disappeared. The question is: What kind of democracy do we need and what form should it take? How can we ensure that democracy be more than just an empty form, that it have genuine contents?

The Chinese political system is also experiencing important changes, one of which is the change in the nature of the party. In the 1980s, the goal of political reform was party-government separation. After the 1990s, this is no longer a popular slogan, and in concrete practice and institutional arrangements, the unity of party and government has become a more commonly seen phenomenon. I call this the staticization of the party.

The origins of this trend are worth careful analysis. According to traditional political theory, a political party represents mass interests, and through struggles and debates in parliament, in other words through procedural democracy, this becomes the state common interest, the expression of sovereign public will. In China, the multi-party cooperative system led by the CCP[9] is also based on the representative nature of the parties. But under conditions of market society, when state organs directly participate in economic activities, different branches of the government wind up intermingled with special interests, and the "neutral state" of the early reform period is currently undergoing transformation. Since the party can keep a certain distance from economic activity, they can, from a relatively autonomous "neutral" position express the will of society. For example, anti-corruption activities mainly rely on party mechanisms for efficient implementation. Since the 1990s, the national will has basically taken shape through the goals of the party, as was the case with the "three represents," "harmonious society," or "scientific development." These slogans no longer directly express the particular representative nature of the party, but instead directly plead for the interests of all of the people. In this sense, the party has become the inner core of sovereignty.

Yet the staticization of the party includes two challenges. First, if the frontier between party and state disappears completely, what force or mechanism can guarantee that the party will not—like the state—be captured by the interests of market society? In addition, the universal representativity of the traditional party (including the neutral character of early socialist countries), was achieved through its clear political values, and if the party is staticized then this means the weakening and the transformation of the party's political values.

If the construction of a "neutral country" is closely related to the political values of a political party, then under new conditions, what is the mechanism that will ensure that China can maintain its representativity? How will the voice of the common people find expression in the public realm? How to carry out adjustment of basic line and policies of the state and the party through genuine freedom of expression, consultative mechanisms and constant exchange between officials and the people? How to broadly absorb domestic and international strength to create the broadest type of democracy? These are questions that cannot be avoided in discussions of the self-reform of the party. When reflecting on the question of political reform in China, we need to consider these questions so as to imagine China's democratic path. Concretely speaking, I argue that there are three aspects to consider: First, in the twentieth century China went through a long and very deep revolution, and Chinese society's demands for justice and social equality are very strong; how should this history and this tradition be transformed into democratic demands under current conditions? In other words, what is the mass line or mass democracy in the new era? Second, the CCP is a vast political party that has gone through enormous changes and is increasingly absorbing state mechanisms. How do we make this party system more democratic? How, when the role of the party is changing, do we guarantee that the state can represent universal interests? Third, how, on a social basis, can we create new political forms allowing mass society to achieve political capacity and defeat the "depoliticizing" trends emerging from neoliberal marketization?[10]

China is an open society, but workers, peasants, and ordinary citizens lack adequate space and guarantees for public participation. How should China allow the voice and demands of society to be expressed in the context of state policy and thus constrain the monopoly capacity and demands of capital—this is the crux of the issue. Freedom for capital or freedom for society; there's a big difference. These are all concrete questions, but contain the embryos of important theoretical questions, for example: What is the direction of people's China's political reform under conditions of globalization and marketization? How under conditions of openness can we engineer Chinese society's autonomy? Against the backdrop of the universal crisis of democracy, the universal importance of this exploration is obvious.

In the wake of China's economic growth, China has sought broader international cooperation and markets. China's presence in Africa and other regions has prompted a good deal of discussion and uneasiness in the West. One wonders whether China, as it deals with economic globalization, can not only create another path of development, but also avoid dealing with the rest of the world in the Western fashion?

Capitalism is by nature expansive; its need for resources is expansive whether in a single country or on the world stage. For this reason I feel that China's modern internationalist traditions should be brought out anew—not the internationalism that was meant to export revolution, but the one that genuinely cared for and respected the existence, development, and social rights of third world countries, and that sought a road to peace, democracy and common development in the world setting.

Questions of international position are related to changes in domestic relations. What kind of commercial culture and political culture does China want to develop? How will China be different from American hegemony? China should be different from early capitalism. The market plays an important role in culture and politics, but we cannot allow market logic to become ruling logic. From the point of view of the economic structure, the position of the laborers should see an important rise, and the ecology and natural environment should be improved. Moving away from the emphasis on political and economic relations is something that is rarely discussed. The current structural crisis is a crisis in the old mainstream model, and now is the time to create a new model of politics. The 1990s are over. The year 2008 was a signal.

This change is dramatic, and to some degree the product of luck, but it is not fortuitous. The problem well may be that Chinese society has not yet adapted to its new status in international society; the accumulated contradictions experienced by Chinese society in the process of marketization and the risks faced in the process of globalization were similarly unprecedented. As a proposition, let's say that the true meaning of the "end of the 1990s" is a search for a new kind of politics, a new path and a new direction.

Excerpt from *The Economy of Rising China and Its Contradictions*

From *Reading and Writing the China Dream Project* (readingthechinadream.com)

1 汪晖, “中国崛起的经验及其面临的挑战,” 文化纵横 (Beijing Cultural Review), 2010.2: pp. 24–35.
2 For an example of Wang's thoughts on Tiananmen in English, see Wang Hui and En Liang Khong, "After the Party: An Interview with Wang Hui" in *OpenDemocracy* https://www.opendemocracy.net/en/after-party-interview-with-wang-hui/. Wang emphasizes the class dimensions of the conflict.
3 By "developmentalism," Wang Hui refers to a neoliberal view of economic growth that stresses development above all else.
4 The new scientific development model was endorsed by CCP authorities in October, 2005, at the meeting of the fifth plenum of the 16th Central Committee and was meant to be a corrective to "blind developmentalism."
5 On this theme, see Barry Naughton, "Chinese Institutional Innovation and Privatization from Below," *The American Economic Review* 84.2 (May 1994), pp. 266–70.
6 Land certificates are associated with the New Left, and are seen as means to compensate peasants for undesirable land, allowing them to migrate to the cities and allowing the state to restructure the rural sector. See Cui Zhiyuan, "Partial Intimations of the Coming Whole: The Chongqing Experiment in the Light of the Theories of Henry George, James Meade, and Antonio Gramsci," *Modern China* 37.6 (2011): pp. 646–60.
7 This set of policies undertaken by the Hu-Wen regime signaled a renewed state interest in the basic livelihood of the people.
8 Such as the Naxalite insurgency. More broadly, see Tilak P. Gupta, "Maoism in India: Ideology, Programme and Armed Struggle," *Economic and Political Weekly* 41.29 (Jul. 22-28, 2006): pp. 3172–76.
9 Although China is routinely labeled a "one-party state," in fact there exist a number of smaller legal political parties, most of them holdovers from the Republican period. None of these parties possesses any real power, however.
10 The "depoliticization" of politics is a theme Wang Hui has stressed for some time. It refers to the process by which technocratic rule replaces genuine political debate to the detriment of democracy and representation. See Wang Hui, "Depoliticized Politics, from East to West," *New Left Review* 41 (2006): pp. 29–45.

STATE-SOCIETY RELATIONS AND THE DISCOURSES AND ACTIVITIES OF A MOVEMENT

DINGXIN ZHAO 赵鼎新

In my study, I compared the language and forms of activity used during the 1989 Movement with those used during the May Fourth Movement of 1919 and the December 9th Movement of 1935–36, the two largest student movements of Republican China.

In 1989, why did Chinese students take Hu Yaobang's sudden death and his memorial service as opportunities for political action? Why did Chinese students often cut their own fingers and use the blood to write slogans? Why did three students kneel in front of the Great Hall of the People to hand in a petition? In short, why did the 1989 Beijing Student Movement have a particular pattern of activities and what was the impact of those activities on the dynamics of the movement? So far, scholars have approached this type of question from a cultural perspective.[1] For example, to prevent other Beijing populations from joining the demonstration, students often set up picket lines and made anyone who wanted to join a march show his or her student identity card. This type of activity is commonly interpreted as a reflection of the students' sense of elitism, an ethos which in turn is seen as rooted in Chinese culture.[2] This explanation, which attributes a cultural manifestation simply to culture itself, can be misleading.

For instance, in studying protest activities in China during the twentieth century, I found that the rhetoric and activities of the 1989 Movement were actually truer to traditional Chinese culture than those of earlier student movements. In relation to the above example of student elitism, for instance, I found that the students of the May Fourth Movement of 1919 had actually praised workers as sacred (*laogong shensheng*), tried to earn their own living through labor (*bangong bandu*), and mobilized workers and merchants to form a broad coalition. I also found that during the December 9th Movement of 1935–36 students launched a rural crusade in the south to mobilize China's peasantry into an anti-Japanese coalition.[3] Yet if we believe that the patterns of a social movement are determined by culture, the 1989 Movement should appear less, not more, traditional than those two earlier movements, since Chinese culture has only become more modern over the course of the twentieth century. The finding, therefore, poses a puzzle.

HISTORICAL BACKGROUNDS OF THE TWO EARLIER STUDENT MOVEMENTS

The May Fourth Movement of 1919, the December 9th Movement of 1935–36, and the 1989 Movement are the three largest student movements in the history of twentieth-century China. They all started in Beijing and spread across the nation. The May Fourth Movement was the first major student movement in modern China. After 1917, China's new intellectuals and students had initiated a vast modernization drive that aimed to strengthen the country through science and democracy. This modernization drive to a great extent paved the way for the rise of the movement. The movement, however, was named after the incidents of May 4, 1919: on that day, over three thousand Beijing students marched in the streets in an anti-Japanese demonstration protesting the Shandong resolution of the Versailles Peace Conference. As merchants, workers, and other urban residents joined the students, anti-Japanese protests soon spread to many other Chinese cities. Eventually the government of Northern China had to dismiss three pro-Japanese officers and refuse to sign the Versailles Peace Treaty. The impact of the May Fourth Movement was profound. Politically, it contributed to the rise of the Chinese Communist Party (CCP) and the reorganization of the Nationalist Party (Guomindang). Culturally it facilitated the rise and dominance of vernacular literature and mass education and the decline of Confucianism and traditional ethics.

While the May Fourth Movement was at once pro-democratic and nationalistic, the December 9th Movement was mainly a nationalistic reaction to Japanese aggression. By 1935, Japan had occupied the whole Dongbei region (Northeastern China) and a large part of Hebei province. Beijing was virtually encircled by Japanese troops. On December 9, 1935, thousands of Beijing students marched to urge the government to resist the Japanese invasion. The movement spread to most of urban China in 1936. The impact of this movement was also monumental. It helped the CCP rebuild its urban base, which had been destroyed by the Guomindang.

It also split the governing elites and led to the Xi'an Incident.[4] A series of chain reactions during and after the movement led to the establishment of a united front between the Guomindang and CCP to fight against the Japanese invasion, paving the way for the communist victory in China.[5]

PATTERNS OF ACTIVITY DURING THE 1989 MOVEMENT

While this study investigates the impact of state-society relations on the patterns of social movement activity, I do not claim that social movement activities are completely shaped by state-society relations. In comparison with the May Fourth Movement of 1919 and the December 9th Movement of 1935–36, the 1989 Movement has three distinctive features. The movement was much more pro-Western in appearance; it bore the strong imprint of the Cultural Revolution and of the communist style of mass mobilization more generally; and finally, culturally embedded rhetoric and movement activities figured much more centrally in the 1989 Movement than in the two earlier student movements. In what follows, I will briefly introduce each of these patterns, relating the last to state-society relations in China during the 1980s.

PRO-WESTERN CHARACTERISTICS OF THE MOVEMENT

During the 1989 Movement, Chinese students flashed the V-sign to indicate victory, built a Statue of Liberty turned "Goddess of Democracy" in Tiananmen Square, held countless press conferences to attract Western attention, provided Western and Hong Kong journalists with easy access to their headquarters, and routinely listened to foreign broadcasts for news and feedback.[6] This list of pro-Western attributes can be expanded. The movement's pro-Western nature was also reflected in its language. English banners such as "For the People, By the People," "Absolute Power, Absolute Corruption,"[7] "Give me Democracy or Give me Death," "Glasnost," and "People Power" appeared everywhere. This pro-Western attitude was new to China. Although both the May Fourth and December 9th Movements were anti-Japanese, students also expressed their grievances with other foreigners. These movements took place between the world wars, hence nationalism became a major feature of the movements. The May Fourth students advocated Westernization only because they believed that democracy could save China from foreign aggression. By the time of the 1989 Movement, however, colonialism was seen as part of the distant past; intellectuals and students were no longer so concerned with saving China. Instead, they felt great pain as a consequence of the strong state that their predecessors had dreamed of and fought for. They had also witnessed the decline of the Soviet Union and a new wave of worldwide democratization. State socialism was no longer treated as a viable model; capitalism and democracy had again become the twin engines of the world system. The pro-Western nature of the movement revealed fundamental changes in the international environment and in the mood of Chinese intellectuals and students.

THE IMPRINT OF COMMUNIST MASS MOBILIZATION

Communist education had imprinted a set of habits and iconic images on students. For example, during the 1989 Movement students sang "The Internationale" whenever they felt that their action was heroic and tragic. Although "The Internationale" is part of a legitimate set of symbols under the regime, students sang the song frequently because the song is rebellious in spirit and singing it was a standard way to express this type of emotion, one that students had learned through revolutionary dramas and films.

The hunger strike was arguably the single most important form of protest during the 1989 Movement. The strike led to the success of the movement, both in terms of the scale of mobilization it achieved and of the worldwide attention it generated. It also sowed the seeds for martial law and the final military crackdown. Significantly, the tactic was not used during the May Fourth and December 9th Movements but was popularized only during the Cultural Revolution.

Between May 16 and 26, 1989, around 172,000 students from various provinces went to Beijing by train.[8] Students also went by other means of transportation. Thus, in late May, Tiananmen Square was filled by energetic newcomers who were reluctant to leave. These students went to Beijing not just to support the movement but to take advantage of the opportunity to get a free trip to visit the capital. This practice was made popular in the Cultural Revolution, which students in 1989 were excited about.

THE TRADITIONALISM OF THE 1989 MOVEMENT

What is most stunning and hard to explain about the 1989 Movement is that its language and activities were actually more traditional and moralistic than those of the May Fourth and December 9th Movements.

In premodern China, kneeling in a public place was a major way by which the Chinese proclaimed their discontents and appealed to the public for support. Indeed, we see that during the May Fourth Movement students knelt in front of workers and merchants to try to mobilize them. Nevertheless, kneeling had never been as significant a movement tactic as it became during Hu Yaobang's funeral on April 22, 1989. Never before had kneeling brought out the emotions of hundreds of thousands of students and triggered a Beijing-wide class boycott.

The same was true of staging protests during funerals. During the May Fourth Movement, the funeral protests at Tianjin and Shanghai were only minor activities[9]. During the December 9th Movement, Beijing students did hold a memorial service and demonstrate on the street for Guo Qing, a high school student who had died in prison. However, when the government suppressed this activity, no further radical actions followed.[10] The 1989 Movement, by contrast, started after Hu Yaobang's sudden death and for its first week centered on mourning activities.

Students of the 1980s also brought back some of the rhetoric that their predecessors during the May Fourth era had vehemently attacked, and which had gradually disappeared from China's political discourse. Traditional Chinese virtues such as loyalty, filial piety, and images of extended family were under severe attack during the May Fourth Movement,[11] yet during the 1989 Movement, students and Beijing residents frequently used language drawing on these elements to mobilize emotions. One frequently encountered slogans that centered on extended family relations, such as: "Mama, we are not wrong!"; "Mama: I am hungry, but I won't eat!"; "Grandpa Zhao, Uncle Li, come save our big brothers and sisters!"; and "Your big brothers have been very anxious!" In addition, one also encountered language that emphasized very traditional Chinese values: "Fasting to the death is only a small deed!";[12] "Loyalty [to the country] and filial piety cannot be obtained at the same time"; and "It is not because there is no retribution, it is because the time has not yet come! When the time comes, retribution will definitely come from the people!" (*Bushibubao, Shijianweidao! Shijianyidao, Renminbibao*).[13]

It is quite tempting to explain this difference in terms of the core issues of each of the three movements. This works partially for the May Fourth Movement. There is no doubt that the iconoclastic nature of the movement delegitimized the use of traditional rhetoric and tactics. However, this explanation does not work for the December 9th Movement, because it was almost purely nationalistic, and there is little reason to expect a nationalistic movement in the 1930s to be less traditional than a pro-democratic movement in the 1980s.

STATE-SOCIETY RELATIONS IN THE THREE STUDENT MOVEMENTS

China during both the May Fourth Movement of 1919 and the December 9th Movement of 1935–36 had a fragmented state, divided elites, strong opposition parties or intermediate associations, and a state legitimized primarily by its capacity for national defense, while communist China during the 1980s had a relatively unitary governing elite that held much tighter control over society, despite the fact that a large proportion of the urban population judged it by its moral and economic performance, not by its ideology.

In the 1980s, public perception of the basis of state legitimation shifted from leftist ideology back to performance.[14] After the ideological legitimation of the state declined, moral and ritual performance once again became a popular criterion by which the people would judge their government.

Nevertheless, although a crisis of ideological legitimacy could be widely felt in urban China during the 1980s, no rival political organizations or parties existed then, as had been the case during the earlier student movements. Moreover, in the late 1980s most of the top-level government offices were still controlled by CCP veterans who had joined the party long before the communists took power. These veterans were aware of China's economic backwardness and its other problems. However, they also believed that these problems did not result from communism or authoritarianism but rather from inexperience. They realized that reform was an absolute necessity, but they never intended to give up what millions of their comrades had died for. They were confident because they had an armed force controlled by veteran senior officers, most of whom were veterans themselves. Thus, the legitimation crisis actually had no catastrophic impact on the higher echelons of the state leadership. Western analysts have highlighted the factional nature of Chinese government during the 1989 Movement. But the crucial fact is that no top state leaders really supported the students during the movement. Their differences were more over strategies to calm down the movement. This contrasts sharply with what happened during the May Fourth and the December 9th Movements, when powerful governing elites openly supported the students.

More independent forms of organizations emerged during the 1980s as China's reform deepened. However, the new associations were still at a very rudimentary stage of development and not comparable to organizations during the republican era. Therefore, during the 1989 Movement, all the movement organizations emerged with no prior history, and student mobilization was facilitated more by the ecology of the campuses and Tiananmen Square than by the strength of organizations.

When the government was challenged ideologically and morally, the challenge resonated widely. However, when the government invoked ideological or legal dimensions of state authority to control the movement, its measures only antagonized people. To adopt a game theory analogy, the whole situation was as if the state elites treated the game as chess and the people took it as *Chinese* chess. Since the chessmen for the two games are similar, each side remained unaware of the situation. Therefore, each player kept making moves that violated the other player's sense of the rules of the game, as if continuously applying Garfinkel's "breaching experiments" to each other. Both sides became increasingly irritated; eventually, the chessboard was overturned.

STATE-SOCIETY RELATIONS AND PATTERNS OF MOVEMENT ACTIVITY

Because China in the 1980s had a less fragmented state and weaker intermediate associations than had existed during the May Fourth and the December 9th Movements, the 1989 Movement was unable to organize so freely and raise demands so directly. In this setting, the students sought to avoid head-on repression by twisting or hiding their real demands and goals behind legitimate forms of collective action. Many activities during the 1989 Movement can be straightforwardly explained as strategies that aimed to create a "safe space" to lower the possibility of repression.[15]

If I were a social psychologist, I would certainly attribute the domination of cultural activities during the 1989 Movement to the emotional nature of the movement. The logic is straightforward: when people act emotionally, they tend to act out what they are most familiar with, according to those behavioral codes that have already been imprinted in their minds and to which they have become habituated.[16]

Someone who had visited Tiananmen Square during the movement was likely to encounter several independent protest activities either simultaneously or sequentially, and a huge crowd of sympathetic bystanders mingling inside and looking for something interesting. Those who acted on the stage might follow traditional, modern, or foreign scripts of social movements. Obviously, what mattered here was the psychology of those who were watching the protests.

During the 1980s, moral performance was a major source of state legitimation. Therefore, people were more receptive to morally (culturally) charged activities and got angry when the government reacted improperly to these activities. Thus, when on April 22 three students knelt on the steps of the Great Hall of the People, Li Peng's failure to come out to receive their petition immediately triggered a citywide class boycott. In fact, many other activities took place around the same time, but none of them were able to capture the hearts of students and shape the future of the movement.

In my interview, an informant was a very radical student leader, and yet he had wished that Li Peng would come out and meet them. As Pye has noted, coming out and receiving a petition in such a circumstance was a ritual that even a mandarin of imperial China had to fulfil.[17] Contrary to most students' expectations, Li Peng did not come out. On that day, what my informant and the journalist acted and cried out was actually a general sentiment—a sentiment of total disappointment in the government. They had this sentiment not because the government was not democratic (even though some of them were fighting for democratization) but because a leader of the government failed to perform a proper ritual, a ritual upon which the state was now basing its legitimacy. It was out of this sentiment that most Beijing students participated in a general class boycott the following day.

Since moral performance was the basis of state legitimacy, activities that morally discredited the government posed a more fundamental challenge to the state and thus were able to mobilize more people. Therefore, during the hunger strike, almost all the people in Beijing, even those working in state institutions, eventually supported the students. Most Beijing residents also joined the mass resistance to the army after martial law was imposed. Most of them, especially those from peripheral government institutions, did not stand up to fight for a democratic China. Instead, they protested a central government that kept silent while students were dying of hunger and that tried to use troops to repress students. In short, many people participated in the movement because they were angry; they were angry because the government's actions violated the people's common notion of how a good government should act.

STRENGTH OF MOVEMENT ORGANIZATIONS AND PATTERNS OF MOVEMENT DYNAMICS

In comparison with the two earlier student movements, the 1989 Movement broke out in an organizational near vacuum. The movement became more and more dominated by spontaneous mass activities.

At the time, China's leading liberal intellectuals comprised the only political force that could have had an impact on the course of the movement comparable to that of the Guomindang in the May Fourth era and the CCP in the December 9th era as organized opposition. These intellectuals, through their books, their speeches at campus conferences, and other activities, had prepared the way for the movement and had won respect among some students. Yet those students who were closest to the leading intellectuals and therefore had a more refined understanding of China's problems and of the goals of the movement were continuously marginalized by those who had gained their credentials through dedicated radical actions. Moreover, out of fear of repression, leading liberal intellectuals had deliberately distanced themselves from the movement in its early stages. By the time that they became collectively involved in the movement, it was already May 14, one day after the start of the hunger strike.

Furthermore, they first participated in the movement as mediators between the government and radical students, seeking to bring the hunger strike to an end. Not only did their efforts prove to be futile, but also the ambiguity of their stance further undermined their already weak standing within the movement. During late May, liberal intellectuals were more and more concerned about the future of the movement. A reflection of this concern was the establishment of the Joint Federation, which claimed to incorporate all the political forces in Beijing. Yet this organization failed to harness the tide of the movement and help it avert a tragic ending. This happened because, unlike the Guomindang and the CCP during the May Fourth and December 9th Movements, the liberal intellectuals in the 1980s had neither substantial organizational resources nor adequate political experience.[18]

Under these conditions, credentials became their only resource; but compared with the Guomindang and the CCP leaders, liberal intellectuals in the 1980s lacked past revolutionary experience as necessary credentials for leadership. In contrast to the newly emergent radical students in the 1989 Movement, the liberal intellectuals joined the movement later and did not participate in the hunger strike, which was generally considered to be the action which showed the greatest amount of dedication.[19] Therefore, all the discussions and decisions made by the Joint Federation turned out to be useless empty talk. As it proceeded, the movement was increasingly driven by emotion and radical action. This finally led the movement into a head-on confrontation with the government—and a tragic outcome.

Excerpt from: Zhao, Dingxin, *The Power of Tiananmen: State-Society Relations and the 1989 Beijing Student Movement*. University of Chicago Press, 2001. Chicago Scholarship Online, 2013. pp. 267–96.

Editor's note: minor adjustments have been made for better readability.

1 Since the 1980s, we have seen the rise of an approach that views people as largely emotional creatures and the rhetoric and activity patterns of social movements as determined by either current "texts" (ideology) or past "scripts" (culture). For example, Keith Michael Baker, *Inventing the French Revolution: Essays on French Political Culture in the Eighteenth Century* (Cambridge: Cambridge University Press, 1990); Lynn Hunt, *Politics, Culture and Class in the French Revolution* (Berkeley: University of California Press, 1984); William H. Jr. Sewell, "Ideologies and Social Revolutions: Reflections on the French Case," *Journal of Modern History* 57 (1985): pp. 57–85; Jeffrey N. Wasserstrom, *Student Protests in Twentieth-century China: The View From Shanghai* (Stanford, CA: Stanford University Press, 1991); Joseph W. Esherick, and Jeffrey N. Wasserstrom, "Acting Out Democracy: Political Theatre in Modern China," *Journal of Asian Studies* 49 (1990): pp. 835–65; and Lucian W. Pye, "The Escalation of Confrontation," in *The Broken Mirror: China after Tiananmen*, ed. by George Hicks (Essex: Longman, 1990), pp. 162–79, on the 1989 Movement have closely followed this approach.

2 Anita Chan and Jonathan Unger "China after Tiananmen," *The Nation*, January 22; Jane Macartney "The Students: Heroes, Pawns or Power-Brokers?" in *The Broken Mirror* (see note 1), pp. 3–23; and Elizabeth J. Perry and Ellen V. Fuller, "China's Long March to Democracy," *World Policy Journal* 8 (1991): pp. 663–85.

3 See John Israel, *Student Nationalism in China: 1927–1937* (Stanford, CA: Stanford University Press, 1966), pp. 134–38 for more details about the event.

4 On December 12, 1936, general Zhang Xueliang detained Chiang Kai-shek, the generalissimo, to try to force him to stop the war with the communists and lead the whole of China to resist the Japanese invasion. This is known as the Xi'an Incident.

5 Chalmers A. Johnson, *Peasant Nationalism and Communist Power: The Emergence of Revolutionary China, 1937–1945* (Stanford, CA: Stanford University Press, 1962).

6 According to Jane Macartney (see note 2), pp. 9–10, "Access to inner sanctums [at Tiananmen Square] was granted only to the Western and Hong Kong press." Moreover, student leader Wang Dan visited Hong Kong reporters almost daily "to feel out their attitude to the students, to find out whether the outside world was interested in the movement."

7 See the photos in Xuese de Limin, *A Bloody Morning* (Hong Kong: Chi Keung Publishing Co.,1989), pp. 48, 68.

8 Wu Mouren, Bao Minghui, Ni Peihua, Ni Peimin, and Wang Qingjia, eds., *Bajiu zhongguo minyun jishi* (Daily accounts on the 1989 democracy movement in China), p. 474.

9 Chow Tse-tsung, *The May Fourth Movement: Intellectual Revolution in Modern China* (Stanford, CA: Stanford University, 1967), pp. 129, 143.

10 Han Xuchang, Yaoerjiu *yundong shiyao* (A history of the December 9th Movement) (Beijing: The College of the CCP Central Committee, 1986),103–08; Israel (see note 3), p. 145.

11 See, for example, Chow (see note 9), pp. 58–59.

12 This is a slightly modified version of half of a traditional Chinese couplet, the other half of which goes: "Keeping one's chastity is the most important matter." The couplet was used to exhort a widow in traditional China to remain faithful to her dead husband.

13 This is the slogan shouted by Chai Ling during early May 1989 (Carma Hinton and Richard Gordon, *The Gate of Heavenly Peace* (Hong Kong: Mirror Books, 1997), 109). It expresses the Buddhist notion of reincarnation, that life is circular and one's status in the next life depends on one's deeds in the current life. It is part of folk wisdom in China.

14 During my interviews, I asked informants the question: "What was your view on the Four Cardinal Principles before the 1989 student movement?" Among the 60 people who responded to the question, 21 (35%) were strictly against them, whereas only 9 (15%) accepted them. The rest (50%) accepted them with reservations. For those who had conditionally accepted the Four Cardinal Principles, most of them said so only because they thought that the state was still effective in certain functions, especially in leading economic development. This finding is also confirmed by other similar studies during the 1980s (see Zhao Yining, "Zhongguo jingji xunqiu ruanzhaolu" (The Chinese economy seeks a soft landing), *Outlook Weekly*, no. 28 (1995): pp. 22–23). Therefore, during the 1989 BSM, at least among intellectuals and students, the Chinese state enjoyed a certain degree of performance legitimacy, but not ideological legitimacy.

15 Sara M. Evans and Harry C. Boyte, *Free Space: The Sources of Democratic Change in America* (Chicago: University of Chicago Press, 1992); Ted R. Gurr, "Persisting Patterns of Repression and Rebellion: Foundations for a General Theory of Political Coercion," in *Persistent Patterns and Emergent Structures in a Waning Century*, ed. by Margaret P. Karns (New York: Praeger, 1986) pp. 149–68; Mark Irving Lichbach, *The Rebel's Dilemma* (Ann Arbor: University of Michigan Press, 1995); Karl-Dieter Opp and Wolfgang Roehl, "Repression, Micromobilization, and Political Protest," *Social Forces* 69 (1990): pp. 521–47; and James C. Scott, *Weapons of the Weak: Everyday Forms of Peasant Resistance* (New Haven: Yale University Press, 1985).

16 Shinobu Kitayama and Hazel Rose Markus, *Emotion and Culture* (Washington, D.C.: American Psychological Association, 1994); H. C. Triandis, "The Self and Social Behavior in Differing Cultural Contexts," *Psychological Review* 96 (1989): pp. 506–20

17 Pye (see note 1), p. 168.

18 China's leading liberal intellectuals in fact often acted as naively and radically as the young students when faced with a crisis situation.

19 This feeling was clearly revealed in Wuer Kaixi's comment on the actions of the twelve leading intellectuals at the beginning of the hunger strike (Hinton and Gordon [see note 13], pp. 121–23): "The problem with intellectuals was that they played the wrong role. They were acting as mediators between the students and government. We forced the government to the negotiation table. This was the first time in forty years and we accomplished it. We, students, acted as an independent political force. And then, we invited intellectuals to join us. They came to the Square to address us as children. The message we got is that we had gone too far and everything had to go gradually. *What have they done to have the right to criticize us?*" (emphasis mine).

DILEMMAS OF TWENTY-FIRST CENTURY GLOBALIZATION: EXPLANATIONS AND SOLUTIONS, WITH A CRITIQUE OF THOMAS PIKETTY'S TWENTY-FIRST CENTURY CAPITALISM

QIN HUI 秦晖

SOCIAL MARKET ECONOMY TYPES A AND B

There can be dramatically different understandings of what we mean by "socialist market economies." In one version, which I will call "social market economy type A," "socialism" means that the common people will hold the government responsible for a high level of common welfare. The fact that the government must provide ever more welfare and security is not the government's "gift" to the people, but rather the people's right, which is the reason that the people support the government. This is what the government should do, and the people do not have to feel grateful (in Sweden the government is responsible for "cradle to grave" welfare and we do not see the people expressing particular gratitude). If the government fails to do this the people will demand accountability, or vote in another government (hence when the Swedish Liberal Party took power they had to provide welfare, even if in theory they were against the welfare state; the people didn't allow them to shirk their responsibility so they had no choice). When we say that the government must "serve the people" and not the people serve the government, this is what "type-A socialism" does, even if the government doesn't constantly flaunt it—because there's no need. If you don't work properly, the boss (i.e., the people) will fire you. Not only must you work properly, but if the boss has further demands, you must also become even more productive (i.e., provide more welfare).

But what is the "market economy" then? In type-A systems what we call the market economy means "the mayor doesn't look for you, the market looks for you."[1] (Note: this does not mean "don't look to the mayor, look to the market;" type-A systems constrain the mayor's ability to abuse his power over the people, but do not constrain the people's ability to call on the "mayor" to be accountable). The government's powers must be limited. Not only do the people grant power to the state, in addition there must be clear boundaries to the state's power. Outside the boundaries (of state power) is our freedom, including freedom of contract and market freedom. In sum, the "socialism" of a "type-A socialist market economy" means that citizens increase their calls for accountability from the government, and "market economy" in this context means that the citizens strictly limit the powers of the government. A government with unlimited powers cannot be part of a market economy.

Economists often say that state enterprises have "soft budget constraints," and in fact soft budget constraints are standard in state enterprises in democracies. In authoritarian situations this problem is not too serious, because in such contexts bureaucrats follow orders from above, and have no trouble employing "hard constraints" against the workers, transforming the state economy into "red sweatshops" where workers work more for less pay. For example, Lenin was enamored of the Taylorite labor system,[2] and believed that one of the advantages of the Soviet economy was that it could universally impose this system. Bukharin[3] even more nakedly argued that the "dictatorship of the proletariat" was not only to foil the capitalists, but was also a "supra-economic strong system that transcended the working class itself." Among his authoritarian measures we find: interdiction of strikes; the "labor army" system; forced unpaid labor; the transformation of labor rights into labor obligations; and the denial of "labor freedom" ("free labor does not accord with the planned distribution of labor").

But if "type-A socialism" tries to do this, it won't work. After the Swedish Social Democrats took power, they nationalized certain enterprises, only to discover that management was hard. In state enterprises in democracies, labor unions are often very strong, and managers in such firms cannot act like they do in China, where managers are promoted if they carry out the central plan. For government officials in democratic countries, their position relies on elections and their position in the company relies on professional certification. The channel (found in authoritarian systems) whereby the "factory manager is recognized by the higher-ups and appointed to the ministry" does not exist. Since there are neither promotion incentives nor capital accumulation incentives, the soft budget constraints in state-owned enterprises are extremely hard to manage. The reason that Eastern European countries, in the early period of rapid change, hastened to deal with state-owned enterprises was less because of the influence of a "new liberal economy" and more because after democratization, the soft budget constraints of state-owned enterprises all became more difficult. To put it more bluntly, after democratization, the plant manager could no longer simply suck up to his bosses but also had to suck up to the workers. Moreover, the factory wasn't his, and with workers and managers all reliant on the state, could the state handle it? Even the "socially owned" enterprises in Yugoslavia encountered the same problem later on.

Since management of state-owned enterprises in type-A socialism is hard, most gradually moved toward "socialist redistribution." Some say this was a "transformation" of the socialist party, which had been bought out by the capitalists. Whether it is a question of state purchase or high taxes, the devil is in the details. For the capitalist, if he can sell his firm at a good price, he keeps the money, so why should he necessarily want to pay high taxes and see the money he made taken away? So, when the Swedish left abandoned their major nationalization plans and moved toward "redistributive socialism," this had nothing to do with the preferences of the capitalists, but was rather the choice of the majority of the voters (most of whom were also workers), and in fact it was simply what was doable within the parameters of the existing system.

For this reason it is natural that some people say that we can't call a "type-A socialist market economy" a socialist market economy, and that it should be called instead "social market economy."[4] But I feel that there is no essential difference between the two. To put it a bit simply, the function of the state and the function of the market both exist, and individual interests and profits, along with public interests and profits, both have a big influence on economic behavior. In this situation, the people's ability to call for government accountability is strong, and the government's power is also strictly limited by the people. The first embodies "socialism" and the second "market economy."

MORE ON THE "TYPE-B SOCIALIST MARKET ECONOMY", AND THE MUTUAL INTERACTION OF TYPES A AND B UNDER GLOBALIZATION: AN UNHEALTHY DEPENDENCY THAT WILL BE HARD TO UNDO

But there is another kind of "socialist market economy" that we will for the moment call type B. This type has two features, the logic of which is completely opposed to that of type A. In the type-B system, "socialism" means that the government has unlimited power, and the people cannot limit that power. And "market economy" means that the government can shirk its responsibilities, while the people cannot call the government to account for its lack of provision of public welfare. The meaning of "socialism" in this system is that there is no way for the free market to exist (either there is no market, or there is a "market" dominated by monopoly and special privilege); the understanding of "market economy" in this system makes the welfare state impossible—if the state accords a bit of welfare to the people they must bow and scrape out of gratitude, and if it gives nothing they cannot make demands. The people are told "don't seek out the mayor, seek out the market," but the "mayor" can abuse the people at will. In sum, from the angle of "socialism" or of "market economy," type B means that the people must "serve the government" even if the state usually puts things otherwise.

In other words, in the above discussion of type-A systems, "socialism" meant that the government's responsibilities are important, and "market economy" meant that the government's power is limited, and "socialist market economy" meant that the government's responsibility continues to grow while its powers continue to decrease. The opposite is true of type B. Here, "socialism" means that government powers are great, and "market economy" means that the government's responsibilities are few, and things will continue to develop in this direction. In this sense, the differences between A and B will grow ever greater. In other words, it's not "convergence" but "divergence."

Comparing A to B, it is increasingly obvious: there are some countries whose governments possess enormous powers and can abuse their people at will while assuming few responsibilities. If they decide not to accord welfare then they don't: they can push back the retirement age, increase the prices for public welfare—they have the final word. In some other countries, the state's power is small, but they have vast responsibilities, and the people ask for reduced taxes (or oppose taxes) at the same time demanding increased welfare (or opposing decreases in welfare). The differences between the two systems are becoming greater and greater. Yet in the context of globalization these two systems have fashioned an extremely interesting exchange: while the people of type-A countries can be very rich, their governments are increasingly poor, to the point that debts are mounting. And while the people of type-B countries are often not rich, even very poor, the governments have more money than they can spend, and use this excess cash in two ways: the government engages in "self-welfare," not only becoming increasingly corrupt, but also spending more on suppressing the people; and it loans money to the type-A countries so that their debt load continues to increase.

But now the economy is global. When I talk about globalization here I don't necessarily mean complete globalization. The system also contains regional internationalism, such as Europeanization, but in any event, the "supra-national" market economy has greatly developed, which means that the people in democratic type-A countries can increasingly fall into the habit of wanting to have their cake and eat it too. The people spend too much and lack the ability to accumulate, but the trade deficits and national debts made possible by globalization allow them to overdraw their global accounts, kicking the can down the road. From the other perspective, type-B countries have become the "world's factories" (or sweatshops), where the people do not spend enough, where there is too much accumulative capacity, where they can "need" other people to overdraw. The economy in type-B countries runs roughshod over the people, affording them little, offering left-over product to others. In this kind of globalized exchange between A and B, both sides have accumulated large numbers of problems which are mutually produced but also produce mutual resentments, to the point of becoming a bad habit that is very hard to break.

But the current crisis is preparing another, unprecedented crisis, as the two completely different "socialist market economies," bound together in an unhealthy codependency through the mechanism of globalization, face a race to the bottom.[5]

LEFTISTS IN THE WEST AND LEFTISTS IN CHINA

Clearly, the government uses its power to attract investment, engaging in all sorts of institutional discrimination against "migrant workers," which seriously distorts the market mechanism between capital and labor. Normally, even in the absence of "socialist" factors like the welfare state and powerful trade unions, Chinese workers, relying only on market conditions, should have a larger space and capacity to negotiate for their interests, but "extra-economic" conditions have made this impossible, at least down to the present time. Pre-1970 South Africa and contemporary China are similar in this respect.

So, even though I am not a leftist, if I were, and I were in Europe, I would of course be anti-globalization, because it has led to capital outflows and the inflow of cheap goods from foreign sweatshops. My unemployment rate is up, my unions are fading, my welfare is dwindling away, and the gap between the rich and the poor is enormous. But if this leftist were in China, why would he oppose the process? The process is completely the opposite in China, right? We see capital inflows and commodity outflows, which creates conditions of change in market equilibrium that are precisely beneficial to Chinese workers, right?

For this reason, if you are someone on the Chinese left, then you should not oppose the process of globalization. Then how do we deal with China's problem of inequality? For this we should encourage the reform of the political system and reduce the power that the political system currently has over workers. The first step should be to ensure that workers obtain the benefits that market forces say they should have, and on this basis we can then "demand welfare accountability," asking for the redistribution that a welfare state should carry out. But if we cannot achieve the benefits that market conditions dictate, is there any point in talking about the second step?

Thus, I think that leftists in Western welfare states should oppose globalization, while leftists in China should welcome it, but at the same time should push for political reform, so that the Chinese working class and the disadvantaged should be able to truly realize the benefits of the changes in the pattern of supply and demand caused by globalization, and thus promote the transformation of type B into type A, so that "socialism" and "market economy" can increase in efficiency and equity.

If we can succeed on this front, then we can at the same time solve the crisis of "unhealthy codependency" between the type-A and type-B countries created by globalization. Our "socialist market economy" will no longer be type B, with its citizens' rate of consumption absurdly low and its rates of accumulation and investment absurdly high, with excess productive capacity, where the people lack protection and the government has more money than it knows how to spend, to the point that it must rely on "other people's overspending" to maintain high growth rates. As for the type-A countries, they will no longer be able to buy our goods without limit, and their tendency to want to "have their cake and eat it too" will diminish and rationality will return. On both sides, the current unhealthy codependency that we see today will give way toward a positive exchange relationship.

THE "HONECKER PARABLE"

In my view, the real questions, in an age of globalization, are not those of "the welfare state and laissez-faire," or even less "capitalism and socialism," but rather the interactions, exchanges, and challenges between the type-A and type-B models of socialist market economies. As globalization accelerates the process of exchange, the bad outcomes of the mutual exchanges between A and B countries will tend to worsen and will infect one another. Bad currency might chase out good currency or good currency chase out bad currency—anything is possible. In the thirty years of reform and opening, while we in China studied Western "market economies," we were also studying "socialism" (modern public welfare and social guarantees). But from another perspective, our "comparative advantage in low human rights" under conditions of globalization also evolved into a trend whereby "our sweatshops destroyed the welfare state," which I once described with the analogy of the Honecker parable:[6]

In 2009, I was in Germany, and had a long discussion with Hans Modrow, the former premier of the East German Communist Party. In the process of unification, Western Germany "absorbed" Eastern Germany, which was a great advance for Germany, although it also brought serious problems. After the destruction of East Germany's former low-wage industrial system, there were limits to new industrial development, and East Germany faced the problem of "deindustrialization" to a certain degree. Despite great advances in the service sector, the unemployment rate remained higher than in the West. Modrow, who was in the opposition, was unhappy. Why? Because after unification, West Germany used a huge "unification tax" and the convertability of the Eastern and Western marks at par to create conditions whereby salaries in both Germanies were basically the same, as were high welfare, strong unions, and labor power—everything was like in West Germany. As a result, East Germany was no longer particularly attractive to capital. So even if the government tried hard to convince Western German capital to invest and renew East Germany, the results were limited. West German capital preferred massive investments in China to produce vast numbers of German cars, and didn't want to rebuild East German car factories.

I asked Modrow whether he had ever thought of another possibility, that after German unification, the East might have swallowed the West? He said it was impossible, because the system in East Germany was a clear failure, and in democratic terms, there were 60,000,000 votes in the West and 16,000,000 in the East.

I said, what if we think of a third possibility. Imagine that twenty years ago, East Germany had suppressed democratization and kept the Berlin Wall. East Germans had no freedom, low-wages, and low human rights, and there was no policy of on-par conversion of East and West German marks. What if Honecker toured the West, visiting Las Vegas and the Moulin Rouge, discovering that the developed world was great, after which he developed a great interest in market economies, and decided to abandon utopia to make money. He left the politics the same but changed the economy to be part of West Germany's. He opened the doors wide to Western capital, demanding in return that the West keep the doors open to accept East German products. He would use authoritarian means to provide the best investment opportunities: whatever piece of land you decide you need he would get it for you; workers had to toe the line and could not protest; if people's homes were in the way of a business deal he would get rid of them; he could decide on allotment of rights to enterprises; there would be no need to deal with anyone, labor unions and agriculture unions were not allowed; he would reward anyone who came to invest and get rid of anyone who got in the way of investment...What do you think would have happened had that come to pass? Modrow said it was impossible, as did all the German people I asked about, who found it equally unimaginable. Still, what would have happened?

The answer is simple. If the state had insisted, the East German people would have stood for it, and the results might have been completely different from what they are now. Western capital would no longer head for China, or Romania, and West Germany wouldn't be employing Turkish workers. They would have swarmed into East Germany, and sweatshops would have sprung up all over East Germany, which would have poured tons of cheap commodities onto the Western markets, completely renewing East Germany's original industries. East Germany would immediately have had an economic miracle, and the "deindustrialization" and high unemployment rates would have appeared in West Germany. With the flight of capital from West Germany, labor would have lost its bargaining power, unions would have declined, welfare would have diminished, and the people's capitalism—built over more than a century—the "social market economy" and its welfare state, would no longer exist. Of course, East Germany would experience serious social problems, such as inequality, alliances between the state and merchants, rampant corruption, environmental pollution, etc. But if the East Germans could withstand all of this, then what would have happened to West Germany? I said, if East Germany didn't change, then West Germany would have only three choices: one would have been for West Germans to build their own economic wall, refusing unification, preventing capital from leaving the country and external commodities coming in. In fact, this is an extreme version of the common practice of trade protection. But in doing so, they would have paid a high moral price, because they had originally proposed tearing down the Berlin Wall. And, in fact, it would not have worked, because West Germany could not use the measures that East Germany had employed to maintain the wall: East Germany shot her citizens who tried to cross the wall. Was West Germany going to execute her capitalist entrepreneurs?

The second was if they didn't build this Berlin Wall, they would have to reduce their conditions to those found in East Germany, because otherwise competition was impossible under conditions of unification. West Germans would have had to learn to be "migrant workers," welfare and human rights would have suffered important declines, the welfare state would have given way to sweatshops, and bad currency would have driven out good currency. If Western Germany had done that, it would be as if East Germany had carried out the unification, because the West would have assimilated to the Eastern system.

The third possibility was that the changes to the Western German democratic system would have been unacceptable to the people, whether it was the reduction of freedom or of welfare, resulting in a great social mobilization which would have refused the importation of the East German system. But if West Germany had suffered major social chaos, East Germany might have used extraordinary means to unify West Germany.

But the real question is, if East Germany had swallowed West Germany, then at no level of meaning would it have signified socialism's victory over capitalism; instead it would have been simply sweatshops' victory over the welfare state, "savage capitalism's" victory over democratic socialism. I asked Modrow: let's set aside for the moment the reaction of the "left" to this scenario, but you, as a leftist, would you like to see this kind of "victory?"

He didn't give a straight answer, and just repeated that it was impossible. Of course, everyone knows that this did not happen in Germany, which is why I call it a parable—the Honecker parable. But elsewhere in the world, is this unhappy scenario merely a "parable"? The fact that it isn't has come to constitute a bigger challenge to freedom and welfare than the internal "debate over laissez-faire and the welfare state."

Neither the left nor the right seems to be aware of "world trends." If you say that we (i.e., in China) do not understand your type-A socialist market economy enough, I might answer that you (Westerners) understand our type-B system even less, and those that try end up engaging in wishful thinking. Of course, in the past, when globalization had not progressed to this point, this failure of understanding was perhaps not all that critical, but today, it is time to take it seriously.

Excerpt from *Dilemmas Of Twenty-First Century Globalization: Explanations and Solutions, with a Critique of Thomas Piketty's Twenty-First Century Capitalism* by Qin Hui

From *Reading and Writing the China Dream Project* (readingthechinadream.com)

Note: subheadings have been added by the editors.

1 Translator's note: Qin Hui is playing on two expressions commonly used in China to describe the change from a planned economy to a market economy. In a planned economy, an enterprise would "seek out the mayor, not the market" (不找市场找市长), while in a market economy the enterprise would do the opposite (不找市长找市场). The Chinese words for "mayor" (*shizhang* 市长) and "market" (*shichang* 市场) are very similar, so the expression is a pun, or a play on words. "Mayor" here simply means the "government." The basic notion is that in a planned economy, the rules are set by the government; in a market economy, the rules are set by the market.

2 Frederick Taylor (1856–1915) was a leading proponent of scientific factory management.

3 Nicolai Bukharin (1888–1938) was a Bolshevik politician and political theorist.

4 Translator's note: The "social market economy" generally refers to the modern German capitalist welfare state and its variations.

5 See Qin Hui, "My Views of the Globalization Crisis: The Interaction of Two Inchworm Effects 我看全球经济危机：两种尺蠖效应的互动," *Leader* 领导者, 2009.2.

6 Qin Hui, "The Honecker Parable: The Counter-Factual Case of East Germany Absorbing West Germany," "昂纳克寓言"：东德吞并西德的"反事实推论," *Thought* 思想 17 (2011).

THE NEW ERA AND ITS INTELLECTUAL ELITE

XUDONG ZHANG 张旭东

Diversity, ambiguity, confusion, and sometimes utter chaos characterize the sociocultural construction of what has been called the New Era (*Xin Shiqi*). It is this sociocultural construction, called variably "the post-Mao era," "the postrevolutionary age," "the eighties," and "the Reforms decade," that constitutes the abstract content I seek to make palpable in this book. As Deng Xiaoping's China established its legitimacy (and to a certain degree its popular mandate) on its promise to embrace a rational, progressive, and affluent world (that is, the "outside world"), it was (and still is) characterized by its imminent need to disassociate itself from the Maoist age ideologically while clinging greedily to state power and handling cautiously the social unconscious, both of which had been so deeply structured by the Maoist discourse. The New Era is thus an essential political invention of Deng's China, designed to make the discontinuity clear while leaving ambiguous room for continuity with the socialist past. As if in ideological self-complicity with the New Era, its intellectual discourse went further by asserting an intellectual autonomy in both cultural and classical terms; it intended to establish a continuum that, despite numerous brutal interruptions and seemingly irrecoverable setbacks, has always been motivated by its own problematic, actualized in the finer formulations by its elite authors and in its privileged texts. If the socioeconomic experimentation of Deng's China, in its characteristic zigzag manner, can be considered as unconsciously aiming at a potential combination of Chinese socialism and contemporary forces of production (not for its claims of building a "socialism with Chinese characteristics," but in terms of a historical alternative, theoretically speaking), then its internal crisis lies in the fact that this regime, out of its political instinct and social limitations, seems unable to achieve the one without neglecting the other. The crisis of Deng's China can be seen as the crisis of Chinese modernism, internalized as a conflict between its content and its form. The intellectual elite of the New Era think they owe their discursive institution, their most precious historical property, to their freedom from the totalitarian past (to a large degree this is true). Yet it is often unclear of what this discursive space was constituted, what situation called for its coming into being, and what conditions of possibility allowed it in the first place.

The relationship between the intellectual mandate and the state patriarchy is an old topic. During the 1980s, as in all of modern Chinese history, this mandate was constantly reinvented and reinforced by the national project of enlightenment. From Yan Fu's 1898 translation of Thomas Henry Huxley's *Evolution and Ethics* to the intellectual campaigns in the 1980s, Maoism seems to be the lone consequential challenge to the selfprivileging intelligentsia that offers to shoulder the vocation of saving the nation and enlightening the people. From a cultural-sociological perspective, the privileges Chinese intellectuals enjoyed during the 1980s had a threefold protection: 1. Protection by the residual, and in a sense revived, gentry-literati tradition, a circulating and empowering social distinction; 2. Protection by the socialist nation-state, which pumps into its intelligentsia an unchallenged technocratic and ideological importance; and 3. Protection by the symbolic capital borrowed from the West, as those "professionals" were the only ones who bad access to and license for such cross-border interplay. These "external" conditions are intimately related to a "protected inwardness" (using the phrase Thomas Mann invented for Richard Wagner) of Chinese intellectuals, which is demonstrated in their elitist aura, their elevated mannerisms, and their textual intricacies and discursive complexities.

The privileges of the intelligentsia need to be viewed in light of their genealogical background and sociopolitical environment. For example, the socialist state, which in theory means to transform its intelligentsia into an organic component of its working class, nonetheless effectively constructs a socioeconomic and cultural-ideological interior in which its intelligentsia dwells. Ironically, the protection of the state guarantees its intellectuals a relationship to a global system that is to be mediated by the political and cultural agencies of the nation-state. Most of the high-profile players during the Cultural Fever came from a handful of elite institutions such as the Chinese Academy of Social Sciences and Peking University. Endowed with such status, Chinese intellectuals tend to speak for the "people" and the "nation" in a transcendental, universalistic posture, often without self-reflexive or self-critical thought about the legitimate violence their privileged position superimposes on social problems and social spaces, on heterogeneous and complex social relations.

As a massive social transformation in which China earned a place in the global market, the New Era has been secretly understood by its most ardent supporters as one of the decisive moments for accumulating national wealth and achieving social differentiation in the history of modern China. From the viewpoint of the sociology of knowledge, the furious accumulation of capital in this period in the socioeconomic sphere is paralleled in the cultural sphere by the intellectual elite's breathless campaigns aiming at accumulating cultural and symbolic capital, and establishing an institution of discourse to sustain the growth and perpetuate the new wealth—be it the enhanced social-political prestige or the exaggeration of the libidinal energy—symbolically. What Karl Mannheim describes as a twofold capitalization of Germany between the 1890s and the 1930s—namely, on the one hand, the transformation of the land-owning *Junker* class into the modern-day German bourgeoisie and, on the other hand, the cultural capitalization by those "whose only capital is their education"[1] —is vaguely recognizable in the Chinese Situation in the New Era. However, there was not a ready propertied class in post-Mao China, where the state remained the sole owner of all capital, including the slim social stratum of the well-educated. Second, the ways in which Germany and China were exposed to the experience of modernity are socially, culturally, and geopolitically different. Third, the international environment has changed immensely between the "age of empire" and our own "postmodern" era—the multi-centeredness or heterogeneity of the modern world allows a different set of intellectual strategies and cultural politics at every level, from national to local to individual. Finally, whereas its German counterpart collectively fought with "desperate intensity"[2] against the "spiritual" crisis inflicted upon them by mass civilization, the partially self-conscious, loosely connected social group of the post-Mao Chinese intellectual elite as a whole was in no position to be preoccupied by such a sense of social, cultural, or spiritual crisis. Rather, they played an active part in the massive project of social-cultural engineering for modernization and lent their elevated voice to the most mass-originated and mass-oriented discourse of social desire for technology, consumption, and pleasure. Unlike the "German mandarins" (Ringer), the Chinese modernists achieved cultural capitalization by identifying themselves with universal progress, not by resisting or critically analyzing the process of modernity.

The political implications of the cultural projects of the Chinese modernists are by no means simple. For many, the intellectual enthusiasm for building a discursive autonomy seen during the Cultural Fever of the 1980s is but a disguised search for a sheltered freedom in both political and existential terms. The obsession with form is often taken as an unambiguous sign of the Chinese intelligentsia's lack of influence on or even access to social construction and state policies. It is understood, often by the modernists themselves, to be a deliberate political gesture, a cultural-political strategy to rise from the social sphere, which is fully penetrated by the state, to the terrain of individuality. Yet I want to acknowledge the subtle presence of a rampant unconscious in the intellectual effort toward formal-discursive autonomy. In a so-called political society, a pronounced devotion to constructing an "autonomous" cultural-discursive institution is not merely directed toward radical technological innovations and political alternativity. It reveals, as well, the intelligentsia's tacit agreement with Deng's social programs or, rather, with the idea of universal progress or evolution that the modernists believe is the *raison d'état* of the New Era. The prudence in committing oneself to long-term, systematic, and "total" restructuring of "Chinese scholarship" can be seen as an implicit vote of confidence, a political conservatism executed in terms of cultural radicalism. The tacit mutual understanding or collaboration between the state and the intellectual endeavor seemed always to have been taken for granted by the participants of the Cultural Fever. This situation cannot be explained fully by the structural relationship between the state and the intelligentsia, although that relationship is among the most important factors to be taken into consideration.

The elite intelligentsia of the 1980s often tended to look beyond the state, only to find a common ground with the state in its own abstract notion of Chinese society as an alternative to both the Soviet model and free-market democracy. Throughout the euphoric decade of the 1980s, the rhetoric of a historical alternative, just like the formulation of a universal modernism, was but a legitimate way for the radical modernist to lay out a vision for the brand-new world. The social-political truth content of this vision might not be overly complicated, however, given the smooth transition toward a "socialist market economy" at that time (the only thing new and seductive in this term was the "market"). The frustration of the idealism of the intellectual elite after the crackdown at Tiananmen Square in 1989 makes explicit the hidden link between material growth, social standardization, and the ontological visions of the Chinese modernists.[3]

Like previous generations of Chinese intellectuals, the post-Mao intellectual elite tended to be a dependent part of the state—the main, unchallenged mechanism of social production and organization. The discursive insurgence in the late 1980s can therefore be viewed as a rebellion against that tradition. Whereas this resistance did not change completely the fact that the ultimate interest, self-realization, and prestige of this privileged group were still largely drawn from, or at least closely linked to, the success of the national project of modernization, it found a new source of power, distinction, and authority in global cultural capital. Until the accumulation of wealth, social specialization, and social differentiation had reached a certain point—a point that seems immanent in any process of modernization—intellectual and cultural activities served as the basis for a sense of a distinct social group coming into itself. Moreover, Chinese intellectuals never, until very recently, possessed the political legitimacy of criticism (which their German counterpart took for granted) when encountering the problems emerging from a society in transition. Their intellectual agendas—unlike technological ones, they are necessarily political—had to take refuge in high culture, that is, in building theoretical systems, engaging in philosophical debates, aesthetic experiments, and historiographical revisionism, and so forth; efforts that were legitimated in the name of the modernization of Chinese culture. Thus, a selection of representative essays was titled *The Cultural Consciousness of Contemporary China*[4]—in fact, any "consciousness" of contemporary China seemed to have to be "cultural."

All these social and intellectual changes further removed the national cultural life from the everyday sphere, although the two kept up a tortuous dialogue through national politics that addressed (as well as distorted and oppressed) both spheres. For most of the 1980s, the public was virtually deprived of any institutional channel for expressing its concerns and sentiments (the "big character poster" was banned after the 1979 *Minzhuqiang*, or the Democracy Wall, movement). The intellectual elite took on a political importance (sometimes self-importance) as the only players in a cultural national theater, so to speak, and, by extension, spokespersons for the people and the nation, its culture, and its history. In this imagined self-image, the breathing room that conditioned the intellectual elite's ideas and voices was the room of legitimation, determined by the functionality of the intelligentsia within the state apparatus. The more productive units in intellectual production—namely, the more privileged, elite institutions—seem to have had an opportunity to bargain with the state for greater autonomy and self-assertion in order to concentrate on their assigned task less burdened by arbitrary and dogmatic elements. These institutions, not surprisingly, were the organizational basis of what was to be known as "Cultural Fever" or the "Great Cultural Discussion" in the second half of the 1980s.

The ideologies of the state and its intelligentsia are by no means always in agreement, however. The modernists also positioned themselves to represent the newly emerging social forces in the marketplace and the private interior. Often this disagreement between the state and the intelligentsia is examined too simplistically. Rather than a spontaneous dissident, the intellectual elite was a social group that had to reposition itself vis-à-vis two interrelated trends: one was growing social experience produced by the economic reforms, which anticipated a changed social structure. The other is the immanent fragmentation of the ideological totality of Mao's China or at least the illusion of it, in the face of increasing recognition that the united front of technocratic reform was reaching a dead end. In other words, the ideological disagreement between the intellectual elite and the state programs lies in subtle differences in the agency of change and the actual changes that were to redefine the subjectivity of the social sphere. This disagreement becomes evident only when the accumulation of capital (material as well as symbolic) and social differentiation have rendered the situation undeniably political and made a new round of position-taking inevitable. This change of fashion in cultural and intellectual life coincided with the onset of the urban (industrial and administrative) reforms in the mid-1980s, which followed an immensely successful rural reform. As I show elsewhere in my work, the increasingly visible impulse of intellectuals to disassociate themselves from the state apparatus and to establish a discursive institution of their own can be best explained by looking at the specific needs of the intellectuals, by analyzing the emergent conditions of possibility that prefigured the cultural-political strategies during the decade of discursive modernism.

When global capitalism was seen as a permanent presence—and a realistic choice—of the Chinese New Era, the insurgence of high culture in the form of new waves and experiments must be turned into the object of a critique of ideology. The cultural history and cultural politics of the New Era, then, are profoundly conditioned by two tendencies: the cultural agencies' increasingly conscious incorporation with global cultural capital and the coming into itself of the Chinese intelligentsia as a group, which found a new social basis, not to mention new symbolic room, for its professional and political life. This disagreement did not require a decisive break with the state and a disassociation from the national project of modernization. Quite the contrary, those two tendencies have been intertwined with, and often carried out through, the practice and rhetoric of the ideology of modernization, which is the orthodoxy of the Deng regime. Whereas different social and political forces were manifested as well as contained *culturally* during the 1980s, they found their less restrained articulation in a differentiated social space—above all in the market—in the early 1990s.

Modernism resides deeply in the sphere of this elite culture. Yet it is disturbing to notice in intellectual endeavors the glaring absence of the other, the everyday sphere, the working class, the peasantry, women, the non-Western world—all those who might well be alienated by a self-indulgent search for aesthetic or philosophical modernity and culturalist "self-expression"—whereas the West, as a privileged other, indeed a future image in abstraction, is always pursued obsessively.

Throughout the 1980s, Western literary, aesthetic, and theoretical discourses were introduced to China, not as ideology, but as knowledge as such, that is, as science. Elitist circles were actively at work in establishing an autonomous terrain mediated and, indeed, protected by a semiotic system based on a scientific, universal standard. This activity is one of the essential elements of the politics of the discursive New Era. These abstractions of particular ideologies were engaged by many intellectuals during the 1980s, in Henri Lefebvre's words, as "reasons and motivations," which are "extremely powerful in and for their consciousness," as "a question of the great ideal, the historic mission, law and civilization."[5] This fetishized system of knowledge production constitutes the object of a dialectical critique of ideology.

The elitist "high culture" is not the only locale in which the social-cultural problematic of the New Era is addressed. The burgeoning of a post-Mao popular culture—TV melodramas, "nonserious" literatures from peasant tales to urban detective stories, ephemeral fashions in music, film, and so forth—assaulted both the official mainstream and the intellectual elite with a changing everyday sphere. One can reasonably be suspicious that too much attention has been devoted to a handful of elite texts from an intellectualist point of view, while too little has been given to the vast field of public and popular cultures. Established through a refusal of the "impure" (Bourdieu), the elite discourse's social origins, its ideological truth content, and its internal power relationship nevertheless provide "systemic" (or systematically coded) materials of study that invite a "vulgar" critique."[6] Chen Kaige, arguably the leader of the cinematic new wave (the so-called Fifth Generation), was not necessarily more "thoughtful" than the pop singer Cui Jian; Ge Fei, one of the most celebrated practitioners of "meta-fiction," is not necessarily more delicate than Wang Shuo, the master of what was dubbed "hooligan literature" (*pizi wenxue*), which swept the Chinese urban literary marketplace; Li Zehou, the influential intellectual historian and Kant specialist, was not always more important than the "River Elegy" (*Heshang*) group, who peddled on television a rival ideology cooked up and presented in wishful and patchy cultural historical commentary.

From the perspective of a larger historical conjuncture, the late 1980s stand as but one empirical platform from which to rethink Chinese modernism and Chinese modernity. In the context of modern Chinese history and its cultural construction, the "unprecedented productivity" proclaimed by the intelligentsia of the New Era is both vacuous and expressive. It is vacuous because more often than not it remains a conspiratorial—although often discontented—partner of the social ideology (the Deng ideology) in which "the eighties" as a cultural category was nourished. The various "fevers" or "crazes" that swept the country in this eventful decade reveal, among other things, the uncritical and often ahistorical tendency of the intellectual discourse. It is nevertheless expressive, however, because its self-assertion is not only an assertion of that ideology, but inevitably also an assertion of the sociohistorical experience and the utopian content of that period. Thus, its charge toward discursive and aesthetic autonomy is simultaneously both a narcissistic preservation of self-identity and a reckless embrace of the unknown world of shocks and experiences that are reproduced as the modernist allegory of contemporary China. The intellectual discourse of the late 1980s entails a Chinese modernism understood as a historical style whose origin can be dated to the May Fourth era, if not earlier. The past decade saw intense discursive and aesthetic innovations that rank the 1980s as one of the most exciting moments in the history not only of the People's Republic but of modern China as a whole. The mode of cultural production particular to this decade is part of the enormous ideological apparatus (the trio of state discourse, the discourse of the intellectual elite, and that of mass culture) through which the myths of post-Mao Chinese society developed into a discursive reality. The New Era as crystallized in its elite discourse can never be read as a mythologized or subjectivized oeuvre of the epoch. It is a historical discourse to be elucidated in terms of the interrelationship between the social and the textual, in which intellectual chaos and ideological ambivalence have their own momentary truthfulness.

Excerpt from Zhang Xudong, *Chinese Modernism in the Era of Reforms* (London: Durman, 1997), pp. 9–17.

Editor's note: minor adjustments have been made for better readability.

1 Fritz K. Ringer, *The Decline of German Mandarins* (Hanover, New Hampshire, 1990), p. 2.
2 Ibid.
3 The more recent intellectual discussions within China seem to add more evidence to this observation. The national debate over the "loss of humanism" in 1994 and 1995 showed the intensified crisis of the intellectual elite as a social group. For an informative collection of articles on this topic see Wang Xiaoming, ed., *In Search of Humanism* (Shanghai: Renwen jingshen xunsilu, 1996).
4 See Gan Yang, ed., *Dang dai zhongguo wenhua yishi* (Cultural consciousness in contemporary China) (Hong Kong: Joint Publishing Co., 1990).
5 Henri Lefebvre, *The Survival of Capitalism* (New York: St. Martin's Press 1973), p. 108.
6 For the idea of a "vulgar" critique of "pure" tastes see the postscript of Pierre Bourdieu's *Distinction* (Cambridge, MA: Harvard University Press, 1984).

ON INDIVIDUALISM IN THE NEW CULTURE MOVEMENT

YANG GUOQIANG 杨国强

As a stage in the course of modern Chinese intellectual history, the New Culture Movement has often been likened to both the Enlightenment and the Renaissance, with such analogies somehow conjoining several Western historical events. These ways of thinking clearly illuminate the diverse orientations and themes inherent to the New Culture Movement. When Chen Boda (1904–1989) later claimed that "the enlightenment in China began with the Hundred Days' Reform of the late Qing," and that "the New Culture Movement led by *New Youth* [made the Chinese enlightenment] a people's cultural movement," he explicitly grouped the New Culture Movement and the Hundred Days' Reform under the same intellectual-historical process.

In contrast to Chen, Feng Dalin once commented that with regard to the "New Culture," "The May Fourth Movement represents the climax of the destruction since the Hundred Days' Reform."[1] Although Feng likewise attributed the New Culture Movement to the same historical process as the Hundred Days' Reform, he did so in a manner intended to be entirely disapproving. Yet both Chen and Feng shared a common understanding on the continuity of the events. In the two decades following the Hundred Days' Reform, a succession of concepts appeared in China: the value of civil rights, sciences, the vernacular press, and arguments concerning "Europeanization"[2] —such as those for "universality" and "universal progress." Under the banners of "Mr. Democracy" (*de xiansheng*) and "Mr. Science" (*sai xiansheng*), these concepts cast the Enlightenment as the European prehistory to the Hundred Days' Reform. Consequently, when the New Culture Movement likened itself to the Enlightenment, it did so as a natural extension of the intellectual legacy of the Hundred Days' Reform. This extension reflects the continuity of history. Nonetheless, as an intellectual movement, the New Culture Movement's distinction from its predecessors and successors does not lie fully in the extension.

The analogy to the Renaissance harks back to an even earlier period than that of the Enlightenment. After the magazine *Xin Chao* (literally "New Wave") chose "Renaissance" as the translation of its title, figures associated with the New Culture Movement often turned to this earlier period in European history as a frame for discussing events in China—a gesture that introduced another dimension of thought into the movement to contemplate the burgeoning subject of the human. In contrast to the Enlightenment's emphasis on rationalism, the entire significance of the Renaissance to the New Culture Movement lay in its humanism. Although democracy and science still dominated the foreground of public discourse, humaneness, humanism, and the yearning for human "liberation" could no longer fit within the scope of the rationalism that the Enlightenment championed.

Before his trip to Europe, Fu Ssu-nien (1896–1950) confessed his thoughts to his friends and colleagues. In an earnest and heartfelt passage, he states: "On the macro and micro levels, I only admit that the human being and the 'self' are true and real; any categories between the human being and the 'self,' including families, localities, and countries, are forms of idolatry. For the sake of the human being, we have to cultivate a 'true self.'"[3] [...] While these words are doubtlessly Fu's rather spontaneous inklings, they can still point to the source and purpose of humanity and humanism in the New Culture Movement. Instead of speaking to the rather boundless themes of democracy and science, the point of focus here was individualism and the individual subject. Thus, the correspondence between European humanism and self-consciousness provided the other lineage of thought within the New Culture Movement, bringing the seemingly remote Renaissance closer to the discourse. Meanwhile, as "any categories between the human being and

'I'" were treated as "forms of idolatry" destined to be abolished and discarded, the individual subject and individualism necessarily stood apart from and in opposition to society. Hence, Luo Jialun (1897–1969) considered this movement an uprising that "uses new attitudes to promote a new society," and he predicted that "destructive work"[4] would inevitably accompany it. Chen Duxiu (1879–1942), on the other hand, termed the movement a "social transformation," advocating for "a declaration of war between the individual and society" based on the "extreme inertia of the established society."[5] Both used individualism to reconstruct the relationship between the individual and society [...].

[...] Thanks to its orientation to the individual subject, this lineage inaugurated a chapter of individualism in modern Chinese intellectual history. At the same time, the humanism of the Renaissance became an idealized platitude, and thus derived meanings that were not present in the first place.

1. CHEN DUXIU: THE INDIVIDUAL AND THE COUNTRY

Chen Duxiu, who was among the first to promote the new thought, was once a Qing state nationalist.[6] His stance shifted to its polar opposite as the new thought was about to transform the society. On the eve of launching the journal *New Youth* (initially *Youth Magazine*), Chen wrote in length to discuss the relationship between "patriotism and self-consciousness," and his main goal was to cast his doubt on the nature of country:

> "The essence of a country is to safeguard the rights of its people and secure their happiness. If the country fails to do so, then its existence will be nothing glorious, and its demise will be nothing regrettable. If China, as a country, can neither defend itself against foreign invasion nor protect its people, if it not only fails to protect its people but inflicts harm on them, and if all governing bodies are in agreement about this, then the people will be in despair."[7]

As a result, "those who hold superficial patriotic views and support the brutalization of the people" were "preposterous if not vacuous." He opposed this "patriotism" with what he termed "self-consciousness" and commented in summary:

> "Alas! Country, country, your rules and laws, without you we won't worry, and with you we won't rejoice. We are not cursing your demise, but it is impossible to not gain this self-consciousness."[8]

The ideological transition of modern China from nationalism to statism/state nationalism took place under the monarchical rule of the late Qing, and the anti-statist consciousness appeared after the monarchy was overthrown. As the discourse of statism was measured against the discourse of civil rights already familiar to intellectual circles, we see a significant conflict. As Chen experienced the shift in his personal beliefs—mirrored by the extreme redirection in his writing—what also received consideration were the changes to the concept of country in the eyes of the Chinese people.

After Chen Duxiu's call to his peers, Zhang Shizhao (1881–1973) drafted an article titled "The Country and the Self," commenting:

> "The political affairs of the country have already greatly depressed the youth. No one knows how far it shall go and whether it can reach an end. Patriotism, as Mr. Chen has correctly predicted, is unfortunately being eliminated by the rising self-consciousness."[9]

Although the country and the "political affairs" carried out in the name of the country were not equivalent, Shen Dingyi (1883–1928) once asserted that, "To the ear of a regular Chinese person, 'country' would call to mind the government, which in turn would make one think of the people working within the government."[10] Regarding Chinese society at the time, statements as such were not only truthful but also concrete. Premised on specific feelings, their aim was not to analyze the definition of "country" but to reveal that the country and its people, once unified by republican ambitions, in reality remained two, and often in opposition. As a result, after the founding of *New Youth*, the familiar set of reasoning based on civil rights (and democracy) continued to be a major subject for Chen, to which he devoted his earnest attention and eloquent argument.

In the intervening years between the waning days of the Qing Dynasty and the birth of the Republic of China, democracy as a theory was transposed into a practical, political realm. What came about included so-called republicanism, (provisional) constitution, presidency, congress, cabinet, judicial independence, and partisan politics, as well as the denunciatory polemics against one another in the name of the law, people, and sovereignty conducted in telegrams, proclamations, and political discourses. From the very beginning, this process had stressed the institutional dimension of democracy, but after the 1911 Revolution overthrew the Qing monarchy with introspective clarity, the Chinese system that resulted from the process was covered over by a densely fissured network. In other words, here was a China where military juntas and warlords replaced scholar-official politics, where politicians emerged outside the bureaucratic ranks, where the old order had collapsed, and the traditional "four occupations" (*simin*) were in a state of dispersion, no longer governed by any unitary system. Therefore, when perceived in its entirety, the institutionalization of democracy eventually had to be something that existed only on paper. Meanwhile, the institutionalized contents of democracy were, in practice, fragmented for instrumentalization and private gains. This was undoubtedly a failed attempt at practicing democracy. But the traces lingering from such a failure would enlighten those in China who witnessed it, encouraging them to identify alternative directions and paths to democracy.

In the New Culture Movement that ensued, the concept of democracy turned from its institutionalizing path to being part and parcel of the spirited intellectual movement. Looking back, one might say that the ascendancy of democracy since the late Qing originated with thought. Hence, it might appear as if the return from practice to thought was rather regressive, but if one were to pay close attention to this newly derived thought, it would be obvious that meaningful transformations had taken place. At the very moment when Chen Duxiu used "self-consciousness" to counter "patriotism," the unity between country and people, which the older generation had regarded as its argumentative premise, was interrupted by the new conceptualization of the next generation. What came next was the understanding that civil rights (democracy), no longer derived from the country (or nation), now belonged to the people. The subjectivity of the people could not but be redefined in the process of the society embracing anti-statism.

Pioneering the expression of anti-statist ideas in writing, Chen interrogated "patriotism" through his concept of "self-consciousness." The public opinion and sentiments supporting such conceptualization undoubtedly stemmed from his observations and perceptions of Chinese society. However, in order to distill and expand from what he had seen and felt, Chen resorted to comparisons with "Western nations":

> "From time immemorial and up till today, Western nations have been thoroughly

individualistic nations. This is true for the United Kingdom and the United States, and isn't it also true for France and Germany? It was what Nietzsche believed in, and wasn't it what Kant also believed in? What ethics, morality, politics, laws, and societies aspire to and what countries hope for can all be boiled down to the principle of upholding individual rights and happiness. Freedom of thought and expression serves the development of individuality; before the law stands everyone equally. The individual's right to freedom is enshrined in the constitution, and no law of the land shall deprive him of the right—that is what we call the human right."[11]

Regarding the hindrance individualism could encounter, he added, "National and social interests might appear to conflict with individualism, but in fact they treat the consolidation of individual interests as their root cause."

In this passage, Chen attempted to explain conclusively Western civil rights through ideas of individualism. As a result, his formulation represents a judgment that rests on insufficient argument and does not consider the subject enough in terms of depth and breadth. Yet, for Chen Duxiu, this comparison still truthfully managed to place the civil rights (democracy) of the Chinese people in the light of "the organization of today's civilized society," as well as to interject "individualism" into both the projected outcome and raison d'être of society.[12] This theorization that begged to differ from the status quo transformed the meaning of "people." It disassembled the aggregate-but-anonymous subject of the civil rights (democracy) as conceived since the late Qing, shattering it to reveal within it concrete individuals with distinct individuality, rights, and thoughts—elements fundamental to the individuals' aggregation. On the flip side, individuality, happiness, rights, and thoughts were posited as the core of any individual existence, and logically, this core made the freedom to pursue them the external way to guarantee individual existence. Through the dynamic formed between the inner meaning and the outer means, the originally passive subject became not merely an active subject but an enterprising and unconstrained one. Chen applied the "individualism" of "Western nations" to reconstruct for the Chinese people a new subject of civil rights (democracy), essentially overhauling the democracy that had long been introduced into China. The new, resulting concept is the democracy of the New Culture Movement that incorporated individualism.

What set Chen apart from the older generation of thinkers was his will against the demarcation between the foreign and the indigenous, which allowed ideas from outside China to enter without having to be retrofitted. He relegated issues such as "national essence," "national conditions," "history," and "the extent of civil society development" to the realm of "mere appearances" and subsequently rid them of their significance. His main goal was to declare uniformity between China and the Western world on both the ontological and qualitative levels. Theoretically speaking, this dismissal of "national essence," "national conditions," "history," and "the extent of civil society development" would result in ontological and qualitative conceptualizations that lacked any local authenticity. At the same time, the dismissal would indicate an indomitable intellectual tendency rising strongly in difficult times, whose urgency and plainness could truthfully reflect the eager mind behind employing Western methods to build for China "a civilized system."

Precisely because Chen did not and could not indigenize the concept of individualism, he was able to interpret the term with such unbridled freedom that led from its source in "Western nations" to much further afield:

"With my hands and feet, I can keep myself fed and warm; with my tongue and mouth, I can convey my own likes and dislikes; with my mind and thoughts, I can act in my personal belief; I shall never let anyone else overstep into my personal bounds, and I shall never enslave others in my service. In my opinion, this is because—on the premise of any person having his autonomy—all conducts, rights, and beliefs should fall into the discretion of each and every individual, and there is no sense in blindly subordinating oneself to others."[13]

In these axioms characterized by their generalizing rhetorical devices, the abstract notion of the individual indefinitely approximates a monadic and exclusive self. Hence, from Chen's perspective, individualism ultimately amounted to a form of self-centeredness. At that time, "Competition for survival is inevitable, so as long as we are still alive, there is no room for retreat." Thus, the realization of individual subsistence, preferences, rights, and beliefs pragmatically became a course of action where "to progress amidst hardships is one's life's vocation."[14] But on a causal level, making the self the anchor of individualism effectively pit individuals against one another in competitions and rendered struggles unescapable. Though Chen acknowledged the egalitarian relationship between the self and others in the sense that one "shall never enslave others in [their] service," this equity rested outside his overall discourse. Therefore, in mere months, Chen argued that the youth should "take up the position to conquer, and not take up the position of being conquered," adding that the conqueror ought to be "courageous and fierce, and not subjugated by force."[15] "Conquering," to him, was nonetheless already a form of "[enslaving] others in [his] service."

In Chen Duxiu's conception, the subject that acted as the foundational building block of civil rights (democracy) carried in fact a sort of self-centric free will; this subject could easily end up perceiving others as rivals. Chen often stood out for his radicality. Consequently, in the many schools of individualism that the New Culture Movement contained, the one that Chen championed was trademarked by a distinct consciousness of the self and a highly competitive spirit. Compared with Cai Yuanpei's readiness to accept the "discourse of mutual aid" and Li Dazhao's modeling of himself after the pacifist Leo Tolstoy amid earth-shattering world conflicts,[16] Chen's argument carried particularly clear and inherent differences. In terms of personal influence, Chen's remarks evidently had a greater impact on people than those of his peers, and in turn had a greater popular appeal.

2. HU SHIH: THE INDIVIDUAL AND THE SOCIETY

Aside from Chen Duxiu, Hu Shih (1891–1962) also embraced the stance of individualism. At the onset of the World War I, Hu—then living in the United States and away from the battlefields—also developed his thought on humankind and distanced himself from the idea of a state that had been made supreme:

"The great problem of today lies in a narrow sense of nationalism, which inculcates that one's own nation must overpower others' nations (for instance, in Germany, the national anthem sings, '*Deutschland, Deutschland über alles, über alles in der Welt!*'). Whoever can achieve this self-interested goal cares not if it entails the destruction of other nations and peoples. As for the so-called morality, law, justice, truth, benevolence, and peace among the subjects of a nation, as well as the diplomacy between nations, these matters are simply put aside, for being the most powerful is understood as the axiom, and the so-called 'international law' means merely might makes right. This is indeed the great problem of today."[17]

The war had not only brought state nationalism step by step to its extreme—it also revealed the aberration of state nationalism as well as its potential to wreak havoc on earth. In the face of such a world, Hu thought, one must raise his vision high above the state:

> "Loving one's nation is no doubt a great deed, but it should be acknowledged that above the nation stands a greater mission and a greater collective whole, namely 'Above all nations is humanity' according to Goldwin Smith."[18]

For his proposed solution, Hu did not head straight towards anti-statism. Despite that, the supremacy of the state that the Hundred Days' Reform brought forth twenty years previously was still successfully dissolved in the light of his consciousness of humanity. As Hu brought the consciousness of humanity back to troubled China and into the still emerging New Culture Movement, the concept—characterized by its universality and generality—was grafted onto issues concerning the Chinese people in its historical, social, and intellectual milieus. The consciousness of humanity then branched itself off into individual consciousness and individualism corresponding to the existence and rights of the individual, without needing to experience excessive and enforced transformations.

The causal understanding of the relationship between the consciousness of humanity and individualism that Hu Shih received in the United States made his thought adjacent to that of the "cosmopolitan" Henrik Ibsen (1828–1905). Despite Ibsen being a playwright, individualism according to Hu still began from "Ibsen-ism":

> "Within Ibsen's plays, there was an evident doctrine concerning the mutually detrimental relationship between society and individual. The society in favor of authoritarianism often mobilizes brute force to crush the person's individuality, suppressing their free and independent spirit. Once the individuality is destroyed and the free and independent spirit is exhausted, the society itself will also stagnate and no longer be alive."[19]

If Chen Duxiu's individualism emanated from the contradiction between the individual and his country, Hu's individualism, by way of Ibsen, showed more spontaneous interest in the antagonism between individual and society.

In the resulting differentiated vision of Hu, society was in reality constituted by "trite habits," "hackneyed thoughts," "extremely unbearable superstitions," as well as so-called "public opinions" deriving from these things. Individuals in the face of society could rely only on themselves as they sought the freedom and independence they rightly deserved. Ibsen once put this idea in a particularly forthright way in a letter:

> "What I chiefly desired for you is a genuine, full-blooded egoism, which shall force you for a time to regard what concerns you yourself as the only thing of any consequence, and everything else as non-existent […]. There are actually moments when the whole history of the world appears to me like one great shipwreck, and the only important thing seems to be to save one's self."[20]

Hu Shih saw behind these sentences that he translated into Chinese, the clear expression of individualism. Moreover, he explained this "egoism, which is really the most valuable kind of altruism," by stating: "Society is made up of individuals, so saving one more individual is equivalent to readying one more for rebuilding society." [...]

The equally distinct individual consciousness here, which reveals itself in the "egoist" qualification of individualism, demonstrates the similarity between Hu Shih's brand of individualism and Chen Duxiu's. But it remains different from Chen's individualism, which is marked by its promotion of fierce competition; Hu's "egoism" considers "only that which is most concerning me in the world is most important," and by disregarding relations both near and distant, it tends toward selfishness and self-interest. Hence, observable differences can be made out between the two. However, since Hu brought in the rhetoric of "altruism" to make his case, as far as Hu's preference is concerned, he did not enjoy such selfishness. But Hu's distaste for selfishness did not necessarily mean it was unconvincing.

If we consider the fact that Hu criticized vehemently the "escapist" self-interest of today's youth in his article published later titled "Non-Individualist New Life," it should be clear that the self-interested side of "egoism" was precisely the most intensely and immediately appealing side to people. Yet, because of such inner contradictions, Hu's conception of individualism lacks the consistency that Chen's conception is capable of maintaining. As a result, less than two years after he brought "Ibsen-ism" to China, Hu already could not but strive to correct the "self-interested individualism" of others. In reality, "self-interested individualism" shared with "self-salvation" not only the source but also the meaning, so the correction he applied only shifted the concept of individualism away from what he aspired it to be.

In this passage, we can observe the shift:

> "In his talk 'Individualism True and False' at the YMCA in Tianjin, Dr. John Dewey (1859–1952) discussed two kinds of individualism: the false kind of individualism is 'egoism'; its nature is self-interested, where it disregards the interest of others for one's own. The true kind of individualism is about 'individuality.' Its character is twofold: first, its thought is independent, and it refuses to rely on the cognition and intelligence of others; second, it takes full responsibility for the consequences of its thoughts and beliefs, unafraid of authorities and prosecutions but acknowledging truth only truth, not personal gain or loss."[21]

If we compare the preceding and following statements, Hu's criticism of the kind of individualism that "disregards the interests of others" is an indication that "only that which is most concerning me in the world is most important" could no longer be the truth. With this limitation in mind, individuals must "[take] full responsibility" for the consequences of their behaviors—this has since become a reasonable and necessary measure. As for the rising individual consciousness in China at the heyday of individualism, this measure provided the theoretical limit and restrictions. With such restrictions, the individualism that had been roaming unbridled thereby came a bit closer to the condition of the real world.

John Dewey provided a more exemplary definition of liberal individualism than Ibsen. As a result, when considered in conjunction with Yan Fu's prescription of "liberties as essence and democracy as function,"[22] Dewey's definition could showcase the shared origin between individualism and democracy. Its kernel of "individuality" was still the self-consciousness of an individual—but because of the existence of individual duties and the objects for which they were responsible, it must be said that, above the individual, there existed a greater being and a higher meaning. The relationship between the two levels, according to Hu Shih, was the relationship between the "small self" (*xiaowo*) and the "big self" (*dawo*) consisting of countless "small selves." Here, he says:

> "The 'small self' is destined for oblivion, whereas the 'big self' will never go into extinction; the 'big self' is unextinguishable. The 'small self' will experience death, but the 'big self' is ever-immortalized, ever-lasting. Although the 'small self' will die, all of its deeds, all of its merits and sins, regardless of the size of their impact will remain within the 'big self.'"[23]

Hence,

> "The current 'small self' of mine has to bear great responsibility for the infinite past of the ever-lasting 'big self,' and it has to bear equal responsibility for the infinite future of the ever-lasting 'big self.' I must repeatedly ask myself, how could I make use of the 'small self' now, so that the infinite past of the 'big self' won't be let down, so that the infinite future of the 'big self' won't be hurt?"[24]

In this discourse, the origin to his conception of the "big self" was clearly the consciousness of humanity that he had long harbored. From Ibsen to Dewey, ideas of liberal individualism came across the seas to fuel the intellectual awakening of individualism in China, providing a rationale for individualism that evolved from being barely integrated to being largely justifiable. When Hu's consciousness of humanity came to resonate with this liberal individualism, thanks to the additional idea of the "big self," the individual self-consciousness that Hu initially appeared to share with Chen Duxiu subsequently revealed its distinction in terms of social ethics.

That said, whether one could "take full responsibility" for the consequences of one's own behaviors, and whether the "small selves" could "be responsible" for the "big self" ultimately depended on one's morality, moral judgment, and moral discipline. Hence, behind the Western European principle of individualism, where rights and duties went hand-in-hand, there lay the prior and inherent supposition that the individual was morally self-aware. In other words, the truthful realization of individualism had to rely on a standardized social morality and a binding moral order. However, most of the figures propagating individualism in China at the time did not possess a strong enough understanding of this dimension of individualism. Thus, as they advocated for individualism in China, their radical, anti-traditionalist propositions catalyzed an intellectual movement that overthrew Confucianism, which had been the de facto guardian of morality in China for the past two thousand years […]. Hu Shih once said:

> "Precisely because the cannibalistic ritual religion of the past two thousand years has borne the trademark of Confucianism, this trademark—whether it is authentic or counterfeit—must be removed, shattered, and burned away!"[25]

[…] The activists promoting New Culture were confident that they could "reject established social morality and honor the truth."[26] To those who observed the world from outside the New Culture Movement, on the other hand, their deepest worries often lay in the moral degeneration of society. Although Western individualism was then entering China, its moral presuppositions had a difficult time to locate their Chinese counterparts in early-Republican China. As Hu and Chen gathered efforts to "mount attacks on Confucianism," their aspired "modern life" could not but become a life that was void of "sages' words of wisdom" and "ancestors' deeds of merit." The resulting lack of "means for nourishment" would cause the imported concept of individualism to be mired in the "cunning, evil, treacherous, and cruel," despite the hope that they had pinned on it, leading the individual astray from any consciousness of self-duty. Eventually, this deviation from any sense of duty would cause the reciprocity between rights and duties to lose its formative momentum. Therefore, even though Hu took Dewey's definition of individualism as authoritative and used it to qualify his own definition, his deep-seated intellectual belief that knowledge could overrule ethics and subsequently morality caused him to lose sight of what Liang Qichao (1873–1929)—one of the two main architects of the Hundred Days' Reform—was able to see. When the world's disarray testified to the fact that knowledge and its sensibility for truth could not overrule morality and its sensibility for goodness, the individualism that appeared as a matter of fact in front of the Chinese people could only be regarded as, in Dewey's terms, defective.

3. LU XUN: THE INDIVIDUAL AND THE MASSES

Compared to Chen Duxiu and Hu Shih, during the New Culture Movement Lu Xun (1881–1936) had less to say specifically about individualism. However, his contemplation of the individual began as early as his sojourn to Japan, which dates to before Chen's and Hu's discourses. Among his writings, the one that best shows his unique and impressive cultural character was his "Concerning Imbalanced Cultural Development" from 1907. At that time, the top echelon of Chinese society was embroiled in the debate over whether to implement constitutional monarchy, and many of the newly established figures were "eager to rally the masses" in order to carry out reforms. Unlike these figures, Lu focused on the individual and their spiritual world. From there, his thinking expanded outward—from the individual to the masses, and from the spiritual to the material. He asked rhetorically:

> "If all ideas were transmittable to the common masses, could the common masses truly be capable of probing the roots of right and wrong? […] If all affairs were reducible to the material, could the material truly be capable of exhausting the essence of life?"[27]

To those in vogue who were "eager to rally the masses," these interrogative sentences that conveyed statements more than questions were in obvious opposition to their beliefs. Rather than following the paths of Ibsen and Dewey as Hu Shih did, in Lu's view, the forerunners of individualism were Friedrich Nietzsche, Max Stirner, Arthur Schopenhauer, and Søren Kierkegaard, among others. Lu especially admired Nietzsche as "a hero of individualism." According to Lu, collectively speaking, they "[developed] individuality" to "exalt the self and glorify the genius," and they attributed the world's "vital energy" (*yuanqi*) to the "courageous and fearless individuals" who were "independent and self-reliant, free of worldly filth, spurning superfluous opinions, and refusing to sink into a vulgar country"—in other words, these were the "*Übermenschen*" and "sages." This distrust of the masses that individualism had brought forth, along with the supremacy of the spiritual over the material, was embodied by Lu's interrogative gestures. In Lu's awareness, both the distrust and the supremacy face and question the same thing: the "imbalances" in the West during the nineteenth century.[28]

In the article, Lu Xun summarized his cultural stance with this statement: "All there is to be discussed can be categorized into two groups of things: that that is non-material and that that is emphatic on the individual." Lu derived both of the "two groups" from the West, but his argument concerning the "two groups" was generated by way of his criticism of the West and his differentiation within the West. Lu Xun's criticism of the West using methods learned from the West, as well as his choice to differentiate within the West, disassembled with clarity the West that many Chinese regarded as monolithic to expose its internal divergences and contradictions. Unlike Chen Duxiu, Hu Shih, and others within the New Culture Movement, who, ten years after Lu's article was published, still heralded the banner of "Westernization" and "globalization," and painted a glorious view of the whole Western world, Lu Xun chose to show his Chinese audience the "imbalanced," "gloom-ridden," and "obstinately conservative" sides of the *fin-de-siècle* West at its acme of worldwide influence. Observed from a cognitive standpoint, Lu's analysis was undoubtedly much more in-depth than his successors. The historical process of the nineteenth century created the nineteenth-century culture; it was thanks to the modernization resulting from the process that the "material" and the "masses" became the center of the gravitational pull, and they remained symbiotic with this modernization. Given the centering of the "material" and the "masses," the *fin-de-siècle* culture that Lu spoke of pointed to a "desolate human world,"[29] where the human and their consciousness had been drowned. As Lu approached the subject by critiquing the "imbalance" created by the "material" and the "masses," he in fact touched on the imbalance and partiality of modernization itself.

Lu's criticism and dissenting view hereafter on "the falsehood and bias of the modern civilization" then has to be regarded as a kind of rebellion against modernity, and its objects of critique often bordered "ideals of equality and freedom" and "ideas about society and democracy."[30] As a result, Lu is to be distinguished from the newly established figures who "looked toward the West in search for the truth." In the seventy or so years since China and the West intersected and conflicted on an unprecedented scale, China has developed from its initial rejection of the "modern civilization" to imitating and admiring the latter, so much that it began to abandon its past to "compete for a different path"[31] toward modernity. The modernizing trajectory in China consisting of imitation, admiration, and competition, along with its accelerating speed of change, forms a contrasting background to Lu's rebellion against modernity. In fact, Lu's difference marks a competing moment in the otherwise largely smooth course of modern Chinese intellectual history. Yet, as Lu's difference lay in his rhetoric "to suppress the material and promote the spiritual, to trust the personal and repudiate the multitudes," his stance lacked any specific proposition that could effectively counter the established historical process. The somewhat vague parallelism employed here indicates that what Lu conveyed toward "modern civilization" could only be a purely negative stance, lacking sufficient substantiation. [...]

Hence, factually speaking, the simple negation could not but also be an abstract negation. As a direct result, those who first recognized the "imbalance" of "modern civilization" were also the first to be trapped in the space between the existing imbalance and the abstract negation of it, with no way of either resolving or getting out of the situation. For Lu Xun, who grounded his thought in theories from the West and used them to address and criticize concrete issues in Western society, the conundrum thus formed was not only acutely impactful but also enduringly unforgettable. Dissimilar to the simplicity and arbitrariness then often associated with other figures' conviction and confidence, being lost meant to admit that one was still searching for his way to address the Chinese question—Lu used the expression "not having a compass even myself" to describe the scenario.[32] Being skeptical entailed that one was in the midst of the current, but neither could one afford to be gullible, nor could one consent to being arbitrary, so that a slither of independence might still be kept. Since not to be gullible or arbitrary would imply the prevailment of reason, acting in these two ways could demonstrate the depth of thinking. That was on the one hand. On the other hand, being lost within and skeptical toward the anti-traditionalist current could bring about a greater sense of stifling and suffering on the spiritual front. Thus, when Lu Xun published his collection of short stories in the 1920s, he titled it *Call to Arms*, and for the subsequent collection, he named it *Panghuang* ("wandering"). Envisaging the brightness of the latter-day, Lu wrote in the preface to *Call to Arms*, "I could not blot out hope, for hope lies in the future,"[33] but for depicting the pale vision still standing, Lu quoted in the preface of *Panghuang* from Qu Yuan, a poet from the third century BCE, "Long, long is my road, and far, far is the journey; high and low, up and down, I'll search with will."[34] [...]

Lu Xun's intellectual experience deepened greatly in the first decade of the twentieth century, which he then carried into the New Culture Movement during the second decade. Within this intellectual movement, the discourse of individualism advocated by and large for the rights of the individual, but Lu alternatively regarded the "non-material" and the "personal" as his intellectual insight, whose focus divergently pointed to the human—as well as the inner aspects of an individual, including "clairvoyance," "individuality," "intention," "subjectivity," "personality," and "spirituality." His individualism, therefore, is defined by spirituality both in content and in aim. In the early years of his thought and vision, the theme for Lu was to encourage people to create an inner world:

> "Therefore, if a nation aims to survive and even compete with its peers, the first and foremost will be to ensure its citizens can establish themselves in the world, and everything else will follow; as for the method for ensuring this establishment, it must be respecting one's individuality and promoting one's spirituality."[35]

During the 1920s, the theme of Lu's proposition remained anchored in the inner world:

> "The most important thing is to reform the national character; otherwise, no matter if the country were a republic, under a dictatorship, or whatever form of government, it would be old wine in a new bottle, and none of it would work."[36]

The connection between the two phases thereby carried on, eventually becoming his life's work.

Thanks to his proposition attentive to individuality and spirituality, since early on, Lu's public image was that of "a warrior defending the spiritual realm,"[37] whose prescience allowed him to "stand aside from the clamor of the masses and maintain one's own view." But this was an image created by the ideal and nestled within it, so looking outside the ideal and into one's real surroundings would lead to these greater questions, according to Lu:

> "Nowadays, if we look around China, where are the people who are the warriors defending the spiritual realm? Who has cried out with a truly sincere voice and led us to a world of goodness, beauty, and robustness? Who has uttered a warm and genial voice to save us from the world of desolation and frigidity?"[38]

Within this world mired in difficulties, the corresponding and contrasting phenomena to the prescient, ideal figure would be the disease troubling the "Chinese national character" and the search for its "root causes."[39] With the prescience being an ideal, its significance was formulated in contrast with the current national character. Reciprocally, as a real social existence, the national character and its disease were only revealed in the light of the ideal prescience. For the "reform" of the national character that has since been transposed into the New Culture Movement, the intellectual labor belonging to the early stage now became the starting point of later thoughts.

The subjectivity of the national character was the ordinary Chinese termed the "common masses." Hence, when Lu Xun devoted his attention to the national character, what he had always focused on was, indeed, the masses. With the "root causes" of the disease of the national character being under investigation, so that "a reform of the national character" could take place, the masses constituting the subjectivity have then been put under scrutiny and diagnosis since the very beginning. They became a passive object without any sense of autonomy, a faceless collective without any distinctive brand, or a thing waiting to be recreated. Moreover, even though the individualism according to Lu and his proposed "reform" of the national character ought to derive from the same vein of thought, if the kernel of this individualism lay in individuality and spirituality, the masses derogatorily dubbed "the blind"[40] and "the onlookers"[41] had to be treated as the opposite to the individual, regardless of its role as the vehicle of the national character. The direct contradiction that ensued between the individual and the masses, on the one side, spiritually distinguished the masses from the individual in his march toward self-realization. It enabled "the 'pompousness' of the individual" and "differentiation" to emerge from the rest and "declare war on the banal crowd."[42] On the other side, the direct contradiction strove to peel off the surface and expose the psychology of the masses, to gaze deeply into the "soul of the nation"[43] that was "incredibly silent" besides being "foolish and frail," so as to "call attention to the need for remedy."[44] However, when the masses were characterized with words and phrases like "cowardice," "selfishness," "greed," "self-deception," and "numbness," as well as "fraud and impudence" and "mutual suspicion and harm," the masses were treated as a passive body on an operating table, exposed in its "darkness" by the writer's scalpel deliberately and without much scruple."[45] The sharp conflict between these two sides revealed a contradiction that, at present and for the foreseeable future, lacked a clear resolution.

Behind the individualism of Chen Duxiu stood the "French civilization" cherished by him; behind the individualism of Hu Shih stood the liberalism introduced by way of Dewey. But behind Lu Xun's "[respect for] individuality and [promotion of] spirituality" stood not a single and complete system of Western knowledge, for it was born out of critiquing the "imbalance" of "today's civilization." Accompanying this isolated stance was Lu's revelation and attack of the nation's "deep-rooted depravity" along with its "ossified tradition."[46] This gesture enabled Lu not only to establish his anti-traditionalist position but bring this position into the New-Culture direction of anti-traditionalism. Most of the figures of the New Culture Movement opposed tradition while presuming to be standing on its outside; Lu differed by understanding very clearly that he came out of the very tradition. Therefore, he was never ashamed to admit that his "spirit is haunted by the toxic and ghostly," which he "strongly detested yet could not remove."[47] The sorts of "darkness" that he depicted in writing, however, was inseparable from his self-reflection. Thus, the self of Lu was constantly in a state of tension. On the work of Fyodor Dostoevsky, he once claimed:

> "Whoever is a great inquisitor must also be a great criminal. The inquisitor impeaches the wickedness of the criminal in court, while the criminal confesses his goodness behind his lectern. The inquisitor uncovers the filth within the criminal's soul, while the criminal

> salvages redeemable radiance from the uncovered filth. In this way, the depths of the soul become evident."[48]

Without doubt, the sense of self-interrogation that Lu Xun extracted from the work of Dostoevsky echoed his personal experience. When Lu wrote down these sentences, it would not have been without the feelings he felt when he turned against tradition as someone who had been influenced by tradition. Therefore, "the depths of the soul" and the equally deep-rooted self-contradiction are two sides of the same coin. The self-contradiction stemmed from his innermost self. Parallel to the self-contradiction was the isolation—as well as the loneliness—resulting from not wholeheartedly entrusting himself to the "modern civilization." Such isolation and loneliness set Lu Xun apart from Chen Duxiu and Hu Shih in the New Culture Movement. Whereas Chen's and Hu's discourses of individualism were coherent on paper, Lu's discourse, because of its very insightfulness and complexity, experienced difficulty in forming a coherent philosophical system. It also demonstrated a symmetrical characteristic: wherever he touched with his brand of individualism, he showed unrivaled profundity as well as unprecedented contradiction. Yet, underneath this profundity lay a thick layer of gray, whereas the contradiction would largely find its home in his critically expressed negation. Thus, on the one hand, topics such as "the individual vs. the masses" and "the material vs. the spiritual" could reveal their contents and meanings with an extraordinary level of clarity—aided by Lu's inclination toward thoughtfulness and intricacy. On the other hand, these topics remained pressured and restrained by the thick layer of gray and by his negative stance, thereby continuing to be dilemmas and problems in China. Although most of Lu Xun's reflections were figurative and approachable with the help of his short stories, the more profound concerns of his reflections often went to humanity and human nature. Thus, compared to Chen Duxiu's and Hu Shih's discourses, Lu's concerns were more fundamental and existed on a metaphysical level.

Edited excerpt from *Exploration and Free Views* (探索与争鸣), 2016, vol. 1, issue (8), pp. 12–22.

1 Chen Boda, "Lun Xin Qimeng Yundong" [On the New Enlightenment Movement]; Feng Dalin, "Cong liu wangfan—Wusi Xin Wenhua Yundong" [Returning from the Current—The May Fourth New Culture Movement], in *Minguo shiqi mingren tan Wusi* [Famous Figures of the Republican Era Discuss May Fourth] (Fujian Education Press, 2011), pp. 215, 66. I still remember thirty years ago, when listening to Mr. Chen Xulu lecture on the metabolism of modern China, when he came to the section on the May Fourth New Culture Movement, he said with some hesitation: The Hundred Days› Reform was an enlightenment, and the New Culture Movement was another enlightenment. For the Chinese people to always be in a state of enlightenment is truly unpromising.

2 *Qingmo choubei lixian dang›an shiliao* [Archival Historical Materials on the Preparation for Constitutionalism in the Late Qing Dynasty], vol. 2 (Beijing: Zhonghua Book Company, 1979), p. 613; Zhang Nan and Wang Renzhi, *Xinhai geming qian shinian jian shilun xuanji* [Selected Commentaries from the Decade Before the 1911 Revolution], vol. 2, Part 1 (Beijing: SDX Joint Publishing Company, 1963), p. 44.

3 Fu Sinian, *Fu Sinian quanji* [The Complete Works of Fu Sinian], vol. 1 (Changsha: Hunan Education Press, 2003), pp. 296–97.

4 Luo Jialun, "Xin Wenhua Yundong de shidai he yingxiang" [The Era and Influence of the New Culture Movement], pp. 29, 31.

5 *Chen Duxiu wenzhang xuanbian* [Selected Essays of Chen Duxiu], vol. 1 (Beijing: SDX Joint Publishing Company, 1984), p. 165.

6 Ibid., pp. 1, 11, 19.

7 Ibid., p. 71.

8 Ibid.

9 Zhang Shizhao, *Zhang Shizhao quanji* [The Complete Works of Zhang Shizhao], vol. 3 (Shanghai: Wenhui Press, 2000), p. 508.

10 Tao Shuimu (ed.), *Shen Dingyi ji* [The Collected Works of Shen Dingyi], vol. 2 (Beijing: National Library of China Publishing House, 2010), p. 390.

11 *Chen Duxiu wenzhang xuanbian* [Selected Essays of Chen Duxiu], vol. 1, p. 98.

12 *Ibid.*, p. 98.

13 Ibid., pp. 74–75.

14 Ibid.

15 *Ibid.*, p. 102.

16 Cai Yuanpei, *Cai Yuanpei quanji* [The Complete Works of Cai Yuanpei], Vol. 2 (Beijing: Zhonghua Book Company, 1988), p. 403; Li Dazhao, *Li Dazhao quanji* [The Complete Works of Li Dazhao], Vol. 1 (Beijing: People›s Publishing House, 2006), p. 254.

17 Hu Shi, written by, and Ji Xianlin, edited by, *Hu Shi quanji* [The Complete Works of Hu Shi], Vol. 27 (Hefei: Anhui Education Press, 2003), p. 531.

18 *Hu Shi quanji* [The Complete Works of Hu Shi], Vol. 27, p. 531.

19 *Hu Shi quanji* [The Complete Works of Hu Shi], Vol. 1, pp. 607–08, 612–14

20 Ibid.

21 Ibid., pp. 707–08

22 Yan Fu, *Yan Fu ji* [The Collected Works of Yan Fu], Vol. 1 (Beijing: Zhonghua Book Company, 1986), p. 23.

23 *Hu Shi quanji* [The Complete Works of Hu Shi], vol. 1, pp. 667–68.

24 Ibid., pp. 707–08.

25 Ibid., p. 763.

26 *Chen Duxiu wenzhang xuanbian* [Selected Essays of Chen Duxiu], vol. 1, p. 129.

27 Lu Xun, *Lu Xun quanji* [The Complete Works of Lu Xun], vol. 1 (Beijing: People›s Publishing House, 1956), p. 184.

28 *Lu Xun quanji* [The Complete Works of Lu Xun], vol. 1, pp. 181, 186–89.

29 *Lu Xun quanji* [The Complete Works of Lu Xun], vol. 7, p. 237.

30 *Lu Xun quanji* [The Complete Works of Lu Xun], vol. 1, pp. 183–84.

31 *Lu Xun quanji* [The Complete Works of Lu Xun], vol. 7, p. 237.

32 *Lu Xun quanji* [The Complete Works of Lu Xun], vol. 9, p. 12.

33 *Lu Xun quanji* [The Complete Works of Lu Xun], vol. 1, p. 7.

34 *Lu Xun quanji* [The Complete Works of Lu Xun], vol. 2, p. 3.

35 *Lu Xun quanji* [The Complete Works of Lu Xun], vol. 1, p. 193.

36 *Lu Xun quanji* [The Complete Works of Lu Xun], vol. 9, p. 26.

37 *Lu Xun quanji* [The Complete Works of Lu Xun], vol. 7, p. 237; vol. 1, p. 233.

38 *Lu Xun quanji* [The Complete Works of Lu Xun], vol. 1, p. 234.

39 Xu Shoushang, *Wangyou Lu Xun yinxiang ji* [Recollections of My Deceased Friend Lu Xun] (Changsha: Yuelu Publishing House, 2011), p. 18.

40 *Lu Xun quanji* [The Complete Works of Lu Xun], vol. 1, p. 182.

41 Ibid., p. 274.

42 Ibid., p. 387.

43 Ibid., p. 5; *Lu Xun quanji* [The Complete Works of Lu Xun], vol. 7, p. 78.

44 *Lu Xun quanji* [The Complete Works of Lu Xun], vol. 4, p. 393.

45 Bao Jing, ed., *Lu Xun guominxing sixiang taolun ji* [A Collection of Discussions on Lu Xun›s Thought on National Character] (Tianjin: Tianjin People›s Publishing House, 1982), pp. 94, 105; *Lu Xun quanji* [The Complete Works of Lu Xun], vol. 4, p. 85; Vol. 9, p. 18.

46 *Lu Xun quanji* [The Complete Works of Lu Xun], vol. 3, p. 35.

47 *Lu Xun quanji* [The Complete Works of Lu Xun], vol. 9, p. 312.

48 *Lu Xun quanji* [The Complete Works of Lu Xun], vol. 7, p. 95.

ON THE ISSUE OF THE INTEGRATION OF LITERATURE UNDER SOCIALIST IDEOLOGY

HONG ZICHENG 洪子诚

I.

In recent years, when discussing the overall characteristics of literature in mainland China from the 1950s to the 1970s, some researchers have often used terms of generalizations such as "homogenization" (一元化, *yiyuanhua*) or "integration" (一体化, *yitihua*). I have also employed such descriptions in some of my own articles and works on literary history. This generalization, it must be said, can be considered valid. However, when using such terms, it is essential to assign them a precise connotation. What I understand by the "integration" of contemporary Chinese literature is, first and foremost, a reference to the process of literary evolution or the formation of a distinctive feature of a particular literary period. In the course of twentieth-century Chinese literature, amid a complex interplay of conflict, infiltration, and the rise and fall of various literary propositions, schools, and forces, "leftist literature" (or "revolutionary literature") had, by the 1950s, become the sole literary reality in mainland China. In other words:

> "China's 'leftist literature' ('revolutionary literature'), having been reshaped by the literature of the liberated areas during the 1940s, saw its literary forms and norms become—through both cultural influence and political institutionalization—the only legitimate literary mode permitted to exist from the 1950s to the 1970s."[1]

Second, "integration" refers to the modes of literary production and organization during this period. This includes literary institutions, organizations, journals and newspapers, as well as the writing, publishing, circulation, reading, and mechanisms of literary criticism. Clearly, a highly organized literary world existed during this time. The establishment of unified standards and centralized management over all aspects of literary production was a deliberate strategy of ideological and cultural governance by the state, which yielded considerable results. Third, another aspect of "integration" refers to the literary forms of this period. This encompasses subject matter, themes, artistic styles, and the tendency toward homogenization of artistic practices across various literary genres. In this sense, "integration" stands in direct opposition to diversity that literary history has embraced at various historical points, as well as to an ideal literary landscape that celebrated pluralistic coexistence.

While the term "integration" may be valid and can effectively capture the structural features of literature during this period, its use should not be taken as definitive or conclusive. In other words, this assessment does not mark the end of research on literature from the 1950s to the 1970s. On the contrary, much work remains to be done, and in some respects, meaningful inquiry has yet to truly begin. Like other widely used concepts today—such as "dominant ideology," "state discourse," or "national narrative"—the term "integration" can, in certain instances, productively describe literary phenomena and texts of the time. But in other cases, its explanatory power is limited. Particularly as such terms evolve into ready-made formulas, an excessive reliance on them may signal a lack of more concrete and in-depth engagement with the literary phenomena themselves. More importantly, it is crucial to main a clear-eyed understanding of the validity and effectiveness of the "integration" framework, including the theoretical premises and perspectives from which it is constructed. While we should acknowledge the analytical insights it can provide, we must also remain alert to its inherent limitations—particularly its potential to obscure other phenomena and issues. Such frameworks and perspectives should not be extended or applied uncritically or without regard for their boundaries.

Therefore, rather than further elaborating on "integration", this article aims to review and reflect on past generalizations, especially those I have made in my own research, to identify potential problems in earlier understandings and applications of the concept.

II.

To begin with, it is important to note that when we use the term "integration" to describe literature from the 1950s to the 1970s, it is sometimes treated as a fixed and static phenomenon. In some of the past writings on the history of contemporary Chinese literature (including *A Survey of Contemporary Chinese Literature*, which I co-authored),[2] a uniform historical context is often presented to the reader. Typically, the first pages of these literary histories usually assert in definitive terms that the founding of the People's Republic of China in 1949, or the convening of the First Congress of All-China Literary and Art Workers (中华全国文学艺术工作者代表大会), marked the beginning of contemporary Chinese literature, signaling a new era in China's modern literary history. This narrative approach, on the one hand, emphasizes the rupture between the two literary periods demarcated by 1949—the birth of a literature with a fundamentally new character. On the other hand, it underscores the inevitability of this transition, its legitimacy, and its conformity to historical laws. In such accounts, the seemingly natural "birth" of this literary world (contemporary literature) and the legitimacy of its emergence are presented as mutually reinforcing. In reality, however, the emergence of contemporary literature, the unfolding of this literary period, and the formation of its "integrated" structure were a protracted and intensely contested process. During this process, the various literary schools and forces that existed in the 1930s and 1940s simultaneously clashed and intermingled, creating a tense dynamic. These tensions manifested in the literary trends and movements of the 1940s to the 1970s as struggles between the "mainstream" and the "non-mainstream," between norms and challenges, between control and resistance. Throughout this period, the expansion and contraction of the literary sphere, and the shifting positions of various literary forces, followed an uneven and fluctuating trajectory.

The emergence of contemporary literature—that is, the effort to establish a unified literary form compatible with the new political and economic system—can be said to have begun as early as the 1940s, specifically after the end of the War of Resistance Against Japan. At that time, the literary scene in China was characterized by a diversity of forms and aspirations. Regarding the question of "where Chinese literature should head," two opposing positions held particular sway. One view, proposed by those often referred to as liberal writers, expressed a hope that the postwar period would bring an end to the persistent disputes and conflicts that had plagued the literary world since the May Fourth Movement. They envisioned a literary scene where writers could devote themselves to their craft and where diverse literary forms could coexist. This was a vision of a literary community grounded in pluralistic values and meanings. Their ideal was rooted not only in their political beliefs and social ideals, but also in their literary commitments. At the same time, this also reflected their confidence in their own creative work and their conviction that they could maintain a competitive edge in an open literary field.[3] Their call to produce "ready-made" literary works of "world-class standard" was, in essence, a challenge directed at leftist writers, from whom an alternative vision for the future of Chinese literature was proposed.

While acknowledging the existence of different literary forms, each expressing distinct values and aesthetic attitudes, leftist writers argued that such fragmentation at the level of "structure of meaning" ultimately stemmed from class divisions and the interests of specific class groups. In modern society, they contended, the various social classes should not, and in fact cannot coexist on equal and parallel terms. This perspective was explicitly articulated in the essays of leading leftist writers in the mid-to-late 1940s, and in the literary campaigns led by leftist forces during the same period.[4] They strongly asserted that revolutionary literature, which embodied the interests of the proletariat, should occupy an absolute dominant position. Their theoretical exposition sought to provide objective and legitimate justification for literature embodying class-based and partisan values, drawing on analyses of economic structures and class relations. This position was to be secured and affirmed through historical practice. To this end, they employed rhetorical categories such as "progressive," "reactionary," and "backward" to classify and rank different writers and literary factions of the time. These distinctions helped identify targets for unity, persuasion, or suppression. Through institutionalized public opinion and organizational means, they worked toward achieving the goal of "integration." In this sense, the emergence of contemporary literature—the realization of literary "integration"—was not a natural evolution but a historically contingent process shaped by organized interventions in the literary world.

Following the convening of the First Congress of All-China Literary and Art Workers (1949) and the establishment of the new regime, leftist literature (revolutionary literature) had, by all accounts, achieved absolute dominance in the literary landscape of mainland China. However, this process of intervention, selection, and conflict did not come to an end. One major reason is that, in the eyes of contemporary cultural radical forces, "integration" is always an unattainable, never-complete goal. Its realization and maintenance are closely tied to the pursuit of an imagined form of pure literature—an ideal that continuously shifts and adapts across different historical periods. As one researcher put it: "With each step forward in the revolution, the targets of struggle change, the vision of the 'future' shifts accordingly, and the historical narratives built around that vision must also be revised."[5] Thus, the work of categorizing literary schools and texts in the name of "integration" was never at rest. From the 1940s dichotomy of the "revolutionary literary front" versus the "reactionary literary front," to the 1950s opposition between the "socialist literary line" and the "anti-socialist literary line," to the 1960s battle between the "proletarian literary line" and the so-called "black line in literature and art," the intensity and sharpness of conflicts only grew more pronounced.

The effort to intervene "historically" to resolve the coexistence of diverse literary positions and form, while maintaining an integrated literary order, requires addressing several key challenges. As previously mentioned, the first is to select canonical texts for this literary structure—that is, to designate "classics" that can demonstratively exemplify its defining features. In the contemporary period, efforts to designate certain writers, works, or schools as "models," "directions," or "standards" are all related to this goal. But the difficulty and complexity lie in the fact that the vast body of literary heritage, along with the existence of diverse modern literary practices, often stands in stark contrast to these designated "classics." They may therefore reveal the intellectual or artistic weaknesses of these so-called "classics," posing a threat to their legitimacy. This presents a paradox for those advocating for literary "integration": if this literature—proclaimed to be the most progressive, beautiful and compelling—refused to draw spiritual and artistic nourishment from the heritage it seeks to replace, its vitality might be diminished; but if it remains entangled with the very literary traditions it seeks to distance itself from, with unclear or ambiguous boundaries, it may undermine the foundation of its own existence and ultimately cause the project of "integration" to collapse. Another issue that needs to be addressed concerns the spiritual orientation and aesthetic sensibilities of writers (and even readers). From the early 1950s onward, a series of ideological reformation campaigns, the promotion of "socialist realism," and the encouragement to "go deep into life," and "go deep among workers, peasants, and soldiers" were all aimed at this objective. At first glance, these efforts seemed effective. At certain times, the apparent consistency of literary beliefs and aesthetic inclinations among writers and readers left a strong impression. Yet this overt success was also questionable. By the mid-1960s, Mao Zedong, in one of his famous directives, stated that "all forms of art" had "many issues, and a large number of people involved, yet the socialist transformation in many sectors has yielded very little to date"; "the social and economic base has changed, yet the arts, one of the superstructural components that should serve this base, remains a major problem." These statements express not only stern dissatisfaction, but also a sense of helplessness and sorrow.

In fact, from a longer historical perspective, the construction and maintenance of an integrated literary configuration in contemporary China has relied less on ideological purification campaigns targeting writers and readers, and more fundamentally—and effectively—on the establishment of a literary production system. This system was comprehensive, tightly structured, and functioned with considerable efficacy. Major shifts in production methods and literary institutions were crucial indicators of the "ruptures" and "turning points" that characterized literature in the 1940s and 1950s.

The establishment of the new institutional framework that gave rise to contemporary literature was primarily manifested in the following aspects:

1. The nature and structure of writers' organizations and associations. In contemporary times, the Writers' Association (作家协会) functioned as the sole official body for writers. This institution, in terms of its nature and function, can be seen as a hybrid of a "pan-political party" organization and a professional guild. While it offered certain protections for writers' rights, its more essential role was to control and manage literary production. It also to some extent reflects the monopolistic nature of professional guilds. However, the kind of autonomy traditionally associated with intellectuals' professional associations had been significantly diminished. Some monopolistic characteristics nevertheless persisted. One indication of this was that, in the 1950s and 1960s, being expelled from the Writers' Association effectively meant losing the right to publish one's work publicly. At the same time, identity labels such as "professional writer," "amateur writer," "literary youth," and "literary enthusiast" emerged to define qualifications and determine hierarchy within the literary system, and regulate the process of entering the literary field.

2. The livelihood of writers. This includes their income, social status, and identity. Issues of social status and identity are both a matter of the writers' self-awareness and social attribution—that is, the stipulations of the system. The transformation of the identity of intellectuals and writers stemmed from changes in the relationship between the state and society after the 1950s. With the unprecedented expansion of state power and resources, a greater portion of the population was integrated into a planned economy model. The primary human resources in society were all allocated to the civil service system, thereby enabling the state to exert comprehensive control over society—including the literary world.[6] Within this model of integration, writers, like teachers, were absorbed into the system as "cadres," erasing the former identity as freelance intellectuals. This restructuring significantly altered both the social status of writers and their sense of professional identity.

3. Literary journals and publishing houses. In the late 1940s, most existing literary journals gradually ceased publication. Even literary journals from the

liberated areas followed a similar pattern. Literary journals that emerged in modern China with an independent character, often tied to distinct literary styles and writers' circles, effectively lost their viability. All literary publications were now required to explicitly define themselves as "official" organs affiliated with institutional bodies. During this period, several attempts to launch journals with distinct stylistic orientations or literary circle affiliations were made, but most ended in failure. Publications under the central authorities such as *Literary Gazette* (*Wenyi Bao*) and *People's Literature* (*Renmin Wenxue*), as well as local literary journals from various provinces and cities, strictly adhered to standardized guidelines and maintained a unified voice, thus effectively ensuring the implementation of literary "integration." Major literary publishing houses in cities like Shanghai and Beijing were either merged, closed, or had their publishing functions redefined during the 1950s. As some researchers have pointed out, "Before 1949, the state apparatus in old China found it difficult, if not impossible, to achieve an integrated system for the governance of knowledge," whereas "after 1949, the situation underwent a fundamental change."[7] From the perspective of publishing and distribution as material infrastructure, private publishing houses and bookstores were gradually eliminated, and a centralized system for publishing and distributing newspapers and books was established at both the central and local levels. In the 1950s and 1960s, People's Literature Publishing House in Beijing, the Writers Publishing House (which at one point operated as a subsidiary imprint of the former), the China Youth Publishing House, and in Shanghai, the New Literature and Art Publishing House (later known as the Shanghai Literature and Art Publishing House) became the authoritative institutions for literary publications.

4. Mechanisms of literary criticism. During this period, professional literary critique and non-professional, politically motivated interventions were intertwined and difficult to distinguish. Some prominent writers also held official positions in literary institutions, and this ambiguity of identity added to the complexity of literary evaluation. The opinions offered by experts (writers and literary critics) on literary works and issues remained important during this time. However, decisive influence was often not wielded by literary professionals. Especially in cases involving "major" issues or significant disagreements in evaluation, final decisions were frequently made outside of the literary community. Certain political authorities did not feel bound by the roles formally assigned to them. The extent to which professional criticism was regarded as "truthful" also depended on the critic's position within the literary system. Naturally, when an issue did not involve major political or ideological agendas, professionals had relatively more freedom to offer their own interpretations. The literary system established in the contemporary period effectively ensured the formation of an integrated literary structure. Of course, this system was not without its fissures. For example, although literary journals had largely lost their relatively independent role as platforms for public discourse, there were moments when certain publications made deliberate efforts to revive this function. The most notable examples were *Literary Gazette*, *People's Literature*, and *Guangming Daily* from Beijing, and *Wenhui Daily* from Shanghai, particularly during the period from 1956 to 1957. Moreover, within this system, individuals with substantial prestige, power, and capability—such as Mao Zedong and Zhou Yang—exerted enormous influence. But their priorities regarding issues of literature, politics, and intellectuals were not always aligned, coupled with varying degrees of control and mobilization over literary resources, this system did not remain fully rigid throughout. This complexity is something we must carefully discern.

III.

Taking into account the complex circumstances of the time, and while recognizing the overarching state of "integration" that defined literature from the 1950s to the 1970s, researchers today are increasingly emphasizing the need to examine the internal shifts and distinctions of that period. Within a specific literary environment, any meaningful understanding of changes in literary forms—as well as the spiritual and psychological frameworks of writers and intellectuals—must begin with uncovering the differences that lay beneath the appearance of uniformity. The "multi-layered" condition within the "integrated" literary structure comes from the fact that the stratification in cultural and literary fields has not completely disappeared in the contemporary era. The circumstances, modes of existence, and interrelations of various cultural elements have naturally evolved during this period, but this did not mean that certain cultural elements have vanished or were extinguished—even if they were greatly weakened or suppressed. Even within the dominant Chinese leftist literature of the contemporary period, there existed a variety of internal components. Contradictions and tensions among different literary forces, their divergent literary propositions and aesthetic orientations all pointed to the limits of this "integrated" framework. Although such conflicts did not fundamentally alter the general landscape of literature during this period, they nonetheless exerted a constraining influence. They reflected not only divergent interpretations of realism among revolutionary writers and the varying emphases of their literary ideals, but also the dynamic interplay—marked by both convergence and tension—between Western modernist techniques and folk traditions in the pursuit of literary modernity during this period. In terms of narrative style and artistic method, the friction between storytelling modes grounded in vernacular and folk traditions and those shaped by the conventions of Western realist fiction further revealed the complexity of this cultural negotiation.

The stance and perspective of the decision-makers in contemporary literature, though following their own internal logic, were not static. Over time, shifts and inconsistencies in their positions contributed to the emergence of a complex, multi-layered literary landscape. The experimental and uncertain nature of the integration process promoted by radical literary forces, along with the challenges they encountered—particularly in determining which human and artistic resources could be harnessed to realize their envisioned new literature—inevitably led to tensions between expectations and outcomes, theory and practice. These were rarely uniform or clearly defined. An evident fact is that, during the Cultural Revolution, although radical cultural forces expressed a highly antagonistic stance toward cultural heritage in theory and in public rhetoric, the human and artistic resources mobilized in the actual production of the "model operas" were inconsistent with these claims. The playwrights, directors, performers, vocal artists, and stage designers involved were all nationally recognized "authorities" in their respective fields (trained and steeped in the very "old arts" being criticized). Moreover, the accumulated expertise of traditional forms like Peking Opera ensured that the production of these "models" was not entirely unmoored or without foundation.

This multi-layered phenomenon generally manifested in two ways. One involved oppositions and conflicts between different literary forms, which formed relationships between "mainstream" and "non-mainstream" (or even "countercurrents"), between "explicit" and "implicit" in specific historical contexts. Works and literary theories that were once criticized, denounced, or ignored in certain periods—as well as secret or "underground" writings (such as those during the Cultural Revolution)—fall into this category. Another form was the multi-layered cultural composition within individual texts. For instance, certain "model operas" exhibited complexity in their cultural origins. The basic political interpretive framework, the limited incorporation of traditional and folk arts, and the pursuit of dramatic flair and entertainment value allowed for the presence of alternative discursive systems beyond the official narrative. Of course, the early underground poetry of the Cultural Revolution period (such as the work of Shi Zhi, who rose to fame in the 1990s) also inherited and retained certain ideological and aesthetic elements of contemporary "mainstream poetry," even as it moved in the direction of transformation.

The attention to and excavation of multi-layeredness will naturally alter or adjust our initial imagination of the literary landscape of this period. However, we must also be cautious of the possibility that new narratives may increasingly diverge from historical facts. If such narratives lead readers to believe that the literature of this period was rich with texts differing from or opposing the orthodox discursive framework, that there was an active intellectual exploration forming a powerful trend, then this may be quite far from the actual situation. One of the important achievements in studies of contemporary literary history in the 1990s was the careful discovery and construction of a "non-mainstream" literary lineage, which helped to revise our previously crude imagination of the era. This deserves positive recognition. At the same time, however, we must remain mindful—indeed, firmly aware—that no matter how much we unearth or recover, this should not obscure the overall "integrated" nature of the period's literary landscape, nor foster an illusion of spiritual elevation among contemporary writers.

There are certain technical issues here that require careful consideration. In the process of constructing this "non-mainstream" literary lineage, a key question could be: Which works and publications can legitimately be included? Two particular challenges may arise in this regard. One involves works that circulated secretly within various circles during the Cultural Revolution, such as hand-copied novels (手抄本文学) *The Second Handshake* (第二次握手), *Fluctuations* (波动), *A Public Love Letter* (公开的情书), and *When the Evening Glow Fades* (晚霞消失的时候), as well as early poems by Shi Zhi, Duo Duo, Mang Ke, Bei Dao, Shu Ting, Gu Cheng, and others. These works circulated through highly informal channels, and their official publication in journals or as books generally came only after the end of the Cultural Revolution. During their hand-copied transmission, alterations made by authors and copyists were inevitable and natural. When these works were officially published, the authors may have (and in some cases certainly did) made substantial revisions. Today, when we categorize such works as "hand-copied novels" or "underground poetry" of the Cultural Revolution, we are in fact basing our assessments on the texts as they were formally published afterward. Another challenge concerns works from the 1950s to 1970s whose ideological or artistic content may have been deemed "problematic" under the literary norms of the time, and were therefore never officially published—some writers even lost their right to publish altogether. There were also authors who, during that period, produced writings that were never intended as literary works or for publication, such as diaries, correspondence, or reading notes. These writings only came to public attention after the Cultural Revolution, either disclosed in newspapers and magazines by the authors themselves or compiled and published by their relatives or friends.

When the writing and publication belong to two distinct literary periods, the situation takes on greater significance. Since the intended aim of this research is to uncover diverse voices and establish the existence of alternative literature beyond the mainstream, during a period often marked as ideologically, emotionally, stylistically, and methodologically uniform and impoverished, confusion on the periods would undermine the foundation of such efforts. This gives rise to a series of questions: Can we rely on the date indicated at the end of a work (or as claimed by the author or others) at the time of its publication to determine its original date of composition? Even if the stated date of composition is credible, a further issue arises: During the often substantial gap between writing and publication, was the work revised or altered—particularly in preparation for official release, by which point it already belonged to a different literary period? If such revisions were significant, can the work still be reliably dated to the originally indicated time? Moreover, if a piece was written during a certain period but remained unread and undistributed—kept privately by the author or others without exerting any influence—can it still be regarded as a literary fact of that period? These are all complex and challenging questions.

IV.

Another question that must be raised when reflecting on the problem of "integration" of contemporary literature is the limitation of the perspective and theoretical basis from which such descriptions of "integration" are made. We are identifying and unravelling this problem of "integration" within the context of imagining a reasonable literary ecosystem characterized by diversity and "pluralistic coexistence." However, such diversity ultimately remains an idealized concept. Mechanisms of suppression exist in all times and places. Even today, as the market and profit gradually become dominant social levers, the kind of suppression that serves to establish a "mainstream" has not disappeared, it simply takes different forms. The criteria for defining the "mainstream" have, of course, changed considerably. Moreover, the limitations of this perspective and theoretical framework lie in the fact that they focus primarily on examining the flaws and failures of leftist literature (revolutionary literature). Yet, the issue of elevating leftist literature as a dominant paradigm and suppressing other literary forms is distinct from the question of that literary paradigm's intrinsic merits and demerits. At the very least, these are not entirely the same issue. In fact, the alienation of leftist literature in the contemporary period should not lead to a wholesale negation of this literary form. Whether or not it offers valuable intellectual and artistic experiences is a separate question that deserves further discussion.

Except from: Hong Zicheng, *The Idea of Contemporary Literature* (当代文学的概念), Peking University Press, 2010, pp. 69–82.

Originally published *in Modern Chinese Literature Studies* (Zhongguo Xiandai Wenxue Yanjiu Congkan), Issue (3), 2000. Translation: You Feng

1 Hong Zicheng, *Preface to A History of Contemporary Chinese Literature* (Beijing: Peking University press, 1999), p. 4.
2 Zhang Zhong, Hong Zicheng, She Shusen, Zhao Zumo, and Wang Jingshou, eds., 当代中国文学概观 / Dang dai Zhongguo wen xue gai guan *A Survey of Contemporary Chinese Literature* (Beijing: Peking University Press, 1986).
3 In a letter to Zhang Zhaohe dated April 30, 1957, Shen Congwen discussed the "blooming" movement among Shanghai writers, noting that some writers were complaining "as if every failure to write or to do well was due to excessive restrictions from above, otherwise many fine flowers would bloom." Shen remarked, "I do not fully understand the issue, but I feel some of these claims are not very fair. Twenty years ago, being able to write did not necessarily mean what one wrote was good. Today, some people say that administrative constraints prevent them from writing, but in fact, even if they resigned from all duties and wrote for three or five years under the same conditions as two decades ago, they would still not produce any truly good works." See Congwen's *Letters to Home* (Shanghai: Shanghai Far East Press, 1996), p. 272.
4 For example, Zhou Yang, "Preface to Marxism and Literature"; Hu Feng, "Placed in the Midst of the Struggle for Democracy"; Quan Lin, "Opinions on the Current Literary Movement"; Zhou Yang, "The New People's Literature"; Mao Dun, "Revolutionary Literature under the Oppression of the Reactionaries: Its Struggle and Development," etc.
5 Huang Ziping, *Revolution · History · Novel* (Hong Kong: Oxford University Press, 1996), p. 28.
6 For the above analysis, see Yang Xiaomin and Zhou Yihu, *The Chinese Work Unit System* (Beijing: Zhongguo Jingji Chubanshe, 1999), pp. 77–79.
7 See Deng Zhenglai, "The Reconstruction of the System of Civil Society and State Knowledge Governance," *Open Times* (Guangzhou), March 2000.

THE DIARY OF HOPE (PARTS 3 & 4)

WANG WEI 王炜

III. THE TIRED CHILDREN OF THE MOVEMENT

Here he is, the conflicted, Europe-weary son of the Movement, who can no longer bear the malaise and revulsions of our present world-order, and so gallops off into the future on the back of an idea… Yes, such men are not merely the bearers of an idea; they are themselves borne along by it… they are, as it were, bound by their naked bodies to this idea… they are dragged on by it through all its terrifying consequences, through every steppe and wasteland, over rock and stone—the briar patch lacerates their limbs…Where, in the end, will they arrive?…I am, after all, a child of the past; I am not yet cured of that servile humility, that grinding self-contempt from which humanity has languished for a millennium and a half, and which we imbibed with our superstitious mother's milk… I dare not say what I have witnessed… But our healthier descendants, in joyful serenity, will contemplate, profess, and assert their own divinity. They will scarcely be able to comprehend the sickness of their forefathers. …It will sound to them like a fairy-tale when they hear that people once…constantly lied and bickered, and endured the most tasteless misery.[1]

The sound once emitted has ceased. The deed is done—
a bygone. We are burdened, split,
not in the event, but in silence.
This is the moment reason is clawed over by all sides,
the understanding that never arrived, sheathed now
in a carapace of knowledge, thanks to all interpretations.
And you—can you keep your form, when each
temporary unity dissolves in acrimony,
and not alter your inner bounteousness? The face,
already caved in, whited out by too much thought;
the thing deemed vital still not understood.
But this is not just a season of fatigue.
It is the orogeny of a total Curtain,
refined from the iron of the last one. As if
this were not the weariness of a moment,
but history's own exhaustion, internalized.
Do we understand it? And from it, derive
an honesty different from the optimism of the factions,
an honest preparation for what cannot be prepared for:
that resurrection, that reappearance?

Rage, Muse! Come now.[2]

1 Heinrich Heine, "Preface to Alexander Weill's Village Tales From Alsatia." Written in Paris on Good Friday, 1847.

2 The original is taken from Victor Hugo's "Nox" (in *Les Châtiments*), and the English translation deliberately uses harsh monosyllables to echo the steely imperative of the Chinese version of the original French, "*Muse Indignation, viens, dressons maintenant.*"

Do we, in the silence,
armed with our aimless integrity
shake hands with our unpleasant memories?
When the Iron Curtain rises,
we can say to those who come after:
it's not that we did nothing to stop it.
But to stop something is to stand still,
and something will not get done.
So those who stopped for this reason
are broken off at their imperfections,
their narratives halted, their thoughts incomplete.
To understand their stopping, and from that place
where they stopped, to begin—
this is more correct, and harder.
Indeed, it's not that to be the best is to die,
yet we must admit—because of those
who stopped, who vanished—we are what stays,
left to finish what might still be done:
the possibility of composing a silent,
multi-layered China.
Though the bickering and lying
hasten its death, some choose to be lawyers
who defend this invisible deed.

Rage, Muse! Come now.

Therefore, to do better than another
is no cause for pride; to do worse, no cause for alarm.
To lose the main thread—that is the thing to fear.
Again and again, do we see in the Burmese,
the Latin Americans, the Russians,
only ourselves, unreachable?
Is everything we learn merely the self-discovery
of our knowledge already had?
Is each person the whole, and yet,
what is it that has closed us off? And inverted us,
shoved our heads in the mud, our legs
planted in the sky, while the New Pharisees
tell us: you are walking freely now, among blue sky,
white clouds, and stars. And so
the whole earth is a sea of trembling feet.

The sun and moon, two immortal wheels,
turn in this expedition that goes nowhere.
Then does servility breed gentleness?
No. Instead, a spiritual rampancy, a terrible
compensation for a self made too small.

Rage, Muse. Come now.

Is this, then, a provincial age?
This tolerance we have lost—what is it?
The only fissure in the closed mind, a wound-
like tolerance, suppressed—how did it twist
into this obsessive form of love? And they,
the over-refined and over-brutalized wise men,
with their theoretical bullshit, help sharpen
the malice of the spiritual butchers. Conscience—
not of one age, not owned by any one group—
is mocked, smeared. And this loss
of sensitivity—not just the numbness to the blighting
of a child or an adult, but the new tide of hate,
surging like the Curtain itself, descending
every hour to harvest us:
to close off the undoneness of another, to sever
their line to the future, and call oneself
the Spirit of the Age, convulsing toward a shared death
in a futureless state of nature.
But what if it is not a dead end?
What if this secret clinical diagnosis
is just the stand-in for a practice
we cannot perform in public?
Is it still possible for us to make a path under the sun,
nothing new, but never yet begun—
to make of it a slow fuse burning in daylight
for the Chinese tongue? Only by taking the feeling
so long hung in negation and disorder,
and forging it into the word for love,
can our language survive, and be heard.

Rage, Muse! Come now.

IV. DEATHS BETWEEN 2000 AND 2020: A RETROSPECT

I:
Here I stand, in this place of repetition,
this too-repeated place, in the face of you.
The sheer material of it all drowns us, the catalogue of disasters
strangling us like a vast Möbius strip.
So, I need something from you, not more evidence.
I should address you as the ancients did: *Genius Loci.*

Genius Loci:
Like so many before and after,
you overestimate yourself. It's true, to stand before me
is to endure repetition. I am its product.
As Voltaire said: "He will repeat himself
until he is understood."
But I am so passive. It is not I who speaks
or performs the repetition; it is something else.
Something else. I have no will, nor duty,
nor power to know it. You underestimate repetition
the way you underestimate love, yet perhaps it is the ambition of repetition,
its Danté-esque vanity, that keeps this thing going,
that ensures someone will always try to know that… something else.

I:
And what is that?

Genius Loci:
I am used to its power, but cannot speak its name.
It is what remains after the fire
of time and the fire of space. And I, I am only
the lowest form of slight existence
of a punctual, infinitely humbled space. Time is an eraser,
used infinitely. I am just the one here who sweeps up
the eraser shavings. Are you going to collect
those shavings, flecked with words no one knows,
and boast, "Look, this is my Inferno"? There is nothing
here waiting for you, nothing intact—or even more intact
after having been destroyed—to give your words substance.
This place is silent.

I:
I didn't know this before. Thank you. Perhaps
this… something else you speak of is of a madman.
And time is the eraser in this madman's hand,
smearing all he has written, a kind of violation.

Genius Loci:
I rely on repetition, you on association, like an echo's
echo. Perhaps you are the one sent by the madman.
You, and poets like you, are the stone,
performing this symbolic exercise over and
again, making me its eternal stand-in.
But what I endure is not the gentle wipe of forgetting,
but a hammering erasure. Every place from the last twenty years
is a dent in my body. Each time the tectonic plates
shattered, each explosion, each flood, a nation
growing in reverse, collapses into me.
This painful embedding is not solid,
but a hollowing out. With every death I am hollowed out
again, the earth that grows on me is eaten away
by blankness. The dead do not queue up to arrive to me, as
I am an impoverished singularity.
I have lost them. These twenty years you speak of
are just a few of the countless times I have lost the human race.

I:
Where did they go?
The ones who left you, where did they go?

Genius Loci:
I do not know. Perhaps they went
to a blankness like the sky, a place that more resembles
an inverted earth, where the formed becomes formless,
the formless, visible—and so, closer to a punishment
incurred by a violent materialization of what stands in
for a truth that will never arrive.
And here, there is nothing. A *genius loci* dragging itself,
birthing more blankness from the void that already is:
What can a convict of the void give you? What can a tour guide
who can't go anywhere show you?
Perhaps you aren't looking for a guide, but for

a common scapegoat. Perhaps I am
the thing that turned to salt when they looked back.
I have no evidence. I only have my debasement.
But I can help you. I can preserve and fix
your most failed parts here, so that when you need
an honest measure, though you have not given up,
you will see your powerlessness is here.
This place—a non-zone of knowing.

I:
I accept failure. We all do.
Our fractured language can only retreat
from the leap into the eternal
to an ever-forming, never-realized resistance to reality.
I admit, this resistance is just a temporary camp,
as the non-zone of knowing expands its map.
Shouldn't we survey this non-zone,
confront it, transform it into a spiritual event,
so that we are not dissolved in the blankness?

Genius Loci:
Don't listen, don't look, say nothing.
Bind yourself, stay put, do nothing,
save being an Odyssean version of the three wise monkeys.
The investigations you say you will undertake
are beyond you. A single, soft roar from "it"
and you would explode on the spot.
Odysseus's cognitive blank was to internalize "it,"
ensuring his own survival.
Twice he hid by claiming to be nothing:
once when interrogated by the giant, once in silence.
Right now, "its" hollowing of you and me,
like a manhunt, has not stopped. Here, the only
thing you can do is accept the lowest of all debasements:
to admit you are nothing.

I:
Are they here, the ones who decomposed
in the foundations of a mountain city?
The ones vaporized in a flash explosion?
(That blast was a slap from Bohai Bay across China's face.)

Is he here? The one smashed into a pile of flesh
one morning by falling rocks?
And him, made into a black, unwanted *sarira*
by a mimicked immolation.
And him, dead in a police car that turned all passersby
into potential clients of a john, a proactive hearse.
And them, fed poison like mother's milk,
as if death would be a reasonable stepfather. Will they
be here with the children who didn't survive the hunger,
with the Young Pioneers who continued their artistic performance
in the flames? And them, still falling,
with those who fell in the Pearl River Delta, falling to earth
repeatedly, as if knocking on the walls between each other.
They were hammered, stabbed, snapped, their
bodies put to the collective use of embroidering a banner on the earth,
a medal the selfish award themselves.
And them, their ashen bodies exposed
in the mud after the flood, like a horrific
photograph developing—are they here too?
Those on the banks of the Yangtze, their lives dammed
by a competently swift and decisive death,
are they here too? Is it because they once
existed, and now do not, that a China
breathing softly within China
is never complete? Are they, all once
Chinese, now just the posthumous children
of a hope that existed since civilization's dawn,
but is now dead—are they all here?

Genius Loci:
You want me to say yes. But they are not.
There are no souls here, man, woman, or child,
who speak mawkish words.
None of them will not exist in your poems,
nor in words and images.
Because of them, words and images
have become a series of blanks, just as
my mind goes blank, over and again, because of them.
This paroxysmal blankness is the negative
correlative of life's heartbeat, a leap from a known silence
to a vaster, unknown silence.

Don't use me as your fulcrum, an imagined still point for your motion.
You won't move anything. You should follow
that ancient negativity—walk along the Styx,
but only on the bank, like those hydrologists you know,
charting its source or its mouth,
not crossing it. Do you really not want to know
where the Styx meets the sea, and what that "sea"
is? Why cross the Styx
and give up that "sea"? You would think going with
or against the current is ordinary life, but to cross something
—like the Styx—is to make history.
So you come to me with these questions that you desire
to ask them too. This is your crossing. But that one
stowaway who did it is obsolete.
The great ambition of crossing the Styx, like crossing the Yangtze,
is obsolete. The unknown is not the other shore.
This repeated literary crossing of yours will not change
the blankness, nor bear a new story. When a
repeating you faces a repeating me, you see
how that placid, steady obsolescence,
that blankness operating through you and me, is realized.

I:
Genius Loci, I object. I object to this bitter blankness.
I suspect it is the result of your world imitating ours,
anti-nature altering nature: a too-real hell.
I suspect it is the threats of those who truly deserve hell
that have frightened the living, those lingering,
philosophical commands that have influenced you. I object
to the idea that the disappeared must also disappear from memory and language.
No, and there is no Dante-esque vanity, only something
we thought we understood, but have not yet begun, not at all!
—To let a pair of great wings, seen only by the eyes of innocence,
made of dazzling, beautiful stars, rise from our
utterly defeated and yet stubborn contemporaneity,
to lift them out of the foul knowledge of this world, and return them
to the hurricane-like, ever-circling, cleansing wind.

BIBLIOGRAPHY

Baker, Keith Michael. *Inventing the French Revolution: Essays on French Political Culture in the Eighteenth Century.* Cambridge: Cambridge University Press, 1990.

Bourdieu, Pierre. *Distinction: A Social Critique of the Judgement of Taste.* Cambridge, MA: Harvard University Press, 1984.

Cai Yuanpei. *Cai Yuanpei quanji* [*The Complete Works of Cai Yuanpei*]. Vol. 2. Beijing: Zhonghua Book Company, 1988.

Chan, Anita, and Jonathan Unger. "China after Tiananmen." *The Nation*, January 22, 1990.

Chen Boda. "Lun Xin Qimeng Yundong" [On the New Enlightenment Movement]. And Feng Dalin, "Cong liu wangfan—Wusi Xin Wenhua Yundong" [Returning from the Current—The May Fourth New Culture Movement]. In *Minguo shiqi mingren tan Wusi* [*Famous Figures of the Republican Era Discuss May Fourth*], 66, 215. Fuzhou: Fujian Education Press, 2011.

Chen Duxiu. *Chen Duxiu wenzhang xuanbian* [*Selected Essays of Chen Duxiu*]. Vols. 1–9. Beijing: SDX Joint Publishing Company, 1984.

Chow, Tse-tsung. *The May Fourth Movement: Intellectual Revolution in Modern China.* Stanford, CA: Stanford University Press, 1967.

Cui Zhiyuan. "Partial Intimations of the Coming Whole: The Chongqing Experiment in the Light of the Theories of Henry George, James Meade, and Antonio Gramsci." *Modern China* 37, no. 6 (2011): 646–60.

de la Peña, Nonny. "Nonny de La Peña in Conversation with Lin Yilin." *Asia Art Archive*, September 18, 2017. https://aaa.org.hk/en/like-a-fever/like-a-fever/nonny-de-la-pea-in-conversation-with-lin-yilin. Accessed October 22, 2025.

Deng Zhenglai. "The Reconstruction of the System of Civil Society and State Knowledge Governance." *Open Times* (Guangzhou), March 2000.

Dewey, John. *Art as Experience.* New York: Minton, Balch & Company, 1934.

Ding Liu, et al. *The 7th Shenzhen Sculpture Biennale: Accidental Message—Art Is Not a System, Not a World.* Lingnan Fine Arts Publishing House, 2012.

Ding Liu, and Lu Carol Yinghua. "Crimes Without a Scene: Qian Weikang and the New Measurement Group." *e-flux Journal*, May 2015. https://www.e-flux.com/journal/65/336470/crimes-without-a-scene-qian-weikang-and-the-new-measurement-group. Accessed October 22, 2025.

Esherick, Joseph W., and Jeffrey N. Wasserstrom. "Acting Out Democracy: Political Theatre in Modern China." *Journal of Asian Studies* 49 (1990): 835–65.

Evans, Sara M., and Harry C. Boyte. *Free Space: The Sources of Democratic Change in America.* Chicago: University of Chicago Press, 1992.

Fu Sinian. *Fu Sinian quanji* [*The Complete Works of Fu Sinian*]. Vol. 1. Changsha: Hunan Education Press, 2003.

Gan Yang, ed. *Dang dai Zhongguo wenhua yishi* [*Cultural Consciousness in Contemporary China*]. Hong Kong: Joint Publishing Co., 1990.

Gupta, Tilak P. "Maoism in India: Ideology, Programme and Armed Struggle." *Economic and Political Weekly* 41, no. 29 (July 22–28, 2006): 3172–76.

Han Xuchang. *Yaoerjiu yundong shiyao* [*A History of the December 9th Movement*]. Beijing: The College of the CCP Central Committee, 1986.

Hasegawa, Yuko. "Ma Liuming: The Politics of Non-Differentiation." In *Ma Liuming: Performances, Paintings, Sculptures*, edited by Eleonora Battiston and Ma Liuming, 27. Bologna: Damiani, 2007.

Heine, Heinrich. "Vorwort zu Alexander Weills *Sittengemälde aus dem elsässischen Volksleben.*" Written in Paris, Good Friday, 1847.

Hong Zicheng. Preface to *A History of Contemporary Chinese Literature.* [pagination missing here for the preface.] Beijing: Peking University Press, 1999.

Hong Zicheng, Zhang Zhong, She Shusen, Zhao Zumo, and Wang Jingshou, eds. 当代中国文学概观 / *Dang dai Zhongguo wen xue gai guan: A Survey of Contemporary Chinese Literature.* Beijing: Peking University Press, 1986.

Hu Shi. *Hu Shi quanji* [*The Complete Works of Hu Shi*]. Vol. 27. Edited by Ji Xianlin. Hefei: Anhui Education Press, 2003.

Huang Ziping. *Revolution · History · Novel.* Hong Kong: Oxford University Press, 1996.

Hung Wu, et al., eds. *Displacement: The Three Gorges Dam and Contemporary Chinese Art.* Chicago: University of Chicago Press, 2008.

Israel, John. *Student Nationalism in China: 1927–1937.* Stanford, CA: Stanford University Press, 1966.

Jin Keyu. *The New China Playbook: Beyond Socialism and Capitalism.* New York: Viking, 2023.

Johnson, Chalmers A. *Peasant Nationalism and Communist Power: The Emergence of Revolutionary China, 1937–1945.* Stanford, CA: Stanford University Press, 1962.

Kitayama, Shinobu, and Hazel Rose Markus. *Emotion and Culture.* Washington, D.C.: American Psychological Association, 1994.

Lan Xiaohuan. *How China Works: An Introduction to China's State-Led Economic Development.* Singapore: Palgrave Macmillan, 2024.

Lefebvre, Henri. *The Survival of Capitalism.* New York: St. Martin's Press, 1973.

Li Dazhao. *Li Dazhao quanji* [*The Complete Works of Li Dazhao*]. Vol. 1. Beijing: People's Publishing House, 2006.

Li Eric X. "A Tale of Two Political Systems." *TED*, July 1, 2013. YouTube video. https://www.youtube.com/watch?v=s0YjL9rZyR0. Accessed October 22, 2025.

Liang Qichao. "Zhongguo Shi Xulun" [On the Narration of Chinese History]. In *Yinbing Shi Wenji* [*Collected Works from the Ice-Drinker's Studio*], vol. 3. Taiwan: Zhonghua Shuju, 1983.

Lichbach, Mark Irving. *The Rebel's Dilemma.* Ann Arbor: University of Michigan Press, 1995.

Lugo, Maria Ana, Martin Raiser, and Ruslan Yemtsov. "What's Next for Poverty Reduction Policies in China?" *Brookings Institution.* https://www.brookings.edu/articles/whats-next-for-poverty-reduction-policies-in-china. Accessed October 22, 2025.

Lu Xun. *Lu Xun quanji* [*The Complete Works of Lu Xun*]. Vols. 1, 4, and 9. Beijing: People's Publishing House, 1956.

Luo Jialun. "Xin Wenhua Yundong de shidai he yingxiang" [The Era and Influence of the New Culture Movement].

Macartney, Jane. "The Students: Heroes, Pawns or Power-Brokers?" In *The Broken Mirror: China after Tiananmen*, edited by George Hicks, 3–23. Essex: Longman, 1990.

Majaca, Antonia. "Odysseus of the Nimble Wits: The Spirits of Totalitarianism and the Cultural Cold War's Entscheidungsproblem." In *Parapolitics: Cultural Freedom and the Cold War*, edited by Anselm Franke, Nida Ghouse, Paz Guevara, and Antonia Majaca, 123–52. Berlin: Haus der Kulturen der Welt and Sternberg Press, 2017.

Naughton, Barry. "Chinese Institutional Innovation and Privatization from Below." *American Economic Review* 84, no. 2 (May 1994): 266–70.

Ni Haifeng, and Pauline J. Yao, eds. *Ni Haifeng: Para-Production.* Hong Kong: Timezone 8, 2009.

Opp, Karl-Dieter, and Wolfgang Roehl. "Repression, Micromobilization, and Political Protest." *Social Forces* 69 (1990): 521–47.

Perlson, Hili. "Artnet Asks: Zheng Guogu—Where Does Spirituality Stop and Humor Start?" *Artnet*, March 25, 2015. https://news.artnet.com/market/artnet-asks-zheng-guogu-280454. Accessed October 22, 2025.

Perry, Elizabeth J., and Ellen V. Fuller. "China's Long March to Democracy." *World Policy Journal* 8 (1991): 663–85.

Plath, Sylvia. *Ariel.* London: Faber & Faber, 1965.

Pollacchi, Elena. *Wang Bing's Filmmaking of the China Dream: Narratives, Witnesses and Marginal Spaces.* Amsterdam: Amsterdam University Press, 2021.

Pye, Lucian W. "The Escalation of Confrontation." In *The Broken Mirror: China after Tiananmen*, edited by George Hicks, 162–79. Essex: Longman, 1990.

Qin Hui. *Chuantong shilu* [Traditional Records].

———. *Tianyuanshi yu kuangxiangqu: guanzhong moshi yu qianjindai shehui de zairenshi* [*Idyllic and Rhapsody: The Guanzhong Model and the Re-understanding of Premodern Society*]. Beijing: Central Compilation & Translation Press, 1996.

———."Dilemmas of Twenty-First Century Globalization: Explanations and Solutions, with a Critique of Thomas Piketty's *Twenty-First Century Capitalism*." *Reading the China Dream*, November 15, 2018. https://www.readingthechinadream.com/qin-hui-dilemmas.html. Accessed October 22, 2025.

———."My Views of the Globalization Crisis: The Interaction of Two Inchworm Effects 我看全球经济危机：两种尺蠖效应的互动." *Leader* 2 (2009).

———."The Honecker Parable: The Counter-Factual Case of East Germany Absorbing West Germany '昂纳克寓言'：东德吞并西德的'反事实推论.'" *Thought* 17 (2011).

Qingmo choubei lixian dang'an shiliao* [*Archival Historical Materials on the Preparation for Constitutionalism in the Late Qing Dynasty*]. Vol. 2. Beijing: Zhonghua Book Company, 1979.

Reuters. "Meituan to Change Delivery Algorithm Rules as China Urges Labour Protection." September 13, 2021. https://www.reuters.com/world/china/meituan-change-delivery-algorithm-rules-china-urges-labour-protection-2021-09-13/. Accessed October 22, 2025.

Ringer, Fritz K. *The Decline of the German Mandarins.* Hanover, NH: University Press of New England, 1990.

Sans, Jérôme, ed. *China Talks: Interviews with 32 Contemporary Artists.* Hong Kong: Timezone 8, 2009.

Scott, James C. *Weapons of the Weak: Everyday Forms of Peasant Resistance.* New Haven: Yale University Press, 1985.

Sewell, William H., Jr. "Ideologies and Social Revolutions: Reflections on the French Case." *Journal of Modern History* 57 (1985): 57–85.

Shen Congwen. *Letters to Home.* Shanghai: Shanghai Far East Press, 1996.

Tao Shuimu, ed. *Shen Dingyi ji* [*The Collected Works of Shen Dingyi*]. Vol. 2. Beijing: National Library of China Publishing House, 2010.

Triandis, H. C. "The Self and Social Behavior in Differing Cultural Contexts." *Psychological Review* 96 (1989): 506–20.

Wang Hui. "Depoliticized Politics, from East to West." *New Left Review* 41 (2006): 29–45.

———."The Economy of Rising China." *Reading the China Dream*, originally published in *Beijing Cultural Review*, no. 2 (2010): 24–35. https://www.readingthechinadream.com/wang-hui-the-economy-of-rising-china.html. Accessed October 22, 2025.

Wang Hui, and En Liang Khong. "After the Party: An Interview with Wang Hui." *OpenDemocracy*. https://www.opendemocracy.net/en/after-party-interview-with-wang-hui/. Accessed October 22, 2025.

Wang Peggy. "Sui Jianguo: The Matter of Endurance." In *The Future History of Contemporary Chinese Art*. Minneapolis: University of Minnesota Press, 2020.

Wang Shaoguang, and Hu An'gang. *The Chinese Economy in Crisis: State Capacity and Tax Reform.* Armonk, NY: M.E. Sharpe, 2001.

Wang Xiaoming, ed. *In Search of Humanism (Renwen jingshen xunsilu)*. Shanghai: Shanghai People's Press, 1996.

Wasserstrom, Jeffrey N. *Student Protests in Twentieth-Century China: The View from Shanghai.* Stanford, CA: Stanford University Press, 1991.

Wu Mouren, Bao Minghui, Ni Peihua, Ni Peimin, and Wang Qingjia, eds. *Bajiu Zhongguo minyun jishi* [*Daily Accounts on the 1989 Democracy Movement in China*].

Xu Shoushang. *Wangyou Lu Xun yinxiang ji* [*Recollections of My Deceased Friend Lu Xun*]. Changsha: Yuelu Publishing House, 2011.

Xuese de Limin. *A Bloody Morning.* Hong Kong: Chi Keung Publishing Co., 1989.

Yan Fu. *Yan Fu ji* [*The Collected Works of Yan Fu*]. Vol. 1. Beijing: Zhonghua Book Company, 1986.

Yang Xiaomin, and Zhou Yihu. *The Chinese Work Unit System.* Beijing: Zhongguo Jingji Chubanshe, 1999.

Zhang Nan, and Wang Renzhi. *Xinhai geming qian shinian jian shilun xuanji* [*Selected Commentaries from the Decade Before the 1911 Revolution*]. Vol. 2, pt. 1. Beijing: SDX Joint Publishing Company, 1963.

Zhang Shizhao. *Zhang Shizhao quanji* [*The Complete Works of Zhang Shizhao*]. Vol. 3. Shanghai: Wenhui Press, 2000.

Zhang Xudong. *Chinese Modernism in the Era of Reforms.* London: Durman Press, 1997.

Zhang Yukun, Xia Yining, and Ding Feng. "In Depth: China's Trillion-Dollar Local Government 'Hidden Debt' Dilemma." *Caixin Global*, September 19, 2023.

Zhao Dingxin. "State Legitimacy, State Policy, and the Development of the 1989 Beijing Student Movement." *Asian Perspective* 23, no. 2 (1999): 245–84.

———."路径不依赖、政策不相干——什么才是中国经济成功的关键" ["Path Independence, Policy Irrelevance—What Holds the Key to China's Economic Success?"]. 2017.

Zhao Yining. "Zhongguo jingji xunqiu ruanzhaolu" [The Chinese Economy Seeks a Soft Landing]. *Outlook Weekly* 28 (1995): 22–23.

IMAGE RIGHTS

Datong Dazhang, *I Saw Death*, 1998
Courtesy of Wen Pulin Archive of Chinese Avant-Garde Art, Beijing

Jiang Jie, *Long March – Xiao Shuxian 2002–Nowadays*, 2002–18
Courtesy of the artist

Kan Xuan, *Ai!*, 1999
Courtesy of the artist

Lin Yilin, *Safely Maneuvering Across Lin He Road*, 1995
Courtesy of the artist

Ma Liuming, *Fen-Ma Liuming I*, 1993
Courtesy of the artist

Wang Guangyi
Study for *Quarantine—All Food is Potentially Poisonous*, 1996
Study for *Cold War Aesthetics*, 2007
Courtesy of Wang Guangyi Studio

Wu Wenguang, *Diary: Snow, November 21, 1998*, 1998
Courtesy of the artist

Xin Kedu – New Measurement Group, *The Analysis (I)*, 1990
Courtesy of Wang Luyan

Zhuang Hui, *Longitude 109.88, Latitude 31.09*, 1995–2008
Courtesy of the artist

Chen Shaoxiong, *72.5 Hours of Electricity Consumption*, 1992
Courtesy of Taikang Art Museum, Beijing

Hong Hao & Yan Lei, *Invitation Letter to Documenta Kassel*, 1997
Courtesy of the artists

Hong Hao & Yan Lei, *Snow Bull*, 2009
Courtesy of the artists

Ni Haifeng, *Of the Departure and the Arrival*, 2005
Courtesy of the artist and Galerie In Situ – fabienne leclerc

Zhou Tiehai, *Will/We Must*, 1996
Courtesy of the artist

Cao Fei & Ou Ning, *San Yuan Li*, 2003
Courtesy of the artists

Han Lei
Kaifeng, Henan Province, 1986
Luochuan, Shaanxi Province VI, 1989
Courtesy of the artist

Living Dance Studio, *Dance with Farm Workers*, 2001
Filmed by Su Ming and Wu Wenguang, edited by Wu Wenguang
Courtesy of Wen Hui

Hiroshi Ohashi (Artistic Director), Wang Molin, Tong Sze Hong, Zhao Chuan, *Lu Xun 2008*, 2008
Courtesy of Zhao Chuan

Rent Collection Courtyard, Sichuan Fine Arts Institute, 2005.
Courtesy of documenta Archiv, Kassel
Photo: Nicolas Wefers

Sui Jianguo, *Kill*, 1996
Courtesy of the artist

Wang Bing, *Man with No Name*, 2009
Courtesy of the artist and Galerie Chantal Crousel, Paris
© Wang Bing

Wang Youshen, *Shining · Kassel*, 1989–2026
Courtesy of the artist

Xiao Lu, *15 Gunshots...from 1989 to 2003*, 2003
Courtesy of the artist

Zhao Yinou
75.2007, 2007
Courtesy of the artist

Zheng Guogu, *Me and My Teacher*, 1993
Courtesy of the artist and Vitamin Creative Space, Guangzhou

Wang Tuo, *The Second Interrogation*, 2022–23
Courtesy of the artist

BIOGRAPHIES

WANG HUI

Wang Hui (b. 1959) is distinguished professor in the School of Humanities at Tsinghua University and director of the Tsinghua Institute for Advanced Study in the Humanities and Social Sciences. As one of the few internationally renowned Chinese thinkers, he has been elected as a foreign member of Academia Europaea (MAE) since 2024. His research interests include Chinese intellectual history, Chinese literature, and social and political theory. He has received the Luca Pacioli Award in 2013 and Anneliese Maier Research Award in 2018. He was the co-editor of the influential Chinese journal *Dushu* (读书) from 1996 to 2007. His recent English publications include *The Rise of Modern Chinese Thought* (2022), *China's Twentieth Century* (2016), *China from Empire to Nation-State* (2015), and *The Politics of Imagining Asia* (2011), among others.

DINGXIN ZHAO

Dingxin Zhao (b. 1953) is emeritus professor at Zhejiang University and director of its Institute for Advanced Study in Humanities and Social Sciences. His research focuses on political sociology, social movements, and historical sociology. After earning a PhD in insect ecology (McGill, 1990), he switched fields to obtain a PhD in sociology (McGill, 1995). He taught at the University of Chicago from 1996 before joining Zhejiang University in 2021. He was a 2009–10 fellow at the Center for Advanced Studies in Behavioral Science.

QIN HUI

Qin Hui (b. 1953) is a distinguished Chinese historian and public intellectual specializing in economic history and peasant studies. He received his Master's from Lanzhou University in 1981 and later was a visiting scholar at the University of Tokyo and a visiting fellow at the Fairbank Center at Harvard University (2003). Formerly a professor of history at Tsinghua University, he retired in 2017 and became a visiting professor at the Chinese University of Hong Kong. His research interests focus on China, globalization, and the "new Cold War." Recently, he has explored China's economy during the Cultural Revolution and is rethinking the lessons of the May Fourth Movement, calling it "the failure of the second wave of global democratization."

XUDONG ZHANG

Xudong Zhang (b. 1965) is a professor of Comparative Literature and East Asian Studies at NYU and the founding director of the International Center for Critical Theory (ICCT). A 2023–24 New Institute Fellow in Hamburg, he serves on the academic advisory committee for Peking University's Institute for Advanced Studies. Zhang has published extensively on critical theory and modernism, particularly comparing Chinese and European modernities. His major English works include *Chinese Modernism in the Era of Reforms (1997)*, *Postsocialism and Cultural Politics (2008)*, and the edited volumes *Postmodernism and China (2000)* and *Whither China (2001)*.

YANG GUOQIANG

Yang Guoqiang (b. 1948) is a professor and doctoral supervisor at the Si-mian Institute for Advanced Studies in Humanities at East China Normal University. His main research area is modern Chinese history, with a particular focus on the study of late Qing intellectuals and the history of social change in modern and contemporary China. His major academic works in Chinese include *The Literati and the World of the Late Qing* (晚清的士人与世相), *Trapped between Past and Present: Chinese Society, Politics, and Culture in the Early twentieth Century* (两头不到岸—二十世纪初年中国的社会、政治和文化), among others.

HONG ZICHENG

Hong Zicheng (b. 1939) is a renowned Chinese literary historian. A 1961 graduate of the Department of Chinese Language and Literature at Peking University, he later became a professor there. As a firsthand witness to the 1949–79 literary scene, he is considered a key founder of the academic study of contemporary Chinese literature. He has authored over twenty Chinese monographs, including *A History of Contemporary Chinese Literature* (中国当代文学史) and *Problems and Methods* (问题与方法——中国当代文学史研究讲稿).

WANG WEI

Wang Wei's (b. 1975) poetry presents the quality of an intellectual epic, weaving through cultural criticism, ethnography, literary history, philosophy, and poetics. It focuses on the spiritual state and existential predicament of people in China today. Wang Wei did not attend university and worked as a journalist in China's border regions; he has always remained wary of the literary establishment in the Chinese-speaking world. His Chinese works include the poetry collection *Memorandum on Light* (光明备忘录), the lecture collection *A Preliminary Discussion on the Muse of Poetry* (试论诗神), among others. He currently lives between Beijing and Zunyi.

SU WEI

Su Wei (b. 1982) is a curator and art-history researcher based in Beijing. His work reconstructs the narrative of contemporary Chinese art history, examining its legitimacy and ruptures in a global context. Using the post-1949 period as a critical entry point, he redefines the continuity of art from its socialist origins to the present by mapping its undercurrents and limitations. He has published a number of articles in local and international art journals including *e-flux Journal*, *YISHU: Journal of Contemporary Chinese Art*, *Journal of Contemporary Art* (Bristol, UK) and *Kunstforum*. He is the editor of *Community of Feeling: Emotional Patterns in Art in Post-1949 China*, forthcoming from Zhejiang Photographic Press.

MI YOU

Mi You (b. 1987) is a curator and professor of Art and Economies at the University of Kassel / documenta Institut, where she leads research on the social, economic, and political conditions of art. She's the author of the book *Art in a Multipolar World* (Hatje Cantz, 2024). Her most recent exhibitions include the 13th Shanghai Biennale (2020–21), *Lonely Vectors* at the Singapore Art Museum (2022), *Clouds, Power and Ornament* at the Centre for Heritage, Arts and Textile, Hong Kong (2023), and *Really? Art and Knowledge in Time of Crisis* at Framer Framed, Amsterdam (2024). She serves as chair of the committee on Media Arts and Technology for the transnational NGO Common Action Forum and is a Berggruen Institute Europe fellow.

ANNA-LISA SCHERFOSE

Anna-Lisa Scherfose (b. 1990) is a research associate in the Department of Art History and Aesthetics at the Kunsthochschule Kassel, where she coordinates the Transdisciplinary Centre for Exhibition Studies (TRACES). She studied art history and sociology in Kassel and Gothenburg and Curatorial Studies at Goethe-University/Städelschule Frankfurt. Scherfose is managing director of BPA// Berlin program for artists. Recent curatorial projects include Britta Thie at Deichtorhallen Hamburg (2025), *BPA// Exhibition* at KW Institute for Contemporary Art, Berlin (2022) and solo presentations at BPA// Raum (2022–2023) in Berlin. Her PhD research explores how artistic networks in the 1990s used the emerging internet to create collaborative infrastructures.

This book is published in conjunction with the exhibition

The China Moment. Contextualizing Individualism in Chinese Contemporary Art.
Organized by documenta Institut at Kasseler Kunstverein
January 24–March 22, 2026

Editor:
Mi You, Su Wei, Anna-Lisa Scherfose

Managing editor:
Anna-Lisa Scherfose

Editorial management:
Adam Jackman, Hatje Cantz

Copyediting:
Hannah Young

Translations:
You Feng, Li Ti, David Ownby, Jacob Zhicheng Zhang

Graphic design:
Rutger Fuchs Amsterdam

Typeface:
Plantin, Graphik

Reproductions:
Lional, DLG Graphic Paris

Production:
Kati Klaeske, Hatje Cantz

Paper:
Circle Offset, 110 g/m²

Printed by:
Westermann Duck Zwickau GmbH
Crimmitschauer Str. 43
08058 Zwickau
Germany

Published by
Hatje Cantz Verlag GmbH
Mommsenstraße 27
10629 Berlin
Germany
contact@hatjecantz.de
www.hatjecantz.com
A Ganske Publishing Group Company

DOCUMENTA INSTITUT KASSEL gGmbH
Untere Karlsstraße 4
34117 Kassel
Germany
office@documenta-institut.de
www.documenta-institut.de

Founding director and academic director: Prof. Dr. Heinz Bude
Managing director: Michael Flörchinger

Chairman of the Supervisory Board: Timon Gremmels, State Minister for Higher Education, Research, Science and the Arts in Hesse

ISBN: 978-3-7757-6168-0 [PRINT]
ISBN: 978-3-7757-6169-7 [EPUB]
ISBN: 978-3-7757-6170-3 [PDF]

Printed in Germany

Cover illustration:
Wang Youshen
Shining · Kassel, 1989–2026
Courtesy of the artist

Cover design adapted from a concept by Workout Services

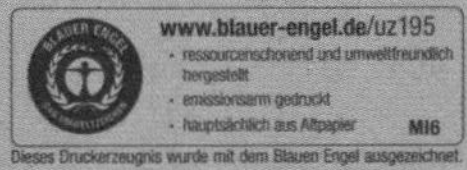